Unabashed
Women

ALSO BY
MARLENE WAGMAN-GELLER

Fabulous Female Firsts: Because of Them We Can

Women of Means: Fascinating Biographies of Royals, Heiresses, Eccentrics, and Other Poor Little Rich Girls

Great Second Acts: In Praise of Older Women

Women Who Launch: Women Who Shattered Glass Ceilings

Still I Rise: The Persistence of Phenomenal Women

Behind Every Great Man: The Forgotten Women Behind the World's Famous and Infamous

And the Rest is History: The Famous (and Infamous) First Meetings of the World's Most Passionate Couples

Eureka! The Surprising Stories Behind the Ideas That Shaped the World

Once Again to Zelda: The Stories Behind Literature's Most Intriguing Dedications

Unabashed Women

The Fascinating Biographies of Bad Girls, Seductresses, Rebels, and One-of-a-Kind Women

MARLENE WAGMAN-GELLER

CORAL GABLES

Cover Design: Jermaine Lau
Art Direction: Jermaine Lau
Interior Layout: Katia Mena

For permission requests, please contact the publisher at:
Mango Publishing Group
2850 S Douglas Road, 2nd Floor
Coral Gables, FL 33134 USA
info@mango.bz

For special orders, quantity sales, course adoptions and corporate sales, please email the publisher at sales@mango.bz. For trade and wholesale sales, please contact Ingram Publisher Services at customer.service@ingramcontent.com or +1.800.509.4887.

Unabashed Women: The Fascinating Biographies of Bad Girls, Seductresses, Rebels, and One-of-a-Kind Women

Library of Congress Cataloging-in-Publication number: 2021936138
ISBN: (print) 978-1-64250-582-5, (ebook) 978-1-64250-583-2
BISAC category code BIO022000, BIOGRAPHY & AUTOBIOGRAPHY / Women

Printed in the United States of America

To unabashed women everywhere.

And to my special women: My mother, Gilda Wagman, my daughter, Jordanna Geller, and my friend Jamie Lovett—the wind beneath my writer's wings.

"Well-behaved women
seldom make history."

—LAUREL ULRICH (1976)

"I decided long ago/ Never to walk in anyone's shadow."

—LINDA CREE AND MICHAEL MASSER (1977)

TABLE OF CONTENTS

"Anyone's Shadow"

"What are little girls made of? Sugar and spice/And all things nice/That's what little girls are made of." When Mother Goose penned her rhyme, little did she realize the heavy load she had placed on female shoulders. To be nice is daunting. And what of those girls who shirked the role of Ms. Goody Two-Shoes? In every age, in every clime, there are those whose DNA does not contain the Pollyanna gene.

Ever since Eve, the original bad girl, went against God's directive against eating from the Tree of Good and Evil, wayward women have had a bad rap. The wages of sin was an angel with a flaming sword who ensured eternal banishment from Paradise. Eve's punishment—as well as that of all her female descendants—was to give birth in great pain. As penance for his participation in Original Sin, her partner—and his male descendants—had to work by the sweat of their brow. No more free rides, thanks to the lady fashioned from Adam's rib. From this biblical couple, the male-female power structure was born.

Throughout the first millennium, the standard of womanhood was to exercise modesty, especially in the sexual arena. The Old Testament admonishes, "Who can find a virtuous woman? For her price is far above rubies." Revered role models remain Madonna (not the Material Girl) and Mother Teresa—hard shoes to fill. In the Medieval era, when the knights rode off on crusades, to ensure their wives didn't play while their hubbies were away, they devised the chastity belt. After all, trust can only go so far. While brides wear white to signify virginity, a prize surrendered on the wedding night, males are allowed free rein to their libido due to the mindset of "boys will be boys." The male adage for sexual conquest—a notch on the crotch—is a much-vaunted trophy. A woman equally liberal with her body is viewed as a slut. Rebel girls viewed the legs crossed mindset as another way for the patriarchy to clip their wings.

Language is symptomatic of societal mores, and English has a plethora of words to describe women who do not walk the prescribed gauntlet. The most derogatory put-downs for those ladies who do not subscribe to the time-honored double standard for sexual transgressions: whore, cougar, frigid (feel free to add your own)—all which have no male equivalent. And no matter how much one peruses *Webster's*, there is no male counterpart for wallflower, or shrinking violet. Other searing adjectives to describe pushy "broads": sassy, shrill, spinster, hag, ditzy, bitch, hormonal. And we have a newer term to describe a bride who places unreasonable demands on her wedding party: Bridezilla. No one seems to feel the need to use the male equivalent of Groomzilla.

Fortunately (or unfortunately, depending on perspective), there have always been badass broads. In Aristophanes's 411 BC play *Lysistrata*, the titular heroine arranged for wives to withhold sex until their soldier husbands ended the Peloponnesian War. As a further measure, the ladies took over the Acropolis, which halted access to the money funding the feud between Athens and Sparta. Another feisty fictional femme was the lady whose name manifested her fiery spirit: Scarlett O'Hara, from Margaret Mitchell's *Gone with the Wind*. Unlike most women in the antebellum South, Scarlett was brash, bratty, and ballsy. She is far more memorable than her archrival Melanie Hamilton Wilkes, the embodiment of virtue—the quintessential good girl. Another woman who gave no fucks was Lisbeth Salander, the tattooed, chain-smoking anti-heroine who favored courtier Goth.

Non-shrinking-violets go through life with upraised middle finger, with an ever-ready retort. Much to the chagrin of those who looked askance at gender equality, there were always women who did not abide by the premise that, when playing a game, everyone accepts the same rules. And for their daring to listen to a different drummer, for their audacity of treading the road less traveled, condemnation was swift. Society put them in pillories of social ostracism, marking them with figurative scarlet letters.

Liberal ladies often use ink as a means to fight against a hostile status quo that does its utmost to keep different femmes in line. Dorothy Parker, the Jewish girl from Jersey, had no tolerance for the constraints of a Victorian mindset. As a prolific drinker in the era of Prohibition, she smoked, and slept with whomever caught her fancy. In the 1920s, a decade when the Ku Klux Klan had its largest membership, she wrote the short story "Arrangement in Black and White" to skewer racism. Her take-me-or-leave-me philosophy (which expression summed up her romantic history) can be explained in Parker's words, "But I shall stay the way I am/Because I do not give a damn."

Unabashed Women pays homage to the anti-Martha-Stewarts—those who do not define themselves by their prowess in the kitchen or the bedroom, those who pried themselves from the shadows. Although they paid a price for their "ballsy" behavior, they, in the words of Mr. Sinatra, had the satisfaction of being able to say, "I did it my way."

The Mother Goose counterpart for little boys is, "What are little boys made of? Snips and snails and puppy dog tails/That's what little boys are made of." The ladies who made leaps into the flames are an amalgam of the sugar and the spice. The most memorable of the Shakespearean heroes were great men with fatal flaws that made them relatable, human. The ladies profiled in *Unabashed Women* serve as their female counterparts; their prickly personalities did not earn them the title Ms. Congeniality, though it freed them of cookie-cutter corsets. They left their historic imprints because they dared to be different and difficult. In the final analysis, badness is in the eye of the beholder.

The list of feisty females is legion, including the nineteenth-century British author Charlotte Brontë. Jane Eyre, although madly in love with Mr. Rochester, spurns his proposal to live with him as his mistress in his estate, Thornfield Hall. The protagonist's response (an eyebrow-raiser in its time): "I am no bird; and no net ensnares me. I am a free human being with an independent will; which I now exert to leave you." Similar to Ms. Eyre, the unabashed women were no birds.

Although the ladies who populate these pages come from different eras and far-flung locales, a common thread binds them: the refusal to let their light be dimmed by another. Martha Gellhorn, the journalist wife of Ernest Hemingway, wrote, "Why should I be a footnote to someone else's life?" Françoise Gilot, the painter and common-law wife of Pablo Picasso, declared, "I'm not here just because I've spent time with Picasso."

In fairy tales, bliss arrives in the guise of a prince; in literature, Heathcliff's passion extends beyond the grave; in film, Ricky Blaine's devotion to Ilsa is the litmus test of adoration. However, songwriters Michael Masser and Linda Creed argue that the greatest commitment has to be to one's self, a philosophy shared by those who forge their own paths. Their lyrics, immortalized by Whitney Houston, state, "I decided long ago/Never to walk in anyone's shadow."

CHAPTER 1

"Quand Même?"
(1844)

"Slow down? Rest? With all eternity before me?"

—SARAH BERNHARDT

Used a letter holder named Sophie made from a human skull? Check. Accessorized with a stuffed bat? Check. Slept in a coffin? Check. The woman who could answer in the affirmative to these questions was also the possessor of the honorific "Divine."

The flamboyant nineteenth-century actress's name is employed by mothers to criticize their melodramatic daughters: "Who do you think you are? Sarah Bernhardt?" However, no matter how histrionic, no matter how eccentric, no one could emulate the famed star in eccentricity, in talent, in hubris.

Sarah Bernhardt's onstage and offstage lives rivaled one another in showmanship. She was the illegitimate daughter of Youle Bernhard, a Jewish woman from Amsterdam who became a sought-after courtesan when she arrived in Paris, and a father who was most likely an officer from Le Havre. Sarah spent her early years with a foster family in Brittany, and later attended a convent near Versailles. A drama queen when thwarted, on one occasion she threw herself in front of a carriage; on another, out a window. Youle did not involve herself in Sarah's life other than to make her contribute to the family's income by working as a teenage courtesan.

The Duc de Morny, the half-brother of Napoleon III, one of Youle's lovers, perceiving Sarah would be as much a drama queen onstage as off, arranged for the fifteen-year-old to attend the prestigious Paris Conservatory for Dramatic Arts. Two years later, she transferred to the Comédie-Francaise; after watching her first production, she pronounced, "The curtain of my life has risen." She failed to attract notice, partially because she was considered unfashionably thin. A wit remarked that Sarah was so skinny that, when she got into a bath, the water level went down. As Alexandre Dumas *fils*, novelist and Sarah's friend, observed, "You know, she's such a liar that she may even be fat." Critics panned her performances, and further salt entered the wound when Youle told her, "See! The whole world calls you stupid, and the whole world knows that you're my child!"

The performance that captured the public's interest took place in 1893, at an event that played out behind the theater's curtain. Régine, Sarah's younger sister, was with her at an annual ceremony to honor Molière, and accidentally stepped on the train of veteran actress Madame Nathalie. Angered, the older woman shoved Régine against a pillar. Sarah's knee-jerk reaction was to scream, "You miserable bitch!" and slap Nathalie on both cheeks. Sarah refused to apologize, and in the first publicity coup of her career, she tore up her contract. The incident made her the talk—and toast—of Paris.

Sarah depended on wealthy lovers for support until she joined the Théâtre de l'Odéon, run by a father and son; she slept with them both. Her performances made her a star in the theatrical firmament. When she played the Queen of Spain in Victor Hugo's play *Ruy Blas*, the aged writer knelt down, kissed her hand, and uttered, *"Merci, merci."* The tribute was genuine, not merely the result of their earlier affair, in the course of which he had gifted her a human skull. She took a brief hiatus in 1864 for the birth of her son Maurice, whose father may have been a passing Belgian dalliance with Prince de Ligne.

Although a consummate narcissist, Sarah still possessed a soul. During the 1870 siege of Paris, she transformed the Odéon into a field hospital, filling the stage, dressing rooms, and auditorium with cots for the injured and the dying. She persuaded her well-heeled stockholders (the name she gave to her lovers who supported her lifestyle) to supply medicine and food, and convinced one to donate his overcoat. She also thumbed her nose when it came to religion. Sarah had been raised as a Catholic, and as a child, she had entertained an inspiration to be a nun. Indeed, one of her prized possessions was a rosary, a gift from Pope Leo XIII. Nevertheless, in an age of virulent anti-Semitism, she adhered to her Jewish roots. Caricatures circulated of her with a Star of David and bags of money, denoting her as a money-grubbing Jew. The only truly embittered disagreement she had with her beloved son was over the Dreyfus Affair, when she defended the Jewish officer charged with treason.

Due to her surging popularity, the Comédie-Francaise arranged her return, and she transformed into its shining star. The newspaper *Le Figaro* declared that everyone was coming to Paris to gaze upon its two main attractions: the newly erected Eiffel Tower, and Sarah Bernhardt. Sigmund Freud wrote of her performance, "my head is reeling," and he hung her photo in his office. D. H. Lawrence compared her to "a gazelle with a beautiful panther's fascination and fury." Mark Twain observed, "There are five kinds of actresses. Bad actresses, fair actresses, good actresses, great actresses—and then there is Sarah Bernhardt." The Divine (her honorific) leading lady also served as muse: Oscar Wilde wrote *Salomé* for her; Marcel Proust portrayed her in his novel *In Search of Lost Time*; Aubrey Beardsley drew her portrait as Salomé holding John the Baptist's severed head. One naysayer was the Irish playwright George Bernard Shaw, who later admitted his acrimony was because she had reminded him of his Aunt Georgina.

From 1880 onwards, Sarah toured Europe and America, and she took along her menagerie of pets—dogs, a snake, and an alligator called Ali-Gaga, who passed away after consuming too much champagne. Adoring fans lavished tributes: Australians danced to "The Bernhardt Waltz"; Argentina presented Sarah with thirteen thousand acres of land; in London, Oscar Wilde laid lilies at her feet. In America, reporters bombarded the famed thespian: What was her waist size? Did she feed live birds to her lion cub? In New York, Sarah made her way to a theater through a crowd of worshippers who demanded she sign their shirt cuffs. At one point, to avoid the throng, her younger sister Jeanne, camouflaged in

Sarah's outlandish clothes, hoodwinked the public so the prima donna could make her getaway. She took the opportunity to visit Thomas Edison, likewise smitten, who gave her a tour of his laboratory. In return, he persuaded her to make a recording on his new invention: the phonograph.

However, not everyone was in Camp Bernhardt. Fundamentalist preachers pronounced her sinful. Ever resourceful, when a Texas theater owner refused to rent his place for her performance, she set up her own tent in a field. Ladies in the audience returned home with the hems of their dresses frayed by the cornstalks.

The woman who had grown up in a foster home, with money from her roles as an actress and a courtesan, purchased her own home located in the Parc Monceau area of Paris, as over-decorated as her stage sets. She shared the space with Maurice, her menagerie of pets, and a constant stream of visitors. Guests who came through her door were the stuff of legend: Theodore Roosevelt, Oscar Wilde, Louis Pasteur, Victor Hugo, Émile Zola. The hostess also served as a muse; Alexander Dumas *fils* declared after a visit, "but when I get home, how I can write! How I can write!"

The most-utilized piece of furniture in her home was the Bernhardt bed—lovers were legion. Some of the famous were Victor Hugo, Charles Haas (Proust's model for his character Swann), Albert Edward, a.k.a. the Prince of Wales, and Gustave Doré. An equal opportunity lover, Sarah also slept with a variety of female paramours.

Along with own her own property, Sarah, who always desired to be at the helm of her ship, commandeered her own playhouse that she unsurprisingly christened the Théâtre Sarah Bernhardt. In a signature exit at the close of a Bernhardt production, in a male role such as Hamlet, she would expertly expire on stage. A critic was so inspired he wrote, "dying as angels would die were they allowed to." In the same show, the audience rose to its feet; their enthusiasm was not diminished by the fact that the star was fifty-six and had played the role of a twenty-year-old.

Despite looking after her exotic animals, grueling schedule, and erotic liaisons, Sarah also took the conventional step of marriage. She fell for a dissolute Greek shipping heir, Aristides Damalas, twelve years her junior, who she described as "pleased with himself as Narcissus." They married in England in 1882, between her engagements in Naples and Nice. He worked as a representative of a Greek delegation stationed in Paris, and due to diplomatic indiscretion, his country reassigned him to a post in St. Petersburg. Acting the part of the devoted wife, Sarah changed her tour engagements and followed him to Russia. Alas, Aristides slipped back into his morphine habit, and one day abruptly deserted to join the French Foreign Legion. When he died from his drug addiction at age forty-two, Sarah referred to herself as "the widow Damalas." Irish writer Bram Stoker said he had partly based his character Dracula on Sarah's husband.

Alongside van Gogh's ear, Bernhardt's leg is the most famous appendage in history. She had suffered an injury when she leapt from a parapet while performing *La Tosca* that resulted in years of chronic pain. According to legend, while enduring an amputation under anesthetic, she had drifted into unconsciousness while singing "La Marseillaise." P. T. Barnum offered her $10,000 for the severed limb to put on display. She refused. "If it's my right leg you want, see the doctors; if it's the left leg, see my manager in New York." Eight months later, at age seventy-one, she starred in *La Dame aux Camelias*, the play that Verdi later adapted as *La Traviata*, where she moved about the stage in a wheelchair that she preferred to a wooden leg. Shortly afterwards, Sarah set off for her ninth and last American tour, to convince the United States to enter World War I. Undaunted, she left for the Front to entertain the troops, where she described herself as hopping about "like a guinea hen."

The immortal thespian's specialty was dying from daggers, betrayal, heartbreak. When the actress herself passed away in her son's arms in 1923, thousands of Parisians gathered at the Théâtre Sarah Bernhardt to pay homage. During World War II, the Germans de-consecrated the playhouse because of Sarah's Jewish roots, and thus it became the Théâtre de la Ville. Her funeral was the largest since that of her admirer, Victor Hugo. Currently, Sarah's leg resides at Bordeaux University medical school; her tomb lies in Père Lachaise Cemetery.

Of all the reams of dialogue that Sarah spoke, perhaps her remarkable life is best encapsulated by words she uttered at age nine, when she leapt across a ditch that none of her friends would attempt. The French translation is "in spite of everything" or "after all," the verbal equivalent of a shrug: "*Quand même.*"

CHAPTER 2

"Girdled the Globe" (1864)

"I have never written a word that did not come from my heart. I never shall."

—ELIZABETH COCHRANE/NELLIE BLY

Some women can fit into one of the following categories: world traveler, fourteen siblings, wife of a millionaire, spent time in a madhouse, owned a pet monkey. In all likelihood, only the nineteenth-century version of Brenda Starr dipped her toes in all of these waters.

The lady who beat a literary character at his own game was Elizabeth Jane, nicknamed Pinky by her mother, Mary Jane. Her father, Judge Michael Cochran, who had risen from mill worker to mill owner, had founded her hometown, Cochran Mills, Pennsylvania. The judge had brought to his second family ten children from his first marriage, and his second wife gave birth to five more. Tragedy struck when Michael passed away when Elizabeth was six, and Mary Jane remarried, then divorced, an abusive alcoholic. With the aspiration of becoming a teacher, Elizabeth enrolled in the State Normal School. Unable to afford the tuition, Elizabeth dropped out and helped her mother run a Pittsburgh boarding house.

In 1885, Elizabeth read a column in *The Pittsburgh Dispatch,* by Erasmus Wilson, that bore the title: "What Are Women Good For?" According to the post, the answer was, not much, other than "to be a helpmeet to a man." Erasmus described working women as a "monstrosity." Infuriated, Elizabeth wrote a scathing rebuttal and signed her letter, "Poor Little Orphan Girl." The newspaper's editor, George A. Madden, taken with the writer's moxie, ran an ad asking the Little Orphan Girl to reveal her identity. When Elizabeth came forward, he asked her to write a column that she entitled "The Girl Puzzle," that called for reform in the divorce laws that were weighted against wives. Madden offered her a full-time position at five dollars a week. Casting about for a nom de plume (she had previously added an 'e' to Cochran), Madden turned for inspiration to Pittsburgh-born Stephen Foster, who had penned "My Old Kentucky Home," the anthem of the Kentucky Derby. The editor landed on another Foster song, "Nelly Bly," though her editor misspelled it as Nellie, thus establishing her byline.

Elizabeth began her journalistic career by going undercover in sweatshops, reporting on the wretched conditions of their female workers. Infuriated factory owners threatened to withdraw their advertisements; consequently, the newspaper only allowed Elizabeth to write articles that fell into the category later known as "the pink ghetto," focusing on topics such as flower shows and fashion. Miserable, she convinced her bosses to make her a foreign correspondent, and she left for Mexico. For several months, she traveled throughout the country, reporting on corruption and poverty. Her acerbic articles infuriated the government and, fearing arrest, she returned to the States. Her experiences were chronicled in a book, *Six Months in Mexico*. Once again obliged to write on entertaining and childcare, Elizabeth quit in protest. Her last act before her departure was to leave a note on Erasmus' desk: "I'm off to New York. Look out for me. —Bly."

In New York, Elizabeth arranged a meeting with Joseph Pulitzer, owner of the *New York World*. Pulitzer agreed to employ her if she infiltrated the Women's Lunatic Asylum, located on Blackwell's Island (currently Roosevelt Island). The famed newspaper tycoon did not provide any plan on how to gain entry, or how to leave once committed. In 1887, the activist became an actress in order to appear a madwoman. Cochrane checked into a boarding house in the working-class Bowery District under the name Nellie Brown. She pretended she was from Cuba, wailed that she was searching for missing trunks, screamed (an act aided by rats scurrying across her pillow), and demanded a pistol. Her guise of insanity was so convincing that her roommate refused to sleep in the same room with her "for all the money of the Vanderbilts." Doctors declared her "positively demented." A few days later, Elizabeth was aboard a ferry, where she observed "two coarse, massive female attendants who expectorated tobacco juice about on the floor in a manner more skillful than charming."

In Blackwell's Island, Elizabeth joined sixteen hundred other unfortunates, and experienced inhumane treatments including filthy garments, rancid food, and sadistic caregivers. Complaints resulted in beatings with a broom. Elizabeth asked, "What, excepting torture, would produce insanity quicker than this treatment?" Baths consisted of three buckets of freezing water poured over her head that gave the sensation of drowning. When she was dripping wet, Nurse Ratchetts forced her into a garment that bore the words "Lunatic Asylum, B. I. H. 6" for Blackwell's Island, Hall 6. When Elizabeth asked for a suitable nightgown, an attendant sneered, "We have no such things here. You are in a public institution. Don't expect anything or any kindness here, for you won't get it." The twenty-three-year-old reporter lived among those who were psychotic and suicidal. Others were there because their husbands wanted them out of the way. One inmate's heavily accented German was mistaken for gibberish, which led to a diagnosis of madness. Even when Elizabeth dropped her act and appeared coherent, no attention was paid. Starving and exhausted, Elizabeth was overjoyed when lawyers from the *New York World* secured her release. Newspapers published Cochrane's exposé as *Ten Days in a Madhouse*; in it, she likened the asylum to a human rat trap, under the headline "Inside the Madhouse." The article recounted how hospital administrators injected their patients with so much morphine that they were rendered comatose. The account shocked the public to such a degree that a month later, the city added a million dollars to the institution's budget and arranged for the facility's facelift.

Bly became a journalistic Robin Hood, exposing the rotten core of the Big Apple. Whenever there was an injustice against women, children, or the poor, Nellie Bly was there. To investigate how females fared in New York City jails, she posed as a thief in order to experience incarceration. Her attempt failed when the police recognized her and gave her preferential treatment. On one occasion, she wrote about the black market, "I bought a baby last week, to learn how baby slaves are bought and sold in the city of New York. Think of it! An immortal soul bartered for ten dollars!"

Future assignments involved meeting the female power players of the day, such as Susan B. Anthony, whom Bly called the "champion of her sex." In articles about Emma Goldman, she portrayed the activist as a person rather than an anarchist. Ages ahead of her time, in a column she posed the marital question "Should Women Propose?" A nineteenth-century Renaissance woman, in her free time, Elizabeth took up elephant training and ballet.

After a stint in a madhouse, what could a famous reporter do next? Elizabeth found her idea in the Jules Verne novel *Around the World in Eighty Days*. She approached Pulitzer with the proposal that she could beat the record of protagonist Phileas Fogg. Although impressed by the concept, Pulitzer told her that her gender would make the trip impossible. Cochrane's response was, "Very well. Start the man, and I'll start the same day for some other newspaper and beat him." The *New York World* conceded. Cochrane added that she would make the trip without a chaperone, and with only one small satchel. Dressed in her trademark black-and-white plaid Ulster coat and hat that resembled Sherlock Holmes's deerstalker cap, Elizabeth boarded the steamship *Augusta Victoria*, bound for England.

In dispatches to the *New York World*, Elizabeth chronicled her experiences, such as the casino in Egypt where she lost money at roulette, the snake charmer in Ceylon, and the instruments of torture in China. Another stop was a visit to Verne and his wife, Honorine, at their home in Amiens, France. Committed to traveling light, her only souvenir was a monkey she christened McGinty, purchased for three dollars in Singapore. The *New York World* experienced a spike in sales covering her voyage. Riding the wave of the journalist's surging popularity, companies issued trading cards and games with her image; a hotel, a train, and a racehorse bore her name.

In a voyage that entailed donkeys, rickshaws, and horses, after seventy-two days, six hours, and eleven minutes, Elizabeth returned, an international celebrity. Thousands of fans greeted her as she stepped off the train; ten celebratory gunshots boomed from Battery Park; boats in New York Harbor sounded their horns. A mountain of congratulatory telegrams awaited, including one from Verne. Cochrane reveled in her reputation that, as an admirer put it, established the American woman as "pushing, determined, and independent." The young woman who embodied Scarlett O'Hara's waist as well as her gumption became America's most well-known woman. A book chronicled her adventures—*Nellie Bly's Book: Around the World in*

Seventy-two Days (1890). Because of her journalistic coup, Elizabeth expected a bonus and editorial recognition, but Pulitzer scarcely acknowledged her feat. Angered at the lack of appreciation, Cochrane quit and embarked on a lecture tour which earned her $9,500—$250,000 in contemporary currency. In 1890, upon the death of her brother Charles, Elizabeth took her widowed sister-in-law and her two children under her wing.

At age thirty, Elizabeth married Robert Livingston Seaman, a millionaire forty years her senior. Fans and friends joked that she was only trying wedlock for the story; however, she abandoned reporting to work with her husband in his steel-container business, the Iron Clad Manufacturing Company, which employed a work force of 1,500. Upon his death, she took over the factory and instituted numerous reforms, including health and recreation benefits, showing more empathy than business acumen. The business floundered, forcing Elizabeth into bankruptcy. Once again experiencing the financial straits of her childhood, she returned to journalism with the *World*, where her columns were dedicated to unearthing corruption. In 1913, Cochrane covered the Woman Suffrage Procession and published the report with the headline "Suffragettes Are Men's Superiors."

The draw of World War I proved a powerful magnet, and she boarded the *RMS Oceanic* for a three-week stint in Vienna; she became the first woman reporting on the Eastern Front. The *New York Evening Journal* published *Nellie Bly on the Firing Line*, a column that carried her reports of the carnage. In the thick of the fighting, she fell under suspicion and ended up under arrest as a British spy. In her final years, as a reporter for the *New York Journal*, Elizabeth took up the cause of abandoned, abused, and missing children and became a "fairy godmother" to an orphaned girl.

Elizabeth Cochrane, immortalized as Nellie Bly, passed away from pneumonia, and her interment took place in the Bronx. One would hope that her last thoughts, rather than returning to the ten days in the madhouse, instead relived her time of glory when she had, as the *New York World* had reported, "girdled the globe."

CHAPTER 3

"Never the Twain Shall Meet" (1876)

"Taxation without representation is a tyranny."
—PRINCESS SOPHIA DULEEP SINGH

When Jack let go of Rose's hand and disappeared into the icy depths of the Atlantic Ocean, *Titanic* fans let out a collective gasp. Those of a less romantic bent were left wondering why the elderly Rose consigned the diamond known as *Le Coeur de la Mer*, The Heart of the Ocean, to a watery grave. The non-celluloid counterpart to the fabulous blue gem reveals another tragic tale.

Princess Sophia Alexandrovna Duleep Singh was the granddaughter of Maharajah Ranjit Singh, the legendary one-eyed "Lion of the Punjab," who ruled the Sikh Empire that extended from the Khyber Pass in the west to Kashmir in the north to Tibet in the east. He rode through his empire with the storied Koh-I-Noor diamond strapped to his sleeve. A century later, the gem became the prize possession of Ranjit Singh. After his passing, at which time several of his wives burned themselves on his funeral pyre, the next maharaja was his son, Duleep Singh. The British seized control and forced the eleven-year-old to relinquish his kingdom to the crown. Four years later, Duleep left for exile in England, where he converted from Sikhism to Christianity. Queen Victoria said of her subject, "I always feel so much for these poor deposed Indian princes." Her pity did not extend to returning his lands or the Koh-I-Noor.

The king without a kingdom married Bamba Müller, who had been born in Cairo, the illegitimate daughter of a German merchant and an Abyssinian slave who placed their child in a missionary ward. In compensation for the confiscation of his birthright, Queen Victoria provided a 2.5-million-pound annual stipend in contemporary currency. The money led to Elveden Hall, a Suffolk estate transformed into a Mogul palace. Sophia was the fifth of his six surviving children, and the Singhs lived in great luxury; gardens held ostriches, leopards, and Indian hawks. Queen Victoria became Sophia's godmother and gifted the child a sumptuously dressed doll known as "Little Sophie." The Prince of Wales paid regular visits. A presentation for debutantes at Buckingham Palace ensured Sophia's social standing.

The idylls of the Punjab Princess came with an expiration date. Her parents' marriage ended due to her father's promiscuity, gambling, and opulent lifestyle. Unable to pay his exorbitant debts, Duleep—who referred to Queen Victoria as Mrs. Fagin after the criminal in *Oliver Twist*—dedicated himself to wresting back his stolen kingdom. When the British government foiled his attempt to return to India, Duleep ran off with Ada, a hotel chambermaid, leaving his family in dire financial circumstances. Upon hearing of his wife's death, he sent a telegram to his oldest son: "Heartbroken—will write next week." The deposed royal passed away at age fifty-five, destitute, in a Paris hotel, a casualty of the Raj. In an act of *noblesse oblige*, Queen Victoria installed her seventeen-year-old goddaughter in "a grace and favor" residence opposite Hampton Court Palace. The shy Sophia was content to dress in the latest Parisian fashions, breed her prize Pomeranians, and participate in the bicycle craze.

The pauper princess became a rebel with a cause through a series of events that made her no longer willing to be an exotic bird in a gilded cage. The initial event that awakened Sophia's political conscience occurred when Northwestern University, near Chicago, rescinded her sister Bamba's acceptance to study medicine—a career denied to women in the United Kingdom—as the public believed that lady doctors were an affront to the natural order of things. A despondent Bamba returned to England and shared her bitterness with Sophia.

Britain had forbidden the members of the Singh family to return to their ancestral homeland, fearing that the presence of the royals could incite dissent against the Raj. Dissent ran high in the country, as its people were not overjoyed with Queen Victoria's proclamation that India was the jewel in her crown. However, when the English planned a spectacular celebration near Delhi for the coronation of Edward VII, three of the Singh sisters secretly sailed for the subcontinent. The siblings rode across their lost lands on horseback and made their way north to the family's old stronghold of Lahore, where they realized the magnitude of what the British had stolen. The trip brought an understanding of why their father had been mired in a bitterness that eroded his soul. When she returned to England, Sophia was a committed anti-colonialist who wrote, "India awake and free yourself!" Sophia likened Britain's subjugation of its colonies to its oppression of women. The connection was made manifest after Lord George Curzon relinquished his post as Viceroy of India—where he vehemently opposed the country's independence—and became the president of the National League for Opposing Woman Suffrage.

Her first step on the crusader path was to sell copies of the *Suffragette* newspaper outside Hampton Court Palace. Her efforts earned her the name "the Hampton Court Harridan." If this were not infuriating enough for the crown, Sophia joined the Women's Tax Resistance League, an act that led to two court appearances. She told the authorities, "When the women of England are enfranchised, I shall pay my taxes willingly. If I am not a fit person for the purposes of representation, why should I be a fit person for taxation?" In response, bailiffs entered her home and left with valuable jewels as payment.

Princess Singh became affiliated with the Women's Society for Social and Political Union, the country's leading suffrage organization. The disenfranchised ladies chained themselves to lampposts, smashed windows, and bombarded parliament with complaints. Their efforts promised to bear fruit until Prime Minister Herbert Asquith sabotaged legislation that would have given women who owned property the right to vote. Infuriated, the spurned ladies turned to more militant measures.

In 1910, on "Black Friday," three hundred suffragettes marched to the seat of the British Parliament, the House of Commons. At the head of the group was the organization's leader, Emmeline Pankhurst; beside her was a diminutive woman, Sophia Singh. She was the focus of curiosity: she was Queen Victoria's goddaughter, a fixture at society parties, had graced the covers of fashion magazines. On this date, Sophia walked with a group who had been warned that, if they persisted, matters could turn ugly. Outside the Commons, police officers turned on the protestors, knocking them to the ground. Home Secretary Winston Churchill had ordered the officers to refrain from making arrests, as he did not want jails filled with rabble-rousing suffragettes, hell-bent on garnering publicity. Rather, the strategy was to tire the demonstrators, forcing them to leave of their own accord. For five hours, the scenario played out; at one point, Sophia charged at an officer who was harassing a demonstrator. Infuriated, Sophia demanded his badge number, and later lodged a formal complaint. Churchill signed a memo with the order to drop any investigation. Similarly, Churchill refused to look into the deaths of two women who had died of injuries sustained during the protest.

The following year, on the day of the King's Speech to Parliament, Sophia joined a march on Downing Street. Dressed as a fashionable matron and holding an expensive fur muff, police officers assumed she was a well-heeled bystander who had come to wave at the prime minister. The officers were shocked when she pushed her way through the crowds and threw herself at Prime Minister Asquith's car, shouting a feminist slogan. After the collision, she pulled from her muff and unfurled a banner that bore the words, "Give Women the Vote." As had her father before her, Sophia proved a thorn in the side of the British. King George V, Victoria's grandson, agitated by Sophia's civil disobedience, asked his staff, "Have we no hold on her?" The police hauled many of the protestors to jail, where the women embarked on hunger strikes. Afraid of being responsible for deaths on their watch, the authorities initiated forced feedings. Since she was Queen Victoria's goddaughter, Princess Singh did not spend time behind bars. Nevertheless, a folder held records of the princess turned protestor.

After World War I erupted, Sophia obeyed Pankhurst's order to suspend the struggle for suffrage in order to support the war effort. The outbreak of fighting provided an additional horror for Sophia, as her sister Catherine had moved to Germany after her marriage. Sophia raised money for Indian troops deployed on the Western Front, unaccustomed to the frigid temperature. She traded Parisian couture for the Red Cross nurse's uniform and tended to wounded Punjabi soldiers convalescing in Brighton. Although she hardly spoke a word of Hindi, the soldiers were overcome with emotion that their nurse was none other than the granddaughter of the great Maharaja, the Lion of the Punjab. Faced with financial hardship, and with the welcome mat to Hampton Court withdrawn, Princess Singh retreated to the countryside with one of her sisters. In her new lodging, Sophia harbored evacuees from London and provided an air raid shelter—one she never used. Instead, Sophia stayed in her house, blowing cigarette smoke out the window. No longer a clotheshorse, she most often sported a threadbare jacket and

Wellington boots. The only link to her past was her beloved Pomeranians.

The rebellious royal spent her old age in the company of her dogs, "Little Sophie" the only memento of her former opulence. Although she had played many roles in her tempest-tossed life, the one Sophia considered most essential was apparent from her entry in "Who's Who" that she contributed shortly before her death in 1948. Under Interests, she wrote, "The Advancement of Women."

Sophia lived long enough to see the success of both her life's causes, female suffrage and Indian independence. One event Sophia never witnessed was the return of the mythic Koh-I-Noor that had once graced the peacock throne of the Mughal emperor in Delhi. The diamond beyond price remains in the Tower of London. In all likelihood, the next time it makes a public appearance will be at the coronation of the future King Charles III, as an adornment of his consort, Camilla. Perhaps the Koh-I-Noor should be returned to India lest it bring misfortune to the House of Windsor, as it did to the Singh dynasty.

The interplay of two distinct cultures shaped the destiny of Princess Sophia, who, had fate played a different hand, would have been a majestic maharani. Her life disproves the words of Indian-British poet Rudyard Kipling, "Oh, East is East and West is West, and never the twain shall meet."

CHAPTER 4

"I'm No Angel" (1892)

"I used to be Snow White, but I drifted."

—MAE WEST

The leader of the pack for unabashed female sexuality was a lady who predated Mansfield, Monroe, and Madonna. The critic George Jean Nathan dubbed the bodacious blonde the Statue of Libido.

A master of erotic innuendo, Mae came from a working-class neighborhood of Brooklyn, the daughter of an Irish-American ex-boxer, John "Battling John" Patrick West, and his French-born wife, Mathilde ("Tillie"), a corset and fashion model. West was never jealous of her siblings because of her supreme self-absorption. She often commented, "I don't like myself. I'm crazy about myself." Mae was a Mount Everest of egomania, a trait she regarded as a virtue.

The precursor of Dr. Ruth, at age five, Ms. West found her passion at the Royal Theater, where she performed wearing a pink and green satin dress and won first prize in a talent competition. She later recounted, "I ached for it, the spotlight, which was like the strongest man's arms around me, like an ermine coat." Formal schooling went by the wayside in favor of vaudeville, and from the age of eight to eleven, Mae played the role of the moonshiner's daughter, Little Nell, who marched through saloon's swinging doors in search of her drunk father. In her early teens, Mae performed under the name "Baby Mae" and incorporated burlesque into her act. Frank Wallace, a song-and-dance man, was her co-star; the young entertainers secretly married in Milwaukee in 1911. Realizing she was not cut from the cloth of domestic diva, Mae helped her husband find a job with a show that was going on the road for forty weeks, a move calculated to dissolve both her professional and conjugal ties. She kept the marriage under wraps—mink, no doubt—until Frank resurfaced in 1941 and demanded a thousand dollars a month in alimony. They divorced in 1942. Asked if she would ever tie the knot again, Mae said, "Marriage is a fine institution, but I'm not ready for an institution."

The Mae moves, "the cooch and the shimmy," borrowed from a Black Chicago club, along with suggestive songs and double-entendre wisecracks, were too blatant for vaudeville, and Mae took her five-inch stiletto heels to Broadway. In 1926, she wrote a play whose title epitomized her life and career: *Sex*. *Variety* deemed it "the nastiest thing ever disclosed on the New York stage." The production's popularity skyrocketed, compliments of a New York City police raid instigated by the Society for the Suppression of Vice, a nineteenth-century organization dedicated to promoting public morality. The authorities closed her play, and the police arrested Ms. West on a charge of corruption of morals. The judge fined her five hundred dollars and issued a ten-day jail sentence. Afforded preferential treatment, she wore silk underwear instead of the state-issued ones. The publicity proved pure gold, and she proclaimed, "Censorship made me." Under her ample cleavage beat a caring heart, and in a letter to the governor of California, Mae praised the warden at San Quentin, saying, "I hope your Excellency will feel as I do and let Warden Duffy continue making bad men good, while I continue making good men bad." The inmates sent her a collective valentine.

In New Jersey in 1928, Mae came up with her alter ego "Diamond Lil" for a show in which the leading lady reclined in a golden bed, perusing the *Police Gazette*. The play delivered a West witticism—directed at a Salvation Army captain played by Cary Grant—as "Come on up," but it is remembered as, "Come up and see me sometime." The star-author took "Diamond Lil" on a national tour and penned her first novel, *The Constant Sinner*. Lampooned by the conservative press, hounded by censors, West put the roar into the 1920s.

After the Wall Street crash extinguished the lights of Broadway, Ms. West, lured by Hollywood, headed in the direction of her name. Not one to be overawed by the big-boy bosses who ran Tinseltown, she boasted, "I'm not a little girl from a little town making good in a big town; I'm a big girl from a big town making good in a little town."

Although her image suggested she only cared about horizontal positions, she was extremely astute in marketing Mae West. She had honed her act from burlesque, Black music, and dance, and demanded to write her own screenplays. The West persona was chiseled platinum hair, a sin-suggestive strut, and an elongated delivery of lines, stretching each word into as many syllables as possible, ("fas-cin-a-tin"). In a scene from her 1932 debut film, *Night After Night*, Ms. Mae, decked out with diamonds, entered a speakeasy. When the hat-check girl exclaimed, "Goodness, what beautiful diamonds!" the forty-year-old actress purred, "Goodness had nothing to do with them." The quip led to the title of her autobiography, *Goodness Had Nothing to Do with It.*

Ms. West chose as her male lead a "sensational-looking young man" whom she spotted walking along the street. Smitten, she declared, "If he can talk, I'll take him." The unknown actor was Cary Grant, with whom she co-starred in a movie in which she fulfilled her lifelong fantasy—being a lion-tamer. Refusing to use a stunt double in the animal-training scenes, Mae entered the cage replete with boots and whip. In the film, she uttered the famous phrase, "Beulah, peel me a grape," a line based on her grape-peeling pet monkey. The notorious leading lady earned the highest salary of any Hollywood star: $300,000 per picture—an astronomical price in the midst of the Great Depression—thereby proving the truth of her quip "The curve is more powerful than the sword."

What followed was a series of highly popular comedies, such as *She Done Him Wrong*, *Go West Young Man*, and *My Little Chickadee*, in the latter of which W.C. Fields co-starred. A West witticism regarding her screen career was, "I'm the woman who works at Paramount all day and Fox all night."

Mae became a film goddess during the silver screen's golden era, keeping men securely pinned beneath her double-decker stilettos. Her name became an entry in the *Webster's New International Dictionary* when the ogling servicemen of World War II christened an inflatable life jacket after the siren. Men were her domain, and the only women she had close relationships with were her mother and sister. The girl from the blue-collar Brooklyn neighborhood was the highest-paid woman in the United States.

Finally, Mae met some men she did not desire: the censors of the Hays Office—the film industry's watchdog. They were less than impressed with her song "A Guy What Takes His Time" with its lyric, "I don't like a big commotion. I'm a demon for slow motion." Although West's popularity had rescued Paramount Pictures from bankruptcy, they did not protect her from the hounds of Hays. Unlike her contemporaries, she refused to let the men in suits alter her image. Another hound of public purity was William Randolph Hearst, who used his newspaper empire to pillory her in the press. "Isn't it time Congress did something about Mae West?" (Hypocritically, at the time, Hearst was canoodling with his mistress, actress Marion Davies, at his mega-mansion, San Simeon.) Mae's response to the slings and arrows aimed in her direction was, "I believe in censorship. I made a fortune out of it." After the sanitization of her pictures, that did not align with her artistic vision, West bid farewell—no doubt with a ring-bedecked middle finger—to Hollywood.

With her hefty bank account, West purchased a home, a shrine to herself. A nude marble statue of the diva stood on her grand piano; on the wall hung a painting of a reclining Mae in which she had also dispensed with garments. Her bedroom held a plethora of mirrors because "I like to see how I'm doin'."

In her later years, journalists who expected to find the aged star taking refuge in yesteryear, a self-pitying Norma Desmond, were in for a surprise. The octogenarian was still preoccupied with all matters horizontal—at age seventy-eight, she claimed that in one marathon session, she had sex twenty-six times in a single day. However, her alter ego "Diamond Lil" was not a portrayal of the private Ms. West. She lived with her bodyguard, Paul Novak, thirty years her junior, whom she had persuaded to change his name from Chester Rybinski. She took her writing seriously, and despite her image as the symbol of hedonism, Mae led a private life of dogged discipline. Under the sequined, form-hugging, cleavage-baring gowns was an artist who orchestrated her moves and movies. Never a fan of tobacco or alcohol, the five-foot-two star followed an organic diet that included fresh fruits sprinkled with almond powder and honey.

West toured for years in *Catherine the Great*, in which she was the only female actress (a ratio in which she reveled). As the Tsarina, she surrounded herself with an imperial guard of muscular, six-foot-tall young men. Her twilight years were dedicated to mediums and ESP, and she became a devoted follower of astrologer Sydney Omarr. Her aged countenance resembled a wax-colored mask, and her hourglass figure had expanded. Mae did not care that her slinky gowns showed off her expanding girth. "I never worry about diets. The only carrots that interest me are the number you get in a diamond." After twenty-four years of retirement, Ms. West left her mirror-lined bedroom to appear in Gore Vidal's *Myra Breckenridge* where she had a falling-out with fellow diva Raquel Welch. Her last rendezvous with the silver screen was at age eighty-five, when she starred in the appropriately-titled *Sextette*. As proof the lady still possessed spunk and a salacious spirit, she delivered the indelible words in her final film: "Is that a gun in your pocket, or are you just glad to see me?"

Mae's notoriety rests on her movies that sent seismic waves of scandal through a conservative Hollywood. She also gained goddess stature when Salvador Dali created the Mae West Lips Sofa, one of the twentieth century's most iconic pieces of furniture. Another Mae milestone was her appearance on the cover of the *Sgt. Pepper's Lonely Heart Club Band* album. When the Beatles contacted her to ask permission to use her likeness, Mae agreed, but she added the quip, "What would I be doing in a lonely hearts club?" The band placed her next to the image of Lenny Bruce, who also pushed the boundaries of free speech.

"A real star never stops," Ms. West said after her release from Good Samaritan Hospital, where she spent three months recovering from a stroke and a concussion. And she never did stop, until she passed away in her Hollywood home at age eighty-eight. Novak, her companion of twenty-six years, opted for an open casket because he claimed his gal still looked great. The ageless actress died a cult figure who had shown that carnal pleasure was not synonymous with brimstone. For West, the only sin was hypocrisy. An apt metaphor for the incomparable Ms. West could well have been the title of one of her movies, *I'm No Angel*.

CHAPTER 5

"I Do Not Give a Damn" (1893)

"The first thing I do in the morning is brush my teeth and sharpen my tongue."

—DOROTHY PARKER

Legions of literary ladies dream of heading for New York City to become the new Dorothy Parker, the wit with the serrated teeth who achieved renown as the Guinevere of the Algonquin Round Table. Would-be Parker acolytes might reconsider walking in her pumps if they understood the pain behind Mrs. Parker's wisecracks.

The woman who descended on New York City, torching pretension and pomposity, was the daughter of a prosperous "cloak and suitor" (her description), J. Henry Rothschild, and Eliza Annie. When anyone asked if she were a relation of the banking family, her invariable response, "My God, *no*, dear! We'd never even *heard* of *those* Rothschilds!" A premature baby, Dorothy quipped that her birth was the first and only time she didn't arrive late. When questioned about her ethnicity, Dorothy's answer was that she was a mongrel, a reference to her Christian/Jewish parentage. She said that, if she were ever to write her autobiography, it would be entitled *Mongrel*. Her obsession with death can be attributed to her mother who "promptly went and died on me" when Dorothy was five years old. An anecdote illustrated her lack of connection with her siblings. Her brother's friend pointed at her and asked if she was his sister. His response: "No."

Dorothy described herself as "a plain, disagreeable child with stringy hair and a yen to write poetry," and her self-esteem did not improve when her father and despised stepmother, Eleanor, enrolled her in Miss Dana's School in Morristown, New Jersey, followed by a stint at the Convent of the Sacred Heart school in New York. Her insistence that the Immaculate Conception resulted from spontaneous combustion left the nuns unimpressed, and her expulsion, which she referred to as her firing, ended her education.

Her lifelong activism manifested itself on the occasion when she observed a Christmas scene from her window. She recalled, "I think I first knew what side I was on when I was about five years old, at which time nobody was safe from buffaloes. My rich aunt—a horrible woman then and now—had come to visit. I remember going to the window and seeing the street with the men shoveling snow, their feet wrapped with burlap. And my aunt said, 'Now, isn't it nice there's this blizzard. All these men have work.' I knew then that it was not so nice that there were men who worked only in desperate weather."

Henry had made unwise investments, and his death in 1914, hastened by grief at his brother's loss on the *Titanic*, required Dorothy to find employment as a piano player in a dance school. As Europe was girding for war, Miss Rothschild sent out her poem "Any Porch," that skewered the spoiled upper-crust ladies of Connecticut. She was over the moon with her acceptance from *Vanity Fair*, and with characteristic chutzpah requested a full-time job; a few months later, publisher Condé Nast hired her for *Vogue*, another of his magazines. For a salary of ten dollars a week, Dorothy provided advertising captions. Under a photograph of revealing undergarments, she wrote, "Brevity is the soul of lingerie." (The risqué endorsement must have had the nuns reaching for smelling salts.) Writing kept her sane and, with a pen as her sword, she railed against rules regulating female behavior, predating the sentiments of *Sex and the City*. Dorothy married Edwin Pond Parker II, who returned from the World War I an alcoholic; she claimed to have chosen him for his "nice, clean surname." Even after their 1928 divorce, she went by the name Mrs. Parker.

After P. G. Wodehouse's retirement, Dorothy assumed his position and became the youngest, and only female, drama critic at *Vanity Fair*. For the next decade, she savaged playwrights and actors. Of one of the former, she wrote, "The only 'ism' Hollywood believes in is plagiarism"; of a performance by Katherine Hepburn, Dorothy wrote, "She ran the gamut of emotions from A to B." Her legendary wit proved a two-edged sword: *Vanity Fair* fired her when she made a wisecrack at the expense of Billie Burke (Glinda the Good Witch in *The Wizard of Oz*), the wife of Florenz Ziegfeld, Jr., the magazine's top advertiser. Colleague Robert Benchley quit in protest, and the friends rented an office near Times Square they dubbed Park-Bench. Mrs. Parker observed, "The office was so tiny that one square less and it would have constituted adultery."

Due to its proximity to *Vanity Fair*'s offices, Mrs. Parker and Benchley, along with other authors, congregated at the Algonquin Hotel, nicknamed the Gonk. In order to accommodate the literary lights, owner Frank Chase furnished the regulars with a large round table, and Mrs. Parker, the only female core member, became its spokesperson. While proper women of her era rarely uttered sexual innuendoes, during their libelous luncheons, Mrs. Parker remarked of a Yale prom, "If all the girls attending it were laid end to end, I wouldn't be at all surprised." Peripatetic visitors included F. Scott Fitzgerald, Noel Coward, and Harpo Marx. The group became known as the Vicious Circle, and Mrs. Parker—friends called her Dottie—reigned with homicidal humor. Behind her verbal blood sport, Dorothy championed sobering topics, ones not considered the domain of the little ladies of the era. She aimed her poisoned barbs at the Roaring Twenties prejudices: racism, sexism, xenophobia.

In a nod to the cliché "looking for love in all the wrong places," Dorothy's second and third trips down the aisle were with the bisexual actor and writer Alan Campbell. She later proclaimed in public that he was "queer as a billy goat." Lured by the lucre of writing for the silver screen, Alan convinced Mrs. Parker to relocate to the West Coast. Mr. Campbell was the possessor of their contract from Metro-Goldwyn-Mayer; Mrs. Parker was the possessor of her old emotional baggage: fear of loneliness, flirtation with suicide, fealty to alcohol. Of the latter, she explained, "I am not a writer with a drinking problem. I'm a

drinker with a writing problem." Her liquid lunches—
many downed during Prohibition—led to the line,
"One more drink and I'd be under the host."

Mrs. Parker and hubby worked on sixteen screenplays
that she pronounced trite. She was unimpressed by
her five thousand dollars a week paycheck; at the
height of the Depression, the average family income
was $1,500 annually. Her contempt of the rich was
apparent in her quip, "If you want to know what God
thinks of people with money, look at the people he
gave it to." Even her Academy Award nomination
for her contribution to *A Star is Born*, starring Judy
Garland, failed to improve her relationship with
Tinseltown. When Louis B. Mayer sent his assistant
to complain about a missed deadline, she told the
messenger, "Tell him I was too fucking busy—or
vice versa."

Dorothy had once compared love to quicksilver: "The
harder you clutch it, the more it slips through your
fingers," an analogy that echoed her romantic history.
A master of self-sabotage, her three marriages (two
with Alan Campbell) and other romantic relationships
hit road-bumps. Dorothy chose emotionally
unavailable men, or those who had the unwelcome
appendage of a wife. As per usual, Dorothy hid
her heartbreak behind a wisecrack: "Take me or
leave me; or, as is the usual order of things, both."
After becoming pregnant with playwright Charles
MacArthur's baby, she had an abortion. Afterwards,
she flippantly remarked, "That's what I get for putting
all my eggs into one bastard." Although Dorothy had
scoffed at love, the last stanza of her final poem,
"War Song," showed it actually was her Holy Grail:

"Only for the nights that were/Soldier, and dawns that came/When in sleep you turn to her/Call her by my name." Insight as to why Dorothy never achieved a lasting relationship can be gleaned from a phrase she suggested for her epitaph: "If you can read this, you've come too close."

Dismissive of the vacuity of Los Angeles, Mrs. Parker threw herself into radical politics. Years before, the police had arrested her as she protested the execution of avowed anarchists Sacco and Vanzetti. Along with Oscar Hammerstein II, Dorothy founded the Hollywood Anti-Nazi League, the first union for screenwriters. A strong advocate for justice, Parker established a committee to defend the Scottsboro boys, eight Black youths falsely accused of raping two white women in Alabama. Dorothy smuggled herself into Madrid, and her account of its siege, that involved a Luftwaffe bombing, is a tribute to the country's freedom fighters. Friends who did not measure up to her standards for militancy against fascism were immediately dropped. Alan worried that her involvement with left-wing causes would result in their blacklisting by the studios. In response, Dorothy called him a coward, a homosexual, and a "fawn's ass." In 1953, the House Un-American Activities Committee launched an investigation into Mrs. Parker's radical activities. Asked whether she had ever been a member of the Communist Party, Dorothy pleaded the Fifth Amendment. The curtain closed on Tinseltown.

Disillusioned, in homing-pigeon fashion, Dorothy returned to a New York devoid of her old friends such as Benchley, Fitzgerald, and Woolcott (the latter described her as "so odd a blend of Little Nell and Lady Macbeth"), who had drunk themselves to death. Her final years proved the truth of her earlier observation, "We all become the thing we hate the most." Always indifferent to money, Dorothy rented a furnished apartment at the Volney Hotel, on the Upper East Side, a room that would have sent Martha Stewart running for smelling salts. Overflowing ashtrays, unwashed martini glasses, and the droppings from her dog did not help the horror of her home. Mrs. Parker, who claimed she was just a "little Jewish girl trying to be cute," passed away from a heart attack in 1967, at age seventy-three. Her will left instructions for her cremation, and when no one claimed her urn, her lawyer's partner kept them in his filing cabinet for fifteen years. Thus, her remains began a fifty-three-year odyssey.

An activist to the end, Mrs. Parker had instructed Lillian Hellman to give her estate and future royalties to Dr. Martin Luther King, Jr. A year after his assassination, the money went to the National Association for the Advancement of Colored People. Two decades later, the organization interred her in the grounds of their headquarters in Baltimore. A memorial plaque marked the spot with Mrs. Parker's suggested epitaph: "Excuse my dust." When the NAACP relocated in 2020, Dottie returned to her beloved New York; her final resting place is in Woodlawn Cemetery in the Bronx, alongside her parents and grandparents.

What lay behind Mrs. Parker's "attitude" can be understood in the last lines of her poem "Observation": "But I shall stay the way I am/Because I do not give a damn."

CHAPTER 6

"Imperfect in Many Ways" (1899)

"Sorrow lies like a heartbeat behind everything I have written."

—P. L. TRAVERS

What child has not wished for a grown-up to transform the black and white of everyday to Technicolor? Such is the timeless appeal of Mary Poppins, who was the friend of a dancing chimney sweep, arranged for parties held on the ceiling, slid up a banister—exploits that beat a proper English tea. What is surprising is that the exemplary English nanny was the brainchild of an Australian writer whose life gave the lie to the idea of maternal instinct.

The creator of a perennial childhood classic was born Helen Lyndon Goff in Queensland, Australia, the oldest of three daughters. Lyndon, the name she went by, adored her alcoholic bank-manager father, but he was tight-fisted with his approval. When Lyndon showed him a poem she wrote, he responded, "Hardly Mr. Yeats." His passing, when Lyndon was seven, plunged his family into despair and financial destitution. His distraught widow ran out of the house during a thunderstorm, yelling that she was leaving to drown herself in a nearby river. She did not follow through with her threat; however, it cemented in her oldest daughter's mind the story about a woman who would drop from the sky to protect her young charges. More than a spoonful of sugar would have been needed to sweeten such a childhood.

Lacking the funds to attend university, out of place in strait-laced Australia, Lyndon embarked for England in her early twenties, and in a bid to start life anew, she christened herself Pamela Lyndon Travers. She arrived in her adopted country with five pounds in her pocket and a heart filled with great expectations.

When her aspirations of becoming an actress floundered, Lyndon determined to earn her livelihood with her pen. She submitted her work to the weekly journal the *Irish Statesman* (as the Emerald Isle was the land of her father's heritage); its editor, George Russell, introduced Lyndon to Madge, the daughter of Sir Francis Burnand, a playwright and the former editor of the magazine *Punch*. To the accompaniment of raised eyebrows, the women began living together, first in a London apartment, later in a nine-hundred-year-old thatched cottage mentioned in the *Domesday Book*, an arrangement rumored to be a lesbian relationship. What helped fuel salacious speculation was Madge's photograph of Lyndon on an Italian beach that showed her only wearing shorts and a floppy hat.

A champion of the underdog, Lyndon took a trip to Soviet Russia. Her empathy with the poor would be reflected in Mary Poppins's world, where an old woman sings "Feed the Birds"; a role played by the eighty-five-year-old Jane Darwell, whose last screen role had been as Ma Joad in *The Grapes of Wrath.* The trip to Moscow became the subject of her first book, which Lyndon dedicated "to HLG," her birth initials.

During a period of convalescence from pleurisy, the beloved nanny waltzed into her Sussex cottage. She later recounted, "I think the idea of Mary Poppins has been blowing in and out of me, like a curtain at a window, all my life." Her secret power as a writer was her ability to tap into the wistful world of youthful innocence. In a leap of faith, she sent out her manuscript for publication under the name P. L. Travers; it became an immediate critical success, translated into twenty languages. Initially, Lyndon had approached E. H. Shepard, who had provided the illustrations for *Winnie the Pooh*, but when he refused the collaboration, she hired his daughter Mary. On the cover of the original book, Poppins resembled a stiff peg doll; the portrait was in keeping with the text, where various characters stated that she is "not much to look at." Ms. Travers always made the point that her books were essentially Zen stories for adults, as she believed grown-ups needed Mary the most. The nonpareil Mary Poppins brought fame, and Lyndon rewrote her past.

After a decade, with the end of her relationship with Madge, and her family in Australia, Lyndon set her sights on having a child and attempted to adopt her teenage maid. Despite Travers's argument that the girl's parents had more than enough children of their own, and that the girl would no longer have to be a maid, they refused.

Needing a change of scene, Travers visited George Russell in Ireland and immersed herself in its literary milieu. With characteristic chutzpah, Lyndon gathered rowan branches and presented them to William Butler Yeats in Merrion Square. In return, Yeats showed her his canary's eggs. Entranced by Irish folklore, Travers joined in the Dublin literati's embrace of Eastern mysticism, which is how she came under the sway of the twentieth-century Russian guru George Gurdjieff and his sidekick, Piotr Ouspensky. The novelist believed Gurdjieff was a visionary; the other school of thought was that he was an oversexed con man who had fathered seven children by seven disciples. Peddling a mishmash of Hinduism and the occult, the con artists fleeced their wealthy followers. Travers became an adherent of yoga and draped herself in scarves; at Gurdjieff's passing, she sat by his embalmed feet. She later became the second Western woman to study Zen in Kyoto.

In 1940, while in Ireland, Lyndon heard of Joseph and Vera Hone, who were raising their four grandchildren in poverty, and contacted them about adoption. The Hones thought the childless, wealthy writer, author of the world's most nurturing nanny, was the answer to their prayers, and offered her their six-month-old twins. Lyndon insisted she could only take one of the boys, and on the advice of her astrologer, or because she preferred the name Camillus over Anthony, she made her fateful choice. At No. 17 Cherry Tree Lane, medicine tasted like candy; under the surface, life was not as magical in Chelsea. While his twin lived in squalor, Camillus was heir to a life of vacations in the French Riviera, private schools, and a home in luxurious Chelsea. His upbringing also entailed his mother's irritation when he cried at night, and misbehavior resulted in threats to send him to the orphanage at Tunbridge Wells. When the Blitz rained death from the sky, mother and son spent the war years in the American Southwest, living among the Navajos. In addition to the scarves, Lyndon wore flouncy skirts and armloads of silver bangles. Bisexual, she fell for the Irish Francis Macnamara, father of Caitlin, the poet Dylan Thomas's wife.

Ever the mythmaker, Lyndon told Camillus that his father had been a sugar magnate who passed away in the tropics. The lie came to light when Camillus Travers ran into his twin brother, Anthony Hone, in a London pub. No doubt their conversation revolved around stronger language than supercalifragilisticexpialidocious. The twins never bonded; the only commonality they shared, other than appearance, was their antipathy to Lyndon and a love of liquor. Camillus spent six months in prison for driving drunk without a license; both men died of alcoholism.

Worlds collided when, in a home outside Hollywood, on Christmas Eve, eleven-year-old Diane Disney shared with her father her beloved book about a magical nanny. For the next decade, Walt made repeated efforts to acquire the film rights to *Mary Poppins*. While most authors would be over the moon at a chance to have their novel turned into a Disney production, P. L. Travers steadfastly resisted. She maintained that her writing was intended to convey universal truths, rather than portray anthropomorphic animals and sudden bursts of song. In 1959, Lyndon finally relented and received script approval, $100,000 up front, and a 5 percent cut of the gross, which made her a millionaire many times over. On her flight to La-La Land, there was no room on the overhead luggage rack for her suitcase, and a young woman with a baby offered to have hers removed. Travers eyed her baby and asked, "Will the child be a nuisance?"

Travers proved Disney's nemesis, and she bombarded the movie mogul with pages of notes about scenes that were antithetical to her vision. The actors who played Jane and Michael Banks were in for a rude awakening: Julie Andrews, dressed in prim Edwardian clothes, puffed on cigarettes and used words unbefitting a proper nanny; Dick Van Dyke arrived with hangovers not improved by singing "chim chiminy chim chim cheree"; Ms. Travers had little tolerance for the child stars.

Disney deliberately withheld an invitation to Travers for the 1964 premiere, but, ever resourceful, she managed to secure a ticket. The shortest verse in the King James Bible is, "Jesus wept." Travers did the same as she watched the celluloid version of her book. Indeed, Travers was so disenchanted with Hollywood executives that in her will she added the provision that no Americans could ever be involved with anything related to *Mary Poppins*. However, Lyndon longed for a stage production, and she would likely have been pleased with the British production of Sir Cameron Mackintosh's 2004 adaptation; no doubt she would have insisted on endless revisions. The juggernaut allowed Disney to purchase land in Florida for his second theme park and made Travers a millionaire. With her windfall, she purchased a home where her neighbor was actor Michael Caine.

In her later years, Lyndon became a writer-in-residence at Radcliffe and Smith Colleges and received an honorary degree from Chatham College, Pittsburgh, in 1978. Poet Ted Hughes said his wife Sylvia Plath, a Smith graduate, had claimed that Mary Poppins was the fairy godmother of her childhood. Another accolade was achieved on the occasion the queen bestowed upon her the Order of the British Empire.

Ever more cantankerous with age, Lyndon's golden years were lonely. Her Disney fame had waned as her name had been excised from the film, future books were panned if they did not include Mary, and she had few friends. Writing remained her outlet, and Lyndon worked as a contributing editor to the New York-based magazine *Parabola*, where she penned meditative essays devoted to searching for meaning. By the time she reached her nineties, her attention was mainly focused on orchestrating her funeral. Private to the end, Lyndon announced that she did not want her death notice to reveal personal information.

The west wind finally took Travers at age ninety-six. At the conclusion of her final novel, *Mary Poppins Opens the Door*, Mary leaves the children and disappears. P. L. Travers wrote, "The bright shape speeding through the air above them would forever keep its secret. But in the summer days to come and the long nights of winter, they would remember... Mary Poppins herself had flown away, but the gifts she had brought would remain for always." The words can apply to the author herself. What made her so relatable was that she was imperfect in many ways.

CHAPTER 7

"What's So Frightening About That?" (1903)

"I want to push the nose of my sailing boat into every creek and to point my skis down every possible gully of the mountain."

—ELLA MAILLART

There exists a breed of people who hear the dog whistle of travel and are inexorably drawn by the Pied Piper of adventure. Some of the legendary explorers have been the Italian Marco Polo, the Portuguese Ferdinand Magellan, the British Robert Scott. Another was a Swiss woman who journeyed far afield from the white-capped Alps.

Her contemporary Sarah Marquis, who walked ten thousand miles in three years, sometimes existing on grubs and snake blood, said that if Ella Maillart had been a man, their native Switzerland would have lionized their wandering daughter. Ella, nicknamed Kini, was born in Geneva, the only child of Paul, a wealthy furrier, and Dagmar, his Danish wife. A sickly child, Ella spent her bedridden days reading adventure books, poring over maps that whetted her desire for adventure.

When Ella was ten, the family moved to a lakeside villa on Lake Geneva, where the adrenaline junkie learned to sail and ski. At age sixteen, she founded her country's first female field hockey team, the Champel Hockey Club, which she served as captain. Sports were the way Ella countered the boredom she always felt in school. In 1924, she represented Switzerland as the only woman in single-handed yachting at the Paris Olympics. Her skill at skiing was such that, in the years 1931–1934, Maillart was a member of the Swiss National Ski Team.

Drawn more by wanderlust than academia, at age seventeen, Ella dropped out of school in order to concentrate on discovering her life's calling. At loose ends, Ella, accompanied by her childhood best friend, Hermine de Saussure, embarked on Hermine's boat *Perlette* for a six-month voyage, where they sailed from Cannes to Corsica. Her next watery quest was, along with four other women, aboard the *Bonita*, a trip that followed the trail of Ulysses to the Ionian Islands and Ithaca. Upon her return, her father informed her that, as his business was floundering, she needed to become self-supporting. Ella's same-sex sexuality excluded marriage, and she cast about for a career that would make her life a continual holiday—an unrealistic goal, but one Maillart was determined to achieve.

Ella embarked on a number of jobs and journeys and became a familiar figure on the sailing circuit in the 1920s and '30s. On one occasion, the commander of the British Mediterranean fleet received an official reprimand because the entire fleet missed a lights-out order while the Admiral entertained the attractive Ms. Maillard and three other yachtswomen. Her various jobs entailed a stint as a French teacher in Wales and acting in a German mountain film.

During a stay in Berlin in 1929, her encounters with Russian émigrés inspired her to write articles on Russian cinema. Charmian London, the widow of Jack London, also in Germany, contributed fifty dollars toward her trip to Moscow and arranged for Ella to stay with Countess Tolstoy, the daughter-in-law of Leo Tolstoy. Ella made her way to Stalin's Soviet Union despite the fact it was a dangerous venture for anyone, especially an unaccompanied woman. Undaunted, Ella skied on the mountain range Sary-Tor, studied film production, and became fluent in Russian. A rolling stone, she walked across the Caucasus Mountains and discovered the hidden valley of Svanetia. Maillart tried to put together a women's field hockey team in Russia and rowed for the Alimentation Workers' Eight. The trip to the USSR and her trek through the Caucasus whetted her appetite for exploration of the Far East. The Swiss adventurer was a trailblazer who broke the glass ceiling for solo women travelers.

In 1932, Ella stood on a mountain, bicycle by her side, and saw, shimmering in the East, the mysterious expanse of the Takl Makan, the territory belonging to China, closed to foreigners. However, Ms. Maillart's creed was, "Nobody can go? Then I shall go." An introduction to a Paris publisher by a well-known yachtsman she had met on the Riviera helped combine wanderlust with a career as an author. Of her livelihood she said, "I write with my foot." Her Caucasus trek became the subject of her books *Parmi La Jeunesse Russe*, 1932, and *Turkestan Solo*, 1934, that included the episode where she spent time with the Kirghiz and Kazakh tribesmen. In one of her pages, she shared her experiences, "...from the heights of the celestial Mountains, I could see, on a plain far away and further still to the east, the yellow dust of the Takla Makan desert. It was China, the fabulous country of which, since my childhood, I had dreamed." The fly in her travel ointment was that China had erected a bamboo curtain, making it inaccessible to outsiders. Nevertheless, Maillart was of the ilk who only heeded their inner compass.

Three years later, Maillart embarked on a harrowing seven-month, 3,500-mile trek from Beijing to Kashmir to Srinagar, India. Her goal was to get "as far as possible from the world of luxury hotels." By way of supplies, Ella set off with two pounds of marmalade, a rifle, a bottle of Worcestershire sauce, writing paper, and a Leica camera. She understood the threat that the local men regarded foreign women as free for the taking, and as a precaution she brought along syphilis medication against the contingency of rape. Ella also brought along Peter Fleming, a *Times of London* correspondent and brother of Ian Fleming, author of the James Bond novels. She had reconnected with Peter when the French newspaper *Petit Parisien* had sent her as special correspondent to Manchuria, where he was reporting for *The Times*. After Peter informed Ella she could accompany him, Ella replied, "I beg your pardon. It's my route and it's I who will take you, if I can think of some way in which you can be useful to me." In actuality, she would have preferred to travel on her own, but Ms. Maillart, aware that foreigners were barred from the warlord-controlled territory, decided it might behoove her to have a friend in case she ended up behind bars.

Together they embarked on a 3,500-mile trip that took them from Peking through the Taklamakan desert and Sin-kiang to Kashmir. Well versed in the ways of the uncharted road, Ella understood the dangers and took the necessary precautions. She was appalled at Peter's lack of planning, at his refusal to be vaccinated against the typhus rampant in China. Most of their journey was undertaken by foot, and they stayed in traditional hogans and visited the Kumbum monastery in eastern Tibet, as had Alexandra David-Neel, the first Westerner to enter Lhasa when it was off-limits to Westerners. In central Asia, they made their way on a caravan that consisted of 250 camels and thirty horses. Fleming, an amateur adventurer, had the better part of their trek: Ella could walk fourteen miles without eating, pitch a tent, cook outdoors in freezing wind, and sew. She was also willing to wash her companion's clothes, and Peter admitted, "It was she, and not I, who did the dirty work." Fleming was also impressed with Ella's tough-as-nails personality. After suffering a severe burn in an incident with a petrol stove, she sprinkled tannic acid on her wound and soldiered on while she let "the lymph drip on the road." Toward the end of their expedition, every night, Peter chanted, "Sixty *li* nearer to London." In contrast, Ella wanted to linger, as she felt that foreign shores were home. Her reluctance to return to Switzerland was also because Europe was teetering on the brink of war.

She immortalized their trip in her 1937 book, in which she wrote that she "would have liked the journey to last for the rest of my life." Her account of a child and newborn lambs on a yurt floor, covered with animal waste, provided a revealing insight into 1935 Turkestan. Upon his return to England, Peter married the actress Celia Johnson; Ella left on another odyssey, with a companion far different from Fleming.

Annemarie Schwarzenbach was the daughter of a wealthy Zurich family who had ties to the Bismarcks and harbored Nazi sympathies. She rebelled against her parents' politics by adopting a bohemian lifestyle and indulging in lesbian love affairs. She harbored a lifelong, though unrequited, flame for Thomas Mann's daughter, Erika; Mann referred to Schwarzenbach as "a ravaged angel." Another of Annemarie's unrequited passions was for the American author Carson McCullers. An additional passion was for morphine. In 1939, after her father presented Annemarie with a car, Ella was jubilant. "A Ford! That's the car to climb the new Hazarejat road to Afghanistan." Ella also hoped their time on the road would free her lover from the clutches of her drug addiction. The two women had more than their fair share of drama: a high-speed chase with the police in Azerbaijan and an escape from officials near the Iran-Afghanistan border.

The plan seemed to be working. Ella arranged their route so they would stay in off-the-beaten-track villages where drugs were not available. However, in Bulgaria, at a hotel in Sofia, Schwarzenbach relapsed. As they drove into Turkey, silence reigned in the Ford until they reached Istanbul, where Annemarie asked Ella why she cared about someone like her. Ella wrote in her book about their trip, *The Cruel*

"Why do I bother about you... I don't know. I can't say it's because I love you, because I detest you when I see such gifts as yours spoilt as they are." In Kabul, Annemarie relapsed, and the two lovers parted ways. After leaving Annemarie with a pair of French archaeologists, Ella recanted her confession that she did not love the tragic Annemarie. "I think I loved her profoundly."

Ella spent the years of World War II in India, visiting ashrams and gurus, and stayed with Ramana Maharshi, as she chronicled in her 1949 book, *Land of the Sherpas.* After the land dubbed "the rooftop of the world," Maillart settled down in a converted-chapel chalet in Chandolin, one of the highest villages in the Swiss Alps, the first home she had owned. She christened her mountain hideaway Atchalan in a nod to Arunatchala, the sacred hill overlooking the ashram of Ramana Maharshi. In her eighties, she actualized one of her ambitions by visiting the South Pacific and, at age eighty-three, Ella set off for her final expedition in Tibet.

Maillart's home is currently a museum that displays her photographs, drawings, and objects from her sojourns. Visitors can view Ella's Royal Geographical Society Fellows card, the boots she wore on her trek across Afghanistan, and a poster of the timetables of the South Manchurian Railway, dated 1934.

Ella's last adventure was in 1997, undertaken with the Grim Reaper, and, as always, it was an experience she met with bravery. On the subject of death, the world traveler said, "You just stop breathing. What's so frightening about that?"

CHAPTER 8

"Tant Pis!" (1903)

*"We don't see people as they are.
We see people as we are."*

—ANAÏS NIN

The Irish wit Oscar Wilde remarked, "Bigamy is having one wife too many. Monogamy is the same." A French woman did not share his opinion on monogamy and was immune to the gossip that her lifestyle engendered.

An individual destined to have more lovers than she did names, Angela Anaïs Juana Antolina Rosa Edelmira Nin y Culmell was born in Neuilly, a Paris suburb. Her father, Joaquín Nin, was a Cuban pianist of Spanish descent; her mother, Rosa Culmell, was a Cuban singer of French and Danish heritage. Joaquín was eight years his wife's junior, and he did not care to keep his eye from wandering. Other negative attributes were that he photographed his daughter in the nude, and he turned physically abusive when angered. Despite Joaquín's peccadillos, Anaïs was a daddy's girl; hence her devastation, at age eleven, when he left to make music with another woman.

Her husband's abandonment left the family in financial straits, and in a bid for a fresh start, Rosa took her two sons and daughter to New York.

Miserable, Anaïs wrote her father a letter pleading for his return; however, after her mother dissuaded her from contacting him, her letter became a diary entry. Later she recalled of her youthful writing endeavors, "I signed my stories 'a member of the French Academy.' Can you imagine!" Over the decades, the journal grew to a quarter of a million pages, and eventually equated her name with infamy.

Angered when a teacher told her to write in a less literary style, Anaïs dropped out of school at age fifteen. Her exotic looks, long neck, and hazel eyes rimmed with trademark heavy black liner landed her a job as an artist's model. At age nineteen, she appeared on the cover of *The Saturday Evening Post.*

In 1923, the teenager wed Hugh Guiler, a well-heeled American banker, and the couple moved to Louveciennes, near Paris, choosing a two-hundred-year-old villa. The décor was Moorish with walls of apricot, but the centerpiece was always Anaïs, curled up with cushions on the Persian rug. Hugh worshipped his wife and strove to provide what she termed "a dream made real." While he worked at his bank, Anaïs read Freud, took a flamenco class, and slept with her instructor. Anaïs flirted at her husband's business parties; oblivious, Hugh thanked her for putting up with, as he put it, "the Philistines of Mammon." His customary greeting when he returned home was, "What are you doing, Pussywillow?" In the evenings, Hugh dutifully listened to his wife's diary entries.

Anaïs's lifelong desire to become a published writer came to fruition in 1930. Intrigued by D. H. Lawrence's *Lady Chatterley's Lover*, she wrote a lengthy essay on the British author, "D. H. Lawrence: An Unprofessional Study." Next came her novelette, *Winter of Artifice*, a fictionalized story from her diary of a dramatic reconciliation between a father and daughter. Although her book did not deliver money or acclaim, it served as her entry into the charmed circle of Parisian literary lights.

When not sitting at the feet—or whatever anatomical part—of authors of renown, Anaïs had a reunion with the father she had not seen for three decades. Their meeting led to the sins of the Nins when they indulged in a carnal relationship. She committed their liaison to her diary with the words that they coupled "in a nonstop orgiastic frenzy."

The foray into publishing also led to an introduction to Henry Miller, then a penniless American expatriate writer. Two days later, they declared their love for one another in a Montparnasse café; spouses Hugh and June did not prove impediments. They consummated their love on his hotel bed, one shared with legions of bedbugs. Henry took his lover's writing seriously, an unusual thing for a man to do in that era. He also read her diary without a trace of jealousy, even the passages that concerned Anaïs's brief affair with his wife. When June returned to the United States, Henry lived in a guest room at Louveciennes, where he partook of Anaïs's sexual favors; moreover, he copied pages from her diaries that he incorporated in his novel, *Tropic of Cancer*. Oblivious, Hugh bankrolled his Pussywillow's lover.

Impregnated by either Hugh or Henry, Anaïs took medication to abort her six-month-old fetus that resulted in a stillborn daughter. When Miller visited her in the hospital, he shared his latest manuscript, to which she responded, "Here is a birth which is of greater interest to me."

With Europe on the brink of war, the Guilers returned to the States. In New York, Anaïs was determined to leave her mark on the literary firmament. Unable to find a publisher, she purchased her own foot-operated printing machine and spent a month learning its operation. The American public proved receptive, and Edmund Wilson published a review in the *New Yorker* that praised her as a pioneering woman writer. Thrilled as she was by acceptance into the fringe of the American literati, an event that impacted her life awaited.

In 1947, Anaïs noticed an attractive man in a white leather coat while she was in an elevator on her way to a Manhattan cocktail party hosted by heiress Hazel Guggenheim McKinley. The two talked exclusively to one another; he mentioned he was twenty-eight and single; Anaïs neglected to mention that she was forty-four and married. Her interest was further piqued when he divulged that he was the stepbrother of Eric Lloyd Wright, the grandson of famed architect Frank Lloyd Wright. That night she wrote in her diary, "Danger! He is probably homosexual." He was not. Anaïs gleaned the autobiographical tidbit two days later, when she invited the man, Rupert Pole, to dinner at her home; Hugh was conveniently in Havana for business. The next diary entry revealed that he was the most virile man she had ever known. After wiring Hugh that she was taking a road trip with a dear friend, Anaïs accompanied Rupert in his 1941 Ford roadster to his home on the West Coast.

Anaïs's new life entailed six weeks in California with Rupert, followed by six weeks in Manhattan with Hugh. The bicoastal charade required countless falsehoods that she kept straight in a secret "Lie Box." When Rupert begged her to marry him, Anaïs agreed to tie the knot in the Arizona desert. For the next two decades, she maintained this lifestyle that caused her to describe herself as a trapeze artist, swinging from one husband to another.

While most people keep their diaries under lock and key, with the sexual revolution and the feminist movement of the 1960s, Anaïs felt it time to release the journals she had stored in a bank vault in Paris. In 1966, Harcourt Brace published *The Diary of Anaïs Nin*, which revealed every nuance of her libido; Nin finally basked in the spotlight she had always craved. *The New York Times* gave her book a glowing review, and the first printing of three thousand copies sold out within weeks. The appeal of the memoir is the escapades of the expat writers in Paris in the 1930s and the antics of the bohemian poets of the Greenwich Village of the 1960s. The diary entries lifted the veil of the confessional from the interior lives of Gore Vidal, Truman Capote, and Richard Wright. Reading about Nin's illegal abortion, legions of extramarital affairs, and incest left mainstream America with a sense of revulsion; liberals lauded her courage in writing confessional erotica. The author became a sought-after guest lecturer at liberal colleges and transformed into a figurehead for feminists. Anaïs spoke at sold-out lecture tours, giving readings of excerpts that shone a spotlight on a life few could fathom. In 1971, she remarked, "Sometimes I feel like I have about ten million daughters." In tribute, Cacharel named a perfume Anaïs Anaïs. Other accolades: France conferred upon her the Prix Sévigné, *The Los Angeles Times* presented her with the Woman of the Year award, and luminaries such as Christopher Isherwood and Henry Miller tried to secure her a nomination for the Nobel Prize.

When cancer claimed Anaïs Nin at age seventy-three, her obituary in *The Los Angeles Times* remembered her as the wife of Rupert Pole; *The New York Times* listed her widower as Hugh Guiler. Nin named her West Coast husband her literary executor, the guardian of her thirty-five-thousand-page diary. Rupert, in a last act of love, flew a small plane over the coast near Santa Monica to set his wife's ashes adrift. Eight years later, he honored Hugh's final wish by scattering his ashes over the same waters.

A metaphor for Ms. Nin is a quotation from her diary, "I must be a mermaid. I have no fear of depths and a great fear of shallow living." And a fitting epitaph could be her trademark expression, "If I am perverse, monstrous...I am what I am! *Tant pis!*"

CHAPTER 9

"Pentimento" (1905)

"One sits uncomfortably on a too comfortable cushion."

—LILLIAN HELLMAN

In 1968, country singer Jeannie C. Riley sang of the hypocrisy of her hometown who pointed fingers at the widowed Mrs. Johnson though they were guilty of worse transgressions. Sixteen years earlier, a playwright had socked it to a more powerful body than the Harper Valley P. T. A.

The American actress Tallulah Bankhead observed, "They say it's the good girls who keep diaries. The bad girls never have the time." The American author Lillian Hellman disproves the quotation, as she was a bad girl who kept a diary in the form of her memoirs. The woman who became one of the most famous female authors of the twentieth century was Lillian Florence Hellman, born in Louisiana. Her parents, Max and Julia, shared the commonality of German-Jewish roots, but hailed from different social strata. Max had to find his own way in the world, while Julia's family, the Newhouse branch, had made a sizable fortune in the banking industry. After the shoe business Max had established with his wife's money failed, he became a traveling haberdashery salesman. Lillian spent her early years shuttling between upper West End Avenue in Manhattan, where she lived with her rich relatives, and New Orleans, where her unmarried paternal aunts ran a boarding house. (She found the eccentric cast of characters in New Orleans more interesting.) The nomadic living situation was hard on Lillian, an only child, and she turned to books as a refuge. After a scolding, at age fourteen, she ran away from home. She returned after two days, and later recounted that she had learned something "useful and dangerous—if you're willing to take the punishment, you are halfway through the battle." In another anecdote, she said that, in order to buy books, she had pawned a ring that her uncle, Jake Newhouse, had given her for her fifteenth birthday. After she confessed, he laughed off the incident and spoke the words she would incorporate into her play *The Little Foxes*: "So you've got spirit after all. Most of the rest of them are made of sugar water."

After graduating from Wadleigh High School in New York, Ms. Hellman enrolled at the Washington Square campus of New York University for three years before she transferred to study journalism at Columbia University. Although academically inclined, she cut classes to spend time in bohemian Greenwich Village. Eventually she dropped out of school and took a job at the new publishing house of Boni & Liveright.

Ladies with less self-confidence than Ms. Hellman might have despaired of finding love; first, there was her prickly personality; secondly, there was her disfigured nose. In her early teens, Lillian had seen her adored father leave for a dinner date with a lady—not her mother. In a rage, she had thrown herself out of a tree in which she had been playing, which resulted in a broken nose. A future detractor, William F. Buckley, featured her on a cover of the *National Review*, showing Lillian looking into a mirror and asking, "Who is the ugliest of them all?" Instead of offering sympathy, her nanny, Sophronia, admonished her to keep quiet about Mr. Hellman's indiscretion. "Don't you go through life making bad trouble for other people."

On December 31, 1925, Lillian married Arthur Kober, a Jewish press agent from Brooklyn. She said of their decision to marry on this date, "We had a crazy idea that if we'd marry on New Year's Eve, we'd remember it." Within a few years, they moved to Hollywood, and Lillian found a position at Metro-Goldwyn-Mayer reading scripts. She also spent time in France, where she was a part of Gerald and Sara Murphy's expatriate circle, which included Scott and Zelda Fitzgerald. During this period, Lillian was at loose ends and drowned her discontent with alcohol and chain-smoking. Her gravelly voice was the result of her lifelong cigarette habit.

In Hollywood, Lillian met the man who made her forget the significance of her New Year's Eve anniversary, the lover who chased away her blues. Dashiell Hammett, the famous author of *The Maltese Falcon*, was also known for his ability to match anyone in alcohol consumption. He was likewise no slouch in the promiscuity arena, and given his predilection for prostitutes, suffered from bouts of gonorrhea. Hellman was smitten. Lillian's recollections tended to vary; however, the version she usually gave on how her relationship with the man she called Dash began was that, after meeting, they talked in his car till dawn about T. S. Eliot. Although Lillian and Hammett were together—on and off—for the next thirty-one years, monogamy never factored into their relationship. Hellman slept with men who whetted her sexual appetite, a fact that earned her the reputation of a "she-Hammett." Another commonality was their strong sense of social consciousness; Lillian was committed to organizing her fellow screenwriters to unionize. The fact that both were married also did not factor into their romantic equation. Hammett was separated from his wife, and Hellman, preferring the bad boy, obtained a divorce. In 1934, Dashiell dedicated his novel *The Thin Man* "TO LILLIAN." He explained that she was his inspiration for Nora, the book's protagonist. Lillian would have appreciated his comment, as Nora was a breakthrough in the depiction of women in detective fiction: neither victim nor femme fatale.

When Lillian shared her aspiration to be a writer, the extremely private Dashiell joked that she should not write his biography because, considering her egotism, it would end up revolving around Lillian. He suggested she dramatize a case that occurred in nineteenth-century Scotland where a malicious student destroyed the lives of two teachers by falsely accusing them of a lesbian affair. Ms. Hellman, who was then reading scripts for the producer Herman Shumlin, sat in a corner as he read her manuscript. After the first act, Shumlin said it was swell; after the second act, he said he hoped it kept up the pace. After he finished, Shumlin announced that he would produce it. *The Children's Hour* opened in 1934 and transformed Hellman into a celebrity. However, because of its scandalous subject matter, theaters in Britain, Boston, and Chicago banned its production. The play also never made it to South Africa, as Lillian refused to have anything to do with a country mired in apartheid. The play earned Hellman $125,000 from its first run and a $50,000 contract from Samuel Goldwyn for the movie version. The Pulitzer Prize committee considered it too risqué, a decision that outraged New York theater critics. Although she could have ridden the wave of her popularity, conscience called, and Lillian left for Spain to aid the Loyalists fighting against dictatorship. Her form of combating oppression was also apparent in her antifascist play, *Watch on the Rhine*.

Lillian also wrote a play based on her mother's family; her close friend, Dorothy Parker, came up with the title, *The Little Foxes*. Scared of success because of what it did to people, Lillian fled from the Broadway opening. In 1980, Elizabeth Taylor starred in the production, and it went on a national tour. A well-heeled woman, Lillian bought an estate in Westchester County that she converted to a farm where she grew white asparagus.

In 1952, Hellman revived *The Children's Hour*, an arrow directed at McCarthyism that saw red under every bed. 'C' had become America's scarlet letter. Her play was an attack on the era's moral bankruptcy and how unfounded rumors victimized the innocent. A month later, Arthur Miller produced *The Crucible*; his parable was also a bullet aimed at McCarthyism. Although both plays satirized the same target, Hellman's was the more radical, as it also touched on the persecution of those in same-sex relationships.

As with other liberals of the time, Hellman was a committed leftist whose political affiliation resulted in a subpoena to appear before the HUAC (the House Committee on Un-American Activities). The committee's intention was to investigate the film industry in fear it would inject Communist propaganda into movies. In order to save their own skins, people testified before the court and named names. Hellman later denounced them as "Clowns who took to the hills." Some of these "clowns" were Walt Disney, Elia Kazan, and Ronald Reagan.

In 1951, in his appearance before the HUAC, Dashiell repeatedly invoked his Fifth Amendment right; the judges cited him with contempt of court and sentenced him to six months in a federal prison. He emerged in shattered health, and Lillian served as his steadfast nurse. When her Dash passed away in 1960, Lillian shed light on their relationship in an interview. She told a journalist, "We did have two periods of planning to be married. The first time, he disappeared with another lady. That's not really fair—I was disappearing too." Her sexual escapades lasted for the rest of her days. At age seventy-nine, Lillian propositioned a man at a dinner party the night before she died of cardiac arrest.

The HUAC delivered its summons to Ms. Hellman the following year. Although she did not view jail time with a Gandhi-like fortitude, she placed principle above self-preservation. In her finest hour, Lillian told the prosecutors that she would testify about her own activities, but, in a nod to Sophronia, added, "I will not go through life making bad trouble for people." She continued to sock it to the HUAC. "To hurt innocent people whom I knew many years ago in order to save myself is, to me, inhuman and indecent and dishonorable. I cannot and will not cut my conscience to fit this year's fashions." However, she was not above following that year's fashions on another level, and tongue-in-cheek joked with journalists that the Balmain dress she wore that day made her "feel better." Hellman knew that by disrespecting HUAC, she risked imprisonment; as it transpired, the government blacklisted Hellman, making her persona non grata in Hollywood. Her income dropped from $150,000 a year to a pittance. Trapped in a financial straitjacket, she sold her farm and worked briefly as a salesclerk in a department store under an assumed name.

In her later years, Hellman published her memoir, *Pentimento*; one chapter recounts how Ms. Hellman smuggled $50,000 to bribe Nazi guards to free prisoners. The Hollywood movie version, *Julia*, starred Jane Fonda as Lillian and Vanessa Redgrave as Julia. Millions watched on television as Hellman received a standing ovation at the Academy Awards. She had traversed the road from the blacklist to the Academy in the span of two decades.

In her memoir, she explained the Italian term that served as the title of her book. In the preface she wrote, "Old paint on canvas, as it ages, sometimes becomes transparent. When that happens it is possible, in some pictures, to see the original lines. This is called *pentimento* because the painter 'repented,' changed his mind. Perhaps it would be as well to say that the old conception, replaced by a later choice, is a way of seeing and then seeing again. That is all I mean about the people in this book. The paint has aged now, and I wanted to see what was there for me once, what is there for me now." For the woman who often reinvented her life, the title of the memoir can serve as her encapsulated biography, *Pentimento*.

CHAPTER 10

"Salomé" (1906)

"He was my cream, and I was his coffee—
And when you poured us together, it
was something."

—JOSEPHINE BAKER

Balancing a fruit hat inspired by the "baianas," Afro-Brazilian vendors, dancer Carmen Miranda's samba sashayed across the world stage. Fruit must be titillating, as another entertainer, clad in a banana skirt, likewise unleashed seismic shock.

Born in the slums of St. Louis, Missouri, the early life of Freda Josephine McDonald held no indication that she would one day be a global sensation. Her mother Carrie, a washerwoman, beat her and announced that she had been an unwanted child. Her father, believed to be Eddie Carson, a drummer, went AWOL. School ended after the sixth grade in order for Josephine to clean houses and babysit. An employer, Mrs. Keiser, burned Josephine's hands with scalding water as punishment for putting too much soap in the laundry.

One of Josephine's earliest and most horrifying memories occurred at age eleven when, during a riot, infuriated mobs torched Black homes. The child saw the corpse of a pregnant woman and witnessed a man's face disfigured by a gunshot. Along with six thousand other terrified Black families, the McDonalds fled the city.

Desperate for an exit from her oppressive home, she shed the name Freda, and at thirteen married Willie Wells, a man twice her age who she met while waitressing. They argued constantly; on one occasion, Willie hit her over the head with a bottle. The relationship dragged on for a tortuous eight months. Josephine gave matrimony another chance with husband Willie Baker; four years later she filed for divorce, though she kept his name.

Josephine worked as a performer for the St. Louis Chorus vaudeville show, where she stood out by wearing skimpy costumes considered too risqué by fellow performers, even by the liberal standards of the Jazz Age. Her contortionist dances seemed to defy the limits of human anatomy, and her body served as a male magnet. Her first big break was in the 1924 all-Black Broadway musical *Shuffle Along*, which thrust her into the heart of the Harlem Renaissance at the height of its Cotton Club popularity. With characteristic chutzpah, Josephine, who had been delegated to the second line of the chorus, shimmied into the front.

Josephine had countless love affairs, but the only lasting one was with her adopted country. At the age of nineteen, she was recruited by a talent scout to perform in a groundbreaking all-Black revue in Paris. With the promise of a thousand dollars a month and escape from racist America, Josephine embarked for Europe. She never again set foot in St. Louis. Her presence on the continent put the roar in the Roaring Twenties, and she introduced Paris to the Charleston.

In 1925, she made her debut in *Revue Negre* at the Théâtre des Champs-Élysées. Dressed in little more than pearls and feathers, Josephine wowed audiences with her *Danse Sauvage*. A master at shaking her butt, she declared that "people had been hiding their asses too long." Her sexual gyrations and bare-breasted act ushered in France's love affair with the dancer Parisians called "The Bronze Venus." At first, crowds cheered for "La Ba-kir," then, simply, "Jasephine." Her irrelevant humor involved singing "Ave Maria" into a rhinestone-covered microphone, clad in a tutu made of a suggestive string of sixteen rubber bananas. Of her exotic, erotic movements, the poet e. e. cummings, a member of the "Lost Generation" of expatriate writers, wrote, "She enters through a dense electric twilight, walking backwards on hands and feet, down a huge jungle tree...non-primitive and uncivilized." Pablo Picasso dubbed her the "Nefertiti of Now"; Ernest Hemingway proclaimed her "the most sensational woman anyone ever saw." Josephine dolls with banana skirts proliferated all over Europe; women styled their hair in Josephine curls. Cashing in on the craze, Josephine marketed Bakerskin darkening lotion, despite the fact that her own beauty routine included skin-lightening milk baths. And while she took on the role of the exotic in her performances, when Josephine attended the theater, she did so in couture by Balenciaga and Dior. In four films, she starred as a shimmying sexpot, a far cry from the American movies where Hattie McDaniel was typecast as Mammy, a maid in *Gone with the Wind*. Not everyone, however, was in Camp Jasephine. The Catholic Church condemned Josephine's primitive sexuality and hounded her stiletto-heeled footsteps. Censors in Vienna called her to the carpet for her "racy dancing." On her European tours, racists and fascists made her their target. Baker brushed aside the rancor and wallowed in the fact she was one of the richest Black women in the world. The girl who hailed from a St. Louis slum moved in rarified circles: Langston Hughes, Colette, the Pasha of Marrakesh, Juan and Eva Perón, and Princess Grace.

Although Josephine loved Paris, with its racial acceptance, and enjoyed enormous wealth, she was lonely. To fill the void, her hotel suite held various animals, including Albert, a perfumed pig, and Chiquita, a cheetah who sported a diamond-studded leash. Less temporary residents were a Sicilian gigolo, Pepito de Abatino, a self-invented Italian aristocrat who also served as her manager. Living with "the Count" did not interfere with her affairs with an Indian Maharajah, a Swedish prince, and an American actress. Perhaps the root of her promiscuity, and menagerie of pets, lay in her confession that she was terrified of sleeping alone. A third trip down the aisle was with a French Jewish industrialist, Jean Lion. Despite the appeal of his surname for the animal-mad Josephine, the marriage crumbled, as the only diva Jean wanted was of the domestic variety.

When the Nazis goose-stepped into Paris, despite her recent recovery from a near-fatal illness, the It-Girl performed for Allied troops in North Africa, braving landmine-strewn deserts. Fired with patriotic zeal, Baker served as a sub-lieutenant in the Women's Auxiliary of the French Air Force in North Africa. She enlisted in the—as she referred to it her heavily accented French—Rey-zis-tonce, and abandoned her banana skirt in favor of a uniform. One of her missions entailed smuggling military intelligence using invisible ink on her underwear. The cost of capture equated to execution. Josephine said of her activism, "France made me what I am. They gave me their hearts. Surely I can give them my life." For her acts of heroism, she earned the Croix de Guerre, and President Charles de Gaulle pinned the medal of a Chevalier of the Legion of Honor with the Rosette of the Resistance on her jacket.

In 1947, Josephine married her bandleader, Jo Bouillon. A miscarriage ended the dream of giving birth, and Baker turned to adoption. Her plan was to take in children of various nationalities to serve as ambassadors for racial harmony, a homespun version of the United Nations. The youngsters were from Korea, Finland, the Middle East, Venezuela, Algeria, Japan, and Colombia. Their mother insisted they maintain their language, dress, and religions. Her aspiration was to give them the happy home life she had been denied as a child; however, wrapped up in her career and self-absorption as she was, nannies served as nurturers. In order to accommodate her family, that she christened "The Rainbow Tribe," Josephine purchased a fifteenth-century, three hundred-acre castle, Château des Milandes. To finance her ever-escalating expenses, Josephine turned the grounds into a theme park. Although visitors numbered in the thousands, the upkeep outweighed the profits. When their offspring reached a dozen, Bouillon bid adieu.

A French citizen since 1937, she often returned to the States; however, in her homeland, her performances also carried a political agenda. She refused to perform in venues that excluded Blacks, even in the Jim Crow South. Historians credit Baker with the desegregation of Las Vegas casinos. Despite her superstar status, in 1951, during a tour, a number of hotels and restaurants blocked her entry. When the famed Stork Club of New York pointedly ignored her table, the NAACP organized a picket line in front of the high-class establishment, and Baker filed legal charges. The incident generated huge publicity, and she came under the radar of J. Edgar Hoover, who placed her on the FBI watch list.

Through Attorney General Robert F. Kennedy, in 1963, Baker participated at the March on Washington. As the organizers did not include women as keynote speakers, Josephine addressed the crowd before the beginning of the official program. Dissenters opposed to her inclusion argued that the girl from St. Louis had become a woman of Paris, and was out of touch with America's civil rights issues. However, as Josephine was friendly with Dr. Martin Luther King Jr., she was able to become a part of the historic movement. On that occasion, there was no banana skirt, no diamond-studded nails. Baker strode to the stage in her French Air Force uniform, displaying her Legion of Honor medal. From the podium she shared with Dr. King, she spoke for twenty minutes. In contrast to her flamboyant dance routines, her speech was simple yet powerful. She stated, "I have walked into the palaces of kings and queens and into the houses of presidents. But I could not walk into a hotel in America and get a cup of coffee, and that made me mad. And when I get mad, you know that I open my big mouth. And then look out, 'cause when Josephine opens her mouth, they hear it all over the world. I am not a young woman now, friends. My life is behind me. There is not too much fire burning inside. And before it goes out, I want you to use what is left to light the fire in you." Before she concluded, she looked out over the sea of the mixed crowd and said, "Salt and pepper—just what it should be." Sammy Davis Jr.'s jaw dropped as he saw the legend up close, and later he escorted her to her hotel in his limo. After the march, Josephine wrote Reverend King and signed the letter, "Your great admirer and sister in battle."

Contrary to the expression that it is "cheaper by the dozen," the cost of caring for her children, and the upkeep of her chateau, eroded her fortune. Debtors arranged for the sale of Château des Milandes and her belongings; during a rainstorm, gendarmes had to physically evict a hysterical Ms. Baker. Financial assistance from Princess Grace of Monaco and her return to the stage enabled Baker to buy a $100,000 Riviera Villa at Roquebrune-Cap-Martin. She made a triumphant return to the United States and performed to acclaim at Carnegie Hall. The last performance of her fifty-year career took place at the Club Bobina, financed by Princess Grace and Jacqueline Kennedy. Ever the show-woman, Josephine drove a motorcycle across the stage, dressed in full glittery regalia. A few days later, she fell asleep with glowing reviews scattered on her bed. The star never awakened.

France honored its adopted daughter, and she became the first American-born woman to receive full French military honors at her funeral. Twenty thousand people lined the streets to bid farewell to

"Jasephine." While Baker will always be associated with a banana skirt, in a metaphorical sense, she was akin to the seven diaphanous veils of Herod's stepdaughter, revealing, yet hidden, the twentieth-century Salomé.

CHAPTER 11

"Black and White Gold" (1906)

*"Other people tend to value you
the way you value yourself."*

—LEE MILLER

World War II left indelible images: of the Marines raising the flag at Iwo Jima, of the skeletal remains of Hiroshima, of the sailor and nurse embracing in Times Square. Another photograph showcases a woman metaphorically washing away the horror of the Holocaust.

Elizabeth Lee Miller was born in the place referenced in *Sex and the City* when Carrie Bradshaw said, "Charlotte Poughkeepsied in her pants." Later, Lee referred to her hometown as "Pokey." Her father, Theodore, was an engineer; her mother, Florence, a nurse from Canada who had suicidal tendencies. Theodore's hobby was photography, and his special subject was his nude daughter. He called his favorite *December Morn*; it showcased the seven-year-old standing in the snow wearing nothing but bedroom slippers. The practice continued until Lee was in her twenties; sometimes the portraits included Lee's similarly buff friends. During the group sessions,

Florence insisted on chaperoning. The same year, a family friend raped Lee shortly before her eighth birthday, leaving her with gonorrhea that, before the invention of penicillin, required agonizing treatments. A further horror occurred when the teenage Lee watched as her boyfriend drowned in a boating accident. The Millers also had to weather the storm caused by John, Lee's older brother, showing a preference for cross-dressing. Several private schools expelled Lee, and a teacher described her as "an idle student and an active rebel."

After a brief stay at Vassar, Miller departed for Manhattan to study at the Art Students League of New York. While crossing a street, she literally stumbled onto her modeling career when a man pushed her out of the way of an oncoming car. The stranger was *Vogue* media mogul Condé Nast who placed the blonde beauty on his magazine's 1927 cover. The teen became New York's top model, appearing in slinky flapper fashions. Lee also became a fixture on the social scene, and she partied with luminaries such as Josephine Baker, Dorothy Parker, and Charlie Chaplin. At first, Lee was thrilled to be the It-Girl of Manhattan; however, disillusionment arrived after photographer Edward Steichen took a portrait of her for an advertisement for Kotex that stirred up a tempest. Miller fled the bourgeois milieu of the States for the bohemia of Paris.

Montparnasse, her new zip code, was the neighborhood of the Jazz Age Andy Warhol, surrealist photographer Man Ray, who had started life as Emmanuel Radnitzky from Brooklyn. Armed with a letter from Steichen, she showed up at Ray's favorite café, Le Bateau Ivre, where she introduced herself as his new apprentice. Dumbstruck, he told her, "I'm leaving for a holiday in Biarritz." "So am I," was Lee's rejoinder. The interchange marked the end of Ray's long-time relationship with girlfriend Kiki de Montparnasse. The thirty-nine-year-old Ray and the twenty-year-old Lee went on a road trip the next day. And so their affair—and their working relationship—began.

Dozens of celebrities had posed for Ray—Wallis Simpson, Coco Chanel, Virginia Woolf—however, his most magnetic muse was Miller. He painted various parts of her anatomy, and produced *Lee Miller's Legs with Circus Performer*, *Miller's Lips*, *Observatory Time*, and *La Priere*, which showcased her backside. To his chagrin, Lee also posed for others' lenses. Jean Cocteau covered her body in butter and transformed her into a classical statue for his film, *The Blood of a Poet*. Pablo Picasso, one of her lovers, painted six portraits of her. The most memorable portrayed her with a green mouth and a vagina resembling an eye. Cecil Beaton altered her gender and only lusted after Lee by convincing himself that she resembled a "sun kissed goat-boy on the Appian Way." A glass manufacturer produced champagne flutes shaped after her breasts. In the midst of this mix, Theodore Miller arrived in Paris from Poughkeepsie and took pics of his nude daughter in a bathtub. After the muse deserted her mentor, a despondent Ray painted a self-portrait that depicted him with a noose around his neck.

After years of posing for men, Lee declared "that she would rather take a picture than be one," and worked as a fashion photographer for French *Vogue*. On a freelance assignment, Lee went to the Sorbonne medical school, where she acquired a severed breast from a mastectomy operation. She carried her souvenir to the *Vogue* office and set up a shoot, arranging the breast on a dinner plate. The horrified editor, Michel de Brunhoff, put the brakes on the garish undertaking. The genesis of the project was her rebuttal to Ray, who had taken shots of her breasts, cropped so that her figure was cut off at the neck.

Lee married a railroad magnate, Aziz Eloui Bey, and she moved with him to his native Egypt. The relationship had begun in Saint Moritz, where Miller was vacationing with Charlie Chaplin. Smitten, Bey left his wife. As the mistress of a mansion in Cairo and a vacation getaway in Alexandria, Lee oversaw a fifteen-member staff. Her hobbies were snake-charming lessons, camel racing, and desert safaris. Another pastime was scandalizing stuffy Cairo society. "If I need to pee, I pee in the road." "If I have a letch for someone, I hop into bed with him." The Miller camera captured images of the pyramids, the Sphinx, and the desert near Siwa that inspired René Magritte's 1938 painting *Le Baiser*. Despite the luxurious lifestyle, Lee self-medicated with her old stand-bys of booze and promiscuity. She described her interior landscape as "a water-soaked jigsaw puzzle, drunken bits that don't match in shape or design."

To escape the heat and her husband, Lee took off for Paris; at a fancy-dress party, she met the artist and art collector Roland Algernon Penrose. Although he preferred men, he was married to the lesbian poet Valentine Boué; after meeting Lee, the following morning, he had switched his preference. The betrayal of Bey, with whom she had thought she would spend her life, led to her confessing, "My 'always' don't seem to be much, do they?' " Despite their respective spouses, the couple summered in a Cornish farmhouse with pal Henry Moore. Afterwards, they joined Picasso at his vacation home outside Cannes. Fellow surrealist artist guests were so enamored of Picasso, they paid tribute by offering him their women.

The idylls of the surrealists ended the day Hitler invaded Poland, and the lovers headed to Penrose's Farley Farm in East Sussex. In a mix of frivolity and practicality, Lee installed a pink-and-blue air raid shelter at the bottom of their garden. British *Vogue* hired Lee to document war chic, and she snapped shots of women in factory overalls, with turbans restraining their hair. She staged a formal photograph of the poet Dylan Thomas, cigarette in hand; another was of the dancer Margot Fonteyn, wearing a hat and gloves. Although proud of her work, she felt it was superficial. She wrote to her parents, "It seems pretty silly to go on working for a frivolous paper like *Vogue*, tho it may be good for the country's morale it's hell on mine." The war became Miller's muse, and she turned her lens on Blitz-ravaged London, which she portrayed as a surreal dreamscape. Desiring to make a difference, Lee earned accreditation as a war correspondent. After ordering a uniform from the pricey Savile Row, she followed the Allied armies. As she explained, "What's a girl to do when a battle lands in her lap?"

On assignment, Lee took pictures of the Nazi treasurer of Leipzig surrounded by his wife and daughter, all dead by suicide. Another photograph was of an SS prison guard floating underwater in a canal. Besides capturing the carnage of battle, such as the D-Day aftermath, she took candid shots of civilians: French female collaborators with shaved heads, an abandoned child, the corpse of a German woman against the backdrop of a devastated Germany. Accompanied by David Scherman, Miller trailed the Allied advance through Europe after D-Day, including a foray into the trenches. The soldiers must have been taken aback by the woman who looked like a blonde Venus huddled in a foxhole during the siege of Saint-Malo or barreling down the road. The GIs liked her, as she was intrepid under fire and because she could match them swear word for swear word.

After trudging through the newly liberated concentration camps at Dachau and Buchenwald, Lee wrote, "I could never get the stench of Dachau out of my nostrils." On the day Hitler committed suicide, Lee was in Munich, where the Army's 179th Regiment had established headquarters in the dictator's apartment on the Prinzregentenplatz. Lee wiped her boots, thick with the cremated ash of Dachau, on the bathroom mat. Afterwards, she took a bath in the tub, where a photograph of the Fuhrer sat next to the soap dish. She remarked, "Mein host was not at home." Scherman's camera immortalized the image; he also took one of Lee smoking in Eva Braun's bed in her nearby home.

F. Scott Fitzgerald once observed, "There are no great second acts in American life," a sentiment that held true for Ms. Miller. At age forty, she was on a train headed for an assignment in St. Moritz when she had to come to grips with the fact she was pregnant. Lee found the prospect of motherhood scarier than the Front. The bohemian Miller and Penrose took the bourgeois road and married to legitimize their baby, whom they christened Antony. After Penrose's knighthood, Lee became Lady Penrose; she referred to herself as Lady Penrose of Poughkeepsie. Suffering from postnatal depression and post-traumatic stress disorder, she sought solace in a bottle. Putting her yesterday under wraps, she only once agreed to a resurrection of her past. In 1975, she attended Man Ray's London showing of his works at the Institute of Contemporary Arts. The reunion was bittersweet for the former first couple of the Paris Surrealists: Ray was in a wheelchair, Miller a committed alcoholic.

Lee treated Antony as if he were an unfamiliar appendage, and he was embarrassed by his outspoken mother and remarked that what was on her mind was what was in her mouth. Cooking provided a creative outlet, and Lee earned a Cordon Bleu and created culinary oddities: blue spaghetti, green chicken, pink cauliflower. Dinner guests were notables such as Henry Moore and Picasso, who painted one of the tiles above her stove. Shared baths with guests followed. After his mother's 1977 passing from cancer, Antony said of her, "She was way, way beyond difficult. I mean, God, she was impossible."

A mother and child reunion arrived when Antony's wife Suzanna discovered Lee's wartime mementos in the attic. These proved more special than the Picasso paintings that adorned the walls of Farley Farm. The photographs and battle mementos—a gunner's binoculars, a silver drinks tray from Hitler's apartment—served as a diary that helped him understand the mother he had never truly known. The findings changed Antony from a dairy farmer to the curator of Lee's life.

In the fairy tale, the miller's daughter spun straw into gold; the twentieth-century Miller's daughter—through her photographs—created black-and-white gold.

CHAPTER 12

"Antonina's Ark" (1908)

"You can never tell who your enemies are, or who to trust. Maybe that's why I love animals so much."

—ANTONINA ŻABIŃSKI

The modern zoo originated in 1907, when a German animal whisperer opened the eponymous Carl Hagenbeck Animal Park. Hans Augusto Rey, a frequent visitor, spent hours drawing monkeys he later immortalized in his literary creation *Curious George*. A Polish zoo was also a curious place whose owner understood that those who emulate the three proverbial monkeys—see no evil, speak no evil, hear no evil—are complicit in inhumanity.

As the world abandoned its moral compass, a woman who firmly held on to her own was Antonina, raised as a strict Catholic by her father Antoni Erdman, a Polish railroad engineer based in St. Petersburg. Antonina was nine when the Bolsheviks killed her father and stepmother at the start of the Revolution. Her aunt took her to Tashkent, Uzbekistan, where she studied classical piano, and later they left for Poland. Antonina worked in Warsaw's College of Agriculture, where she met Jan Żabiński, a zoologist eleven years her senior. When a position for a zoo director arose, Jan seized the unique opportunity. In 1931, the couple married, and the following year Antonina had a son Ryszard (Ryś,) christened after the Polish word for lynx. At one point, Antonina looked after three household toddlers: her son, a lion cub, and chimpanzee. Ryś's favorite pet was his badger, whom he took for walks with a leash and who used a potty. Antonina made her morning rounds on her bicycle, accompanied by an ostrich and a usually tame camel. Ryś slept alongside Wicek, a lion cub, Balbina, a cat, and other assorted animals.

Eden ended in 1939 when the Nazis invaded Poland. In the Luftwaffe attack, a half-ton bomb rained death on their zoo, killing dozens of the animals trapped in their cages. To compound Armageddon, the animals that managed to escape stampeded into a Warsaw engulfed in flames. Not only were the Poles privy to the Nazi invaders goose-stepping into their capital, they also witnessed a Noah's Ark of camels, llamas, ostriches, antelopes, foxes, and wolves screeching through the streets. In the midst of the bedlam, Antonina stopped a stranger, "Have you seen a large badger?" The zookeepers eventually rounded up their four-footed crew.

Shortly afterwards, Lutz Heck, a zoologist, paid a visit; he knew the couple from before the war, and he was overly attentive to Antonina, who reminded him of his first love, who shared her blonde beauty. Heck had become a Nazi who went on big-game hunts with Reich Marshall Hermann Goering and the Minister of Propaganda, Joseph Goebbels. Lutz ordered their prize specimens deported: the elephant, Tuzinka, to Königsberg, the camels to Hanover, the hippopotamus to Nuremberg. On New Year's Eve, to ingratiate himself with the SS upper echelon, Heck arranged for a party at the Warsaw Zoo. Upon their arrival, Antonina grabbed Ryś and took him to his room to read his favorite book, *Robinson Crusoe*. However, there was no distracting her son from the sound of gunfire and the shrieks of animals in their death throes.

In shock at the depravity, Antonina wondered how such barbarity could happen in the twentieth century as evidenced when the German Governor of Poland declared, "I ask nothing of the Jews except that they disappear." As a patriot, Jan joined the Polish Resistance, where he took the code name Francis after Francis of Assisi, the patron saint of animals. His specialty was sabotaging the enemy's trains by jamming explosives into the wheel bearings that ignited upon movement, and by slipping poison into Nazi sandwiches.

His wife was also committed to defying the murderers in their midst, as she could not be like many of her fellow Poles who turned a blind eye to the plight of the Jews ensnared in the Warsaw Ghetto. Jan and Antonina decided to save as many Jews as they could, well aware that the price of doing so was execution that would leave their son an orphan. In the contingency of capture, the couple carried cyanide capsules.

Comforted by the fact they knew how to handle dangerous animals, Jan and Antonina pulled the wool over the wolves' eyes. Pretending to befriend the invaders, the Żabińskis offered to raise pigs to provide them with meat. The subterfuge allowed Jan to enter the ghetto to gather refuse for hog feed; it also allowed him to smuggle desperate Jews out. While the Nazis emptied the ghetto, Jan and Antonina repopulated their zoo—this time with humans. The Żabińskis hid their refugees in animal cages, in their basement, and in secret tunnels. Their guests who had Aryan features were passed via the underground to safer locations, while those of Semitic appearance prayed to live out the war in hiding.

In one instance, Antonina decided to make the dark-haired Jews look more Aryan, and her guinea pigs were the Kenigswein family. Using cotton balls soaked in diluted peroxide, she rubbed the concoction on their heads, resulting in brassy red hair.

The fact that Heck, on account of his attraction to Antonina, was a frequent visitor made the underground fraught with daily danger. In order to ward off suspicion from the family cook, housekeeper, and unwanted visitors, Antonina gave each of her "guests" an animal code name; for example, she christened the sculptor Magdalena Gross "starling" because Antonina imagined her as "flying from nest to nest to avoid capture." Based on Ryś's comment that the Kenigsweins' dyed hair made them look like squirrels, they took on the code name "squirrels." Ryś found it strange that his animals bore human names, and the strangers in hiding went by animal names. In a home fraught with more dangers than Robinson Crusoe ever faced, Ryś knew if he let the truth of the underground slip out, his parents would be killed. He stopped playing with friends and confided his secrets only to Moryś, his pet pig. It was a never-ending trauma for the child when a German soldier dragged Moryś to be butchered for meat.

The residents referred to their sanctuary as "The House Under a Crazy Star." Feeding the escapees, sometimes as many of fifty of whom were in residence, proved problematic. On one occasion, when German soldiers shot the flocks of crows, Antonina gathered their corpses and her "four and twenty blackbirds" were baked into a pie that she passed off as pheasant pie. Although it was not "a dainty dish to set before the king," it was a welcome treat. Another use of code was when Germans were at the door, Antonina would rush to her piano, where she'd pound out the chords of Jacques Offenbach's "Go, go, go to Crete!" from *La Belle Helene*. Because of all the brushes with the Grim Reaper, one of their guests remarked that they must live under the influence of a lucky star, not just a crazy one.

A fellow freedom fighter, Irena Sandler (code name Jolanta), had dedicated herself to smuggling children from the ghetto in coffins and boxes and placing them with Catholic families or in orphanages. The children had to assume Christian identities, so Irena wrote their real ones on slips of paper that she buried in jars in the hope they would be reunited with parents who survived the war. The Gestapo ended up capturing her, and they subjected her to torture in Pawiak Prison. Irena escaped with the help of the Underground and became one of the Żabińskis' esteemed visitors.

In the spring of 1943, Heinrich Himmler determined to liquidate the Warsaw Ghetto as a birthday present for the Fuhrer. Dedicated heart and soul to the mustachioed madman, he once told a friend, "Believe me, if Hitler were to say I should shoot my mother, I would do it and be proud of his confidence." Himmler's gift became the Warsaw Ghetto Uprising, where the remaining Jews decided to go out in a blaze of resistance. When the Germans set fire to the ghetto, many died in the flames, committed suicide, or surrendered. A few managed to escape, and underground newspapers called upon Christian Poles to shelter the escapees. The Żabińskis opened their doors to many of those looking to escape, though Antonina had her hands more full than usual with the birth of her daughter Teresa. As his own act of retaliation, regardless of the danger, Ryś and another boy painted a towel with big red letters: "Hitler *kaput!*" that they planned to hang over the main gate of the zoo. Jan punished his saboteur-in-the-making with a spanking.

In 1944, as the tide of war blew against the Nazis, the Poles staged a counterattack. Jan bid farewell to his mother, wife, and two children; before he left, he handed Antonina a tin can that held a loaded revolver in case the Germans arrived. The heavy burden of caring for Ryś, his four-week-old sister, and those hiding in the House Under a Crazy Star often left Antonina struggling against depression.

After the news of the Polish Uprising reached Hitler, he ordered Himmler to bulldoze Poland. As Stukas rained death on the city, two SS men barged into the Żabiński home shouting, "*Alles raus!*" The soldiers forced the family outside, their hands raised in surrender; Antonina could only lift one arm, as she was holding Teresa. Although paralyzed with fear, Antonina pleaded in German, saying how noble they were, how she admired their ancient culture. The guns did not lower. A soldier ordered Ryś to go behind the shed, and when he disappeared from view, a single gunshot rang out. Ryś appeared a few moments later with their chicken, Kuba, dripping blood. One of the soldiers smirked, "We've played such a funny joke!"

At her lowest moment during the Occupation, Antonina wrote in her diary of the Nazi nightmare that it was "a sort of hibernation of the spirit, when ideas, knowledge, science, enthusiasm for work, understanding, and love—all accumulate inside where nobody can take them from us." The spiritual hibernation ended with the defeat of the Third Reich, and Jan returned home from a prisoner-of-war camp.

The following year, the Żabińskis began rebuilding their ravaged zoo, reopening it in 1949 with some of the original animals. However, with the Communist takeover of Poland and the back-to-back ravages of Nazism and Stalinism, two years later, Jan resigned as director. In her later years, Antonina wrote several children's books from the perspective of animals. Antonina's dream of a reborn zoo came to pass after the fall of communism; she did not live to see it, as she passed away in 1971. Before Jan died three years later, he told a reporter about how "a timid housewife" mustered the strength to stand up to the butchers. He explained that she was able to do so because "from time to time she seemed to shed her own human traits and become a panther or hyena, able to adopt their fighting instinct, she arose as a fearless defender." The Warsaw Zoo is once again open, and the Żabiński home is now a museum. For her role in saving her beloved animals from the twentieth-century flood, her story can be described as Antonina's Ark.

CHAPTER 13

"Hell on Wheels"
(1908)

"Travel is compost for the mind."
—MARTHA GELLHORN

A song by the Swedish pop group ABBA revolves around lovers, their time together made more poignant by the fight for freedom raging under a starlit sky set against the roar of cannons, the retorts of gunfire. The nonfictional "Fernando" was an eminent American journalist covering a civil war with the woman who shared his bottle and bed.

In 2019, members of English Heritage placed a blue plaque in honor of Martha Gellhorn at her former London home in Cadogan Square, Chelsea, the first to bear the designation "war correspondent." The story of how the American writer received the singular British distinction could well have come from the pen of her acclaimed novelist husband.

From birth, her parents instilled in Martha Ellis and her three brothers a fiery independence. Her father, George Gellhorn, was an immigrant German gynecologist; her mother, Edna, whom she described as her "true north," was an intrepid social reformer.

At age eight, Martha took her first foray into activism when she participated in a suffragette protest, organized by her mother, at the St. Louis Democratic National Convention. Her equally progressive father pulled his daughter from her convent school when he discovered the nuns taught classes on female anatomy with a textbook, making sure they covered the revealing photographs. Although extremely proud of her daughter, Edna harbored misgivings, "Martha is a law unto herself."

Following in her mother's footsteps, Martha attended Bryn Mawr College; bored, she dropped out "to go everywhere, see everything, and sometimes write about it." However, the only niche that could scratch her itch was a position as a foreign correspondent, an aspiration she achieved when she landed a job with the United Press. The periodical fired her after she reported an incident of sexual harassment by a coworker. Undaunted, at age twenty-two, Martha alighted in Paris with two suitcases, a typewriter, and seventy-five dollars. In France, she met her first Nazi, whom she described as "Scrubbed and parrot-brained," a type she had not learned about in Bryn Mawr. In the continent, she sowed some spectacular wild oats. Her sexual sojourn involved mostly married lovers, including an affair with Bertrand de Jouvenel, who had slept with his Mrs. Robinson—the writer Colette, his stepmother.

In 1934, Gellhorn returned to the United States, where she worked as an investigator in Franklin D. Roosevelt's Federal Emergency Relief Administration, reporting on the Great Depression. Her endeavors came to the attention of Eleanor Roosevelt, the person whom Martha most revered, other than her mother. Her travels across America led to the novella *The Trouble I've Seen*, the title an allusion to a Black spiritual. H. G. Wells provided the preface and pursued the author: "I am strongly moved to ask you to pack up come to England and to bed with me." Martha declined. While on assignment in Idaho, Gellhorn rallied workers to break the windows of the FERA to expose a crooked administrator. The tactic proved successful; however, the organization fired her for being a "dangerous Communist." Empathetic, the Roosevelts invited her to live at the White House until she could get back on her feet. For two months, Gellhorn was a guest in the Lincoln Bedroom.

In *Casablanca*, Rick Blaine, seeing his lost love Ilsa, bemoaned, "Of all the gin joints in all the towns in all the world, she walks into mine." The words could well have belonged to Nobel Prize winner Ernest Hemingway. In 1935, either by chance or design, Martha ended up in Sloppy Joe's Bar in Key West, Florida, where she met the acclaimed novelist. He invited the leggy blonde in the little black dress to join him for drinks. Impressed after watching her down glasses of Papa Dobles, a concoction of Bacardi rum and lime, Hemingway was hooked. For her part, Martha was in awe of the author of *A Farewell to Arms*, in which the hero tells a woman, "You're brave. Nothing ever happens to the brave." Ernest—contrary to his name—was married to his second wife Pauline, who had been the other woman in his first marriage.

When Hemingway, in his role as journalist, left to cover the Spanish Civil War, Martha followed suit and arrived in Madrid with a rucksack, fifty dollars, and an assignment from *Collier's* magazine. Her open-sesame to the world of journalism was a letter from President Roosevelt addressed to "All American Foreign Service Officers to provide every assistance to an old friend." In the Hotel Florida, their lovemaking took place against the bombardment of fascist bombs. To drown out the horror, they played Chopin's Mazurka in C Major. They had their first fight the day after, when Hemingway locked her in the room with the comment he "didn't want her mistaken for a whore de combat."

Ernest had lived with his first wife, Hadley, in Paris; his second wife, Pauline, in America; and his third wife, Martha, in Cuba. The couple married in 1940 in Wyoming (roast moose for dinner) and settled in Finca Vigía (Watchtower Farm), a retreat overlooking the hills of Havana. Martha's decorating touch was chintz-covered chairs; she detested the animal heads Hemingway mounted on the walls, souvenirs from his 1934 African safari. On his Royal typewriter in their Cuban getaway, Hemingway wrote *For Whom the Bell Tolls*, bearing the dedication "This book is for MARTHA GELLHORN." Hemingway had patterned the character of Maria after Martha; when the book became a movie, Gellhorn successfully suggested Ingrid Bergman for the role.

During *The Times* the literary power couple were apart, Martha wrote letters to her husband filled with pet names for him and his private part that she nicknamed "Scoobie." Despite the term of sexual endearment, she wrote a friend that, in regard to sex with Ernest, the main thing "is the hope it would soon be over." Martha's first and foremost love was her career, which proved the snake in their Edenic hideaway. She tired of his Kilimanjaro sense of entitlement; he resented her putting her career before him. Steaming, he told Gellhorn's mother that he should have added to his book's dedication to Martha, "If I can find her." When *Collier's* sent her to a London in shambles after the Blitz, he sent her a cable: "Are you a war correspondent or wife in my bed?" After Martha called in a vet to fix some of the tomcats on their property, he claimed it was her psychological desire to emasculate him.

As enraged as the bulls he chased in Pamplona, Hemingway contacted the editor of *Collier's* and offered his services, aware his famous name would take precedent over his wife's. When Martha discovered her husband's duplicity, she was livid. Revenge was sweet when she stowed away aboard a hospital ship and reached the Normandy shore on D-Day. Her irate husband, on the other hand, only witnessed the action through binoculars aboard a tanker in the Channel. Martha alighted on Omaha Beach, the sole woman amidst 160,000 men. Hemingway felt it a worse form of castration than that involving the tomcats. Afterwards, they met up in London's Dorchester Hotel, where a ferocious fight ended in Martha's final farewell to Scoobie. She was the only one of Hemingway's wives to leave him, an act he never forgave. Martha said of his rage, "Hell hath no fury like that of E. H. scorned." Dreading posterity would merely remember her as one of Hemingway's ex-wives, his name became verboten. As she put it, "Why should I be a footnote to someone else's life?" Even while married, Martha had strayed, once with General James Gavin, who had conducted a simultaneous affair with Marlene Dietrich.

Martha lived her mantra that love passes, work remains. The intrepid journalist went to Dachau with the liberation troops and described it as "the circle of Hell." She wrote of the haunting sight, "Behind the barbed wire and the electric fence the skeletons sat in the sun and searched themselves for lice. They have no age and no faces; they all look alike and like nothing you will ever see if you are lucky." Of her nomadic existence as a foreign news correspondent, Martha stated, "I liked having no possessions, no problems, and you never knew if you were going to be alive after the next day and that was immensely interesting." Perhaps her bravura came from her ex-husband's quotation, "Nothing ever happens to the brave." Not one to let age slow her down, in her seventies, she covered civil wars in Central America. The year she turned eighty-one, Martha reported on the US invasion of Panama.

Martha and the opposite sex were akin to a magnet and a nail, and she maintained lifelong relationships with male friends whom she referred to as "trench buddies." One of these was the acclaimed photographer Robert Capa, with whom she had experienced bombing raids in Spain and the violence that followed the birth of Israel. However, her love affairs, including one with her second husband Tom Matthews, a former editor of *Time*, came with an expiration date. She recalled her marriage as "nine invaluable years." Martha's take on holy matrimony was, "For me, marriage is a terrible institution, and it should be suppressed." Nevertheless, the union did foster a relationship with her stepson, Sandy Matthews, whom she preferred over Sandy Gellhorn, whom she had adopted in 1949 from an Italian orphanage. Martha explained that she had embarked on the road of maternity—after a number of abortions—because she did not want to feel like a "dried seed pod." The mother-and-son relationship was rife with tension, as Martha was a doer and despaired of Sandy, who had perfected the art of idleness. Eleanor Roosevelt remarked of the adult Sandy Gellhorn that he suffered from Martha's consuming self-absorption. Her lifelong love affair was with countries, and she traversed the globe with sojourns in Spain, Cuba, Mexico, and England, and a passionate one with the continent of Africa.

Desirous of leaving the United States—which she condemned for its imperialism—she traveled through Cuba, Italy, Mexico, and Kenya, finally settling in Britain, where she spent her last fifteen years in a small cottage in Wales and her apartment in London. Her home served as a salon for writers and foreign correspondents. The flat was spartan, as she preferred to spend her money on her travels. In her eighties, she planned on snorkeling in the Seychelles until her cataract surgery went awry; she had the doctor professionally cursed by a Malagasy medicine man. Well into her twilight years, she continued to chain-smoke, drink, and eat whatever she damn well pleased.

Looking back on a life as colorful as that of a heroine in a Hemingway novel, she reflected, "I'm over privileged. I've had a wonderful life. I didn't deserve it but I've had it." At age eighty-nine, plagued by ovarian cancer and diminished vision that prevented her from using the manual typewriter that had been her life's constant companion, she took the same road as Hemingway and ended her life through suicide. While he had chosen a gunshot to his head, Martha ingested a cyanide capsule. Sandy Gellhorn and Sandy Matthews scattered Martha's ashes in the River Thames so she could "continue travelling." On her old, battered typewriter, Gellhorn had written the words that encapsulated her indomitable spirit, "I do not wish to be good. I wish to be hell on wheels, or dead."

CHAPTER 14

"Coming Up Roses" (1911)

"Men aren't attracted to me by my mind. They're attracted by what I don't mind."

—ROSE LOUISE HAVOK/GYPSY ROSE LEE

Henry VIII described his fifth wife, Catherine Howard, as "a rose without a thorn." Alas, love proved fickle. After charging Catherine with adultery, he ordered her decapitation. In contrast, an American rose— due to a steel-encased backbone—evaded the chopping block.

The stage mother of all stage mothers was Rose Thompson, who made Joan Crawford seem nurturing. At the age of fifteen, recently released from convent school, Rose wed newspaperman John Hovick. She raised her two daughters, Louise and June, as generals girded for battle: against her, against each other, against men.

After John went AWOL, Rose was hell-bent on turning her two girls into vaudeville stars. Regarding legality as a frivolity, she forged birth certificates, making Louise and June appear three years older in order to circumvent child labor laws. The sisters did not learn their actual ages until 1949; another autobiographical tidbit they unearthed was that Rose had christened them both Ellen June.

When Louise was four, the Hovicks departed for Hollywood, where Rose formed a children's act; as Louise was pudgy, Rose focused on the prettier, talented sister. She also entered into two quick, and quickly over, marriages. While money was always high on Rose's priorities, school was not, and her daughters' education ended when they went on tour. Nevertheless, Louise became a voracious reader and immersed herself in the works of Boccaccio, Rabelais, and Shakespeare. Never a domestic diva, Rose doled out a dollar a day to the girls for food, which usually included pie for breakfast. In an act that instilled fear in her offspring, Rose pushed a hotel manager out a window, causing his death. The jury bought her claim of self-defense.

At age "thirteen," June married fellow performer Bobby Reed; the couple took off in the middle of the night, despite the freezing snow. Fearful that her paycheck had eloped, Rose summoned the police, who brought Bobby to the station. When he went to shake his mother-in-law's hand, she took out her gun and twice pulled the trigger. Fortunately for Bobby, the safety latch was on. The police, figuring June was safer with hubby than her mother, released the shaken young man. Her sister's response to her sibling's hidden husband was relief that June had set her sights on Bobby, not Stanley, the boy with whom Louise had shared her first kiss.

With June's defection and the onslaught of the Great Depression, mother and daughter devised a battle plan. While legitimate producers could not fill Broadway seats at five dollars a ticket, owners of the burlesque houses, such as those owned by the Minsky brothers, packed in patrons for a fifth of that price. Classy they were not, what with the men in the audience holding empty milk cartons and raw liver concealed under newspaper. Madame-Mama Rose declared that flesh always sold, and as Louise had morphed into a five-foot-nine long-legged brunette beauty, she found her niche in stripping. As a novice, Louise met the older Tessie the Tassel Twirler, who advised, "In burlesque, you've got to leave 'em hungry for more. You don't dump the whole roast on the platter."

Disdainful of the word "stripper," Louise referred to her new position using the Upper East Side slang term "ecdysiast." Putting the tease in striptease, her signature move was to slowly drop her shoulder strap. Forgoing the name on her actual birth certificate as well as her doctored one, she reinvented herself as Gypsy Rose Lee. She gained renown as the stripper with a brain, as often photographed holding a book as lounging in a bubble bath, and sometimes concurrently. Her routine consisted of removing her clothes while plucking out dressmaker pins and dropping them into a tuba, whose suggestive sound elicited laughs. At the close of her performance, she snuggled into the stage's velvet curtain, tossing her gown to the floor. Never nude, she purred, "Oh, boys, I can't take that off. I'll catch cold."

From 1929 to 1934, Gypsy worked at Minsky's Burlesque in New York City, refining her act, while offstage she indulged in Turkish cigarettes, brandy-laced coffee, and sex. When the police raided the burlesque house on grounds of immorality, her photograph appeared on the front pages of the tabloids. Her quip to the newspapers was, "I wasn't naked. I was completely covered by a blue spotlight." Louise enjoyed the camaraderie of the paddy wagon, and her ensuing notoriety was good for business.

Despite Rose's mantra "Men will take everything they can get and give as little as possible in return," Louise had an affair with Rags Ragland, a comic and consummate womanizer. Another dalliance was with mobster Waxey Gordon, who doubled as her Sugar Daddy. He paid to have her teeth capped; in return, he expected more than a flash of her pearly whites.

Raised in the School of Rose, Louise dipped her finger in someone else's pie. Dwight Fiske, a piano player at the ritzy Savoy-Plaza, sang risqué lyrics for his white-tie clientele. Ever eager to climb the social ladder, Louise traded Minsky's for the Irving Place Theater, the Metropolitan Opera of burlesque. Her salary increased from five hundred dollars a week to a thousand, and Louise "borrowed" Fiske's music for ambience. While using his lines, she affected a posh accent, singing "I'm a lonesome little Eve/All I do is sit and grieve./Like Eve I carry round this apple every night/Looking for an Adam with an appetite." Louise was over the moon at Irving Place, where the clientele included columnist Walter Winchell, of café high society, and British aristocrat the Earl of Gosford. A reporter for the *New Yorker* wrote, "We had to admit we went for Miss Lee, so to speak." Riding the crest of popularity, Louise appeared at a Waldorf Astoria hotel charity function clad in a leotard covered with leaves, the latter of which she auctioned. Patrician patrons refused to accept money made off the garment from a stripper.

One who did not scorn Louise was Eddie Braun, despite there being a Mrs. Braun. He showered Louise with diamonds and attended her matinee performances. Understanding the art of self-promotion, Louise appeared at the opera in a cape encrusted with orchids. Tired of being the other woman, and looking for a way out of burlesque, Louise set out for Hollywood. However, Louise discovered she could not shed her reputation as easily as she did her clothes. The Hays Office, the morality police against smut, did not allow Zanuck to use the queen of burlesque as a headliner for the 1937 film *You Can't Have Everything*. Public morality branded Louise a harlot, and the director received four thousand letters of protest. Bowing to public pressure, the studio stripped her of her stage name; she was once again Louise Hovick.

In a bid for a life that did not include her breasts and backside, Louise tried her hand at wedlock and married Arnold "Bob" Mizzy, a dental supplies manufacturer. The marriage barely outlasted the honeymoon. One impediment to the relationship was Rose's habit of brandishing a gun at her son-in-law. Following in her mother's marital missteps, Louise took her vows three times, although she had the distinction of having a chimpanzee as a ring-bearer for one of her ceremonies.

Divorced and out of work, Mama "*mia*" Rose came to the rescue when she introduced Louise to Chicago-based Michael Todd. He produced shows for the 1939 World's Fair in New York for his film *The Streets of Paris* and decided on Louise as his star. He said of his choice, "That's a no-talent broad worth a million bucks on any midway. I would give my right ball to get her into a show of mine." One of the show's fans, First Lady Eleanor Roosevelt, sent her a telegram which read, "May your bare ass always be shining." Louise cashed in $80,000 in municipal bonds and acquired a stake in the show, and Todd and Hovick generated several films. Not averse to the trappings of fame, Louise arrived for a club date in Las Vegas in a specially-built maroon and gray Rolls-Royce that held twenty-seven pieces of luggage, a guinea pig, five Siamese cats, and two turtles.

A Renaissance woman, Louise joined the ranks of Brooklyn Bohemia through February House, a commune whose members included Salvador Dali, Leonard Bernstein, W. H. Auden, Carson McCullers, Richard Wright, and other stars in the artistic firmament. In a leap from the lascivious to the literary, Louise published *The G-String Murders*, a thriller set-unsurprisingly-in a burlesque house. Her book became a bestseller using backstage slang (breasts were referred to as "Bordens"). Authors Carson McCullers, Janet Flanner, and Carl Van Doren championed Louise, self-anointed as "America's Leading Literary Figure."

With money from *The Streets of Paris* (four thousand dollars a week), Louise purchased a 63rd Street mansion that had once belonged to a Vanderbilt (it has since been owned by Spike Lee) featuring a mink-covered toilet seat, Picassos on the walls, and a vintage Rolls in the garage. Along with the mistress of the manor and her Chinese crested dogs, other residents included June and her daughter April. Another occupant was Erik, Louise's illegitimate son with famed director Otto Preminger. For the sake of domestic tranquility, Mama Rose had her own digs. Realizing her sexual appetite was not satiated by men, Rose ran a lesbian boarding house in a ten-room apartment, financed by Louise. She also managed a lesbian farm at her country home in Highland Mills. As old habits die hard, at a party, Rose pulled her gun on a female guest; her daughter's connections covered up the murder. Rose used terror tactics to extract money from her girls and wore rags to the theater where Louise performed to extort further funds. As added persuasion, Rose threatened to write a tell-all book. In 1954, on her deathbed, Rose unleashed her hatred on Louise: "You'll never forget how I'm holding you right this minute, wishing with all my heart I could take you all the way with me—all the way down!" Move over, Medea. June wrote a memoir of her unique family, aptly entitled, *Early Havoc;* Louise called her own literary confessional *Gypsy;* that became a Broadway musical starring Ethel Merman. The actress lost out in the Tony Awards to Mary Martin for *The Sound of Music* but shrugged it off, "How are you going to buck a nun?"

In 1961, while living in California, Louise purchased a seventeen-room Italian-Renaissance-styled mansion she described as "early Gloria Swanson." Hovick traded her stripper gloves for gardening gloves, at last an Eve not dependent on an Adam. Erik chanced upon his mother working in her garden; she wore a rag around her head, a bikini top, and two aprons—one in front to hold tools and the other in the back, as she said, "to keep the cops away." A serpent appeared in her Eden when she came down with cancer, which she declared was a posthumous present from Rose. Despite a life filled with thorns, for the woman who brought class to the age-old practice of stripping, her indefatigable outlook—to borrow a lyric from *Gypsy*—was "Everything's coming up roses."

CHAPTER 15

"Any Wars?" (1911)

"I must admit I enjoy being in a war."
—CLARE HOLLINGWORTH

Society is well versed in the "trials of the century"—the kidnapping of the Lindbergh baby, the judgement of the war criminals in Nuremberg, the People v. O. J. Simpson. What has slipped through the cracks of history is the woman behind the "scoop of the century."

Patrick Garrett saw a battered trunk, covered in dust and exotic shipping labels, in the attic of his parents' London home. The relic belonged to his great-aunt, who loomed large in family lore. Upon opening the valise, Patrick saw passports, rolls of film, and records of foreign bank accounts. Among the jumble were sepia-toned photographs of long-lost lovers. There were also letters of gratitude that revealed that his relative had been the British Oskar Schindler.

Born in the same year as Lucille Ball, Tennessee Williams, and Ronald Reagan, but destined to tread a far different path, Clare Hollingworth experienced World War I as a child in Britain. She always remembered seeing German bombers flying over her family's farm. Her father, Albert, worked at his shoe and boot factory, but in his time off, he took

Clare and her pony, Polly, to investigate the damage inflicted by a Zeppelin raid. Despite introducing his child to the mysteries of the military, he and his wife Daisy disapproved of "educated women," and sent Clare to study at a domestic science college for "lady wives" in a building that had formerly housed a mental asylum. The result of her lessons was hatred of domesticity. Clare later admitted that it was useful to have mastered how to cook an omelet. As she refused to become a dedicated husband-hunter, her family and town did not know what to make of her. Bowing to pressure, Clare became engaged to "a suitable young man," a betrothal of which both sets of parents approved. Upon her realization that he "was not my dish," she ended their relationship. She further upset her parents with her decision to become a journalist. Clare later told an interviewer, "My mother thought journalism frightfully low, like a trade. She didn't believe anything journalists wrote and thought they were only fit for the tradesmen's entrance."

As her aspiration would entail further education than what she had obtained in domestic science classes, on a scholarship, Clare enrolled in a program of Slavonic and East European Studies in London, followed by a course to study Croatian at the University of Zagreb, then part of Yugoslavia. After graduation, Clare obtained a secretarial position at the League of Nations Union, an organization established in 1918.

In her new job, she met the decade-older Vandeleur Robinson, a mustachioed, bespectacled intellectual. Clare was taken with his knowledge of foreign affairs, so much so she toured the Balkans with him, despite the fact there was a Mrs. Robinson. After his wife divorced him on the grounds of infidelity, he asked for Clare's hand. She only agreed when she learned that marriage did not necessitate relinquishing her maiden name. Clare became the eighth woman in England to hold a passport that did not include a husband's surname.

Hollingworth ended her secretarial stint and volunteered for a relief organization's mission to travel across Germany to the Polish port of Gdynia to rescue refugees fleeing the Nazi takeover of Czechoslovakia and the Sudetenland. The group had chosen Clare as she had a German passport, one left over from a Christmas vacation in Kitzbühel, the Austrian ski resort frequented by the Prince of Wales, author Ian Fleming, and high-ranking Reich officials. Among the thousands she assisted was two-year-old Madlena Korbel, who history remembers as Secretary of State Madeline Albright. Clare also aided Austrians and Germans who had opposed Hitler and helped them cross the border into Poland disguised as peasants. For verisimilitude, she supplied them with chickens to make them seem like farmers. For her daring rescues, the English press dubbed her "the Scarlett Pimpernel," an allusion to the character in Baroness Orczy's novel who helped aristocrats flee the French Revolution. In contrast, British officials were not impressed with some of the communists and other "undesirables" she smuggled into the country, and her employers dropped her from their mission. Upon her return to London, Clare contacted the editor of the *Telegraph*, who offered her a job as an assistant to Hugh Carleton Greene (later Sir

Hugh Greene), brother of novelist Graham Greene, in Poland.

As only diplomats' vehicles were permitted to cross the border, Clare turned for help to her former lover, the British Counsel General John Thwaites, whose car displayed a Union Jack. The trip proved uneventful, and she returned with as much wine, aspirin, and film as possible, since these items were not available in Poland. She was heading back, driving along a steep hillside, when she noticed huge tarpaulins that concealed the scenery from passing traffic. A gust of wind lifted a loose piece of fabric, revealing the presence of thousands of Wehrmacht tanks lined up in battle formation. Hollingworth had chanced upon the greatest scoop in history: the invasion that ignited World War II.

In her Katowice room, Clare contacted the British embassy in Warsaw with the words, "It's begun." After the official skeptically asked, "Are you sure, old girl?" Clare held the receiver outside her window so he could hear the roar of Panzer tanks and German planes. The next morning, *The Daily Telegraph* headline proclaimed "1,000 TANKS MASSED ON POLISH FRONTIER—TEN DIVISIONS REPORTED READY FOR SWIFT STROKE." The British paper *The Guardian* described it as "probably the greatest scoop of modern times." Two days later, Clare heard on the radio that Britain had declared war on Hitler. Anxious for a scoop, Clare slept in a car, where she kept wine and biscuits. She said of those days that you could go anywhere with a T and T, a typewriter and a toothbrush.

"ANY WARS?" (1911)

With the arrival of the Russians, Clare took off for Bucharest, where she remained until 1949. She assured her newspaper that she would not return home to be with her husband. "Good God, no! Oh, no. Not. At. All." Her relationship with Vandeleur was effectively over, and fifteen years later he divorced her on the grounds of desertion. She explained, "When I'm on a story, I'm on a story—to hell with husband, family, anyone else." Her second husband was Geoffrey Hoare, a writer for *The Times*, who polished her articles before she sent them off to her editors. The couple departed for Jerusalem to cover the bloody birth of Israel. She recalled the day of the bombing of the King David Hotel by militant Zionists as one of the few occasions when she tasted fear.

A huge domestic battle ensued in the couple's Paris home when Clare discovered hubby was having an affair. Hollingworth confronted Joan Harrison, the other woman, and threatened to shoot her with her pearl-handled pistol if she ever slept with Geoffrey again. Holding on to her man may have been for practicality as well as romance. Clare depended on Geoffrey to help with her writing, which was not on par with her reporting skills. Perhaps to fend off a divorce, Clare converted to Roman Catholicism. Despite his alcoholism and womanizing, Clare was devastated at Geoffrey's passing; it was the only occasion she ever asked for time off. She confided that she missed him every night in bed, the place where they had drunk beer and discussed current events. Clare admitted she had an affair as a new widow but that it had been a fiasco. She determined that, in the future, men would just be passing ships, though she added that it would have been lovely to have had a boyfriend for a trip to Timbuktu or Togoland. She expressed her philosophy as, "A good gin-and-tonic gives me more pleasure than any man." Proving that maternal instinct does not always hold true, she took pains to never become pregnant. "I would so greatly prefer the noise of the guns in Beirut to children. Am I wicked?"

As part of her journalistic duties, in order to obtain a window into the Royal Air Force, Clare obtained her pilot's license and learned how to parachute. On a night foot patrol behind enemy lines, she was trying to sleep when she heard German voices nearby. "What did I do? Put some more sand over my head and hoped for the best."

A non-celluloid Forrest Gump, Clare Hollingworth interacted with the major events and power players of the twentieth century. She reported on World War II from Eastern Europe, the Balkans, and North Africa, and wrote of the bitter enmity between Arabs and Jews as the curtain closed on the British Empire. Ms. Hollingworth often said she was never as happy as when she was on the road, even though she did so as a stranger to creature comforts. Her bed was sometimes in trenches, once buried up to her neck in sand for warmth against a frigid desert night. Even in the confines of a hotel, she often roughed it by sleeping on the floor so she wouldn't "go soft." In Vietnam, a sniper's bullet narrowly missed her head. For the Algerian Civil War, she entered the Casbah—the epicenter of violence—akin to a suicide mission. Honors often accompanied the horrors, and Hollingworth became the first resident correspondent in Beijing since the imposition of the "bamboo curtain." At age eighty, clothed in her habitual safari attire, she shimmied up a lamppost to gain a better view of the crackdown in Tiananmen Square. Her last major posting covered the death of Mao Zedong and the ensuing power struggle. For fifty years, the five-foot-three-inches-tall Ms. Hollingworth pursued danger, as that was where, she explained, the best stories awaited. An intrepid journalist, she ran to the places all else were running from.

Through her vast networks of connections and bulldog tenacity, Claire acquired interviews with the world's most renowned: Mohammed Reza Pahlavi after he became the shah of Iran in 1941, and his last, in 1979, after the Ayatollah Ruhollah Khomeini swept him from his peacock throne. In 1965, desirous of reporting on the hostilities between India and the newly birthed Pakistan, as reporters were not permitted on the front, she called on a favor from an old acquaintance, Indira Gandhi, then India's minister of broadcasting and information. Other famed meetings were with Henry Kissinger—"I thought very highly of him"—and Margaret Thatcher, with whom she was not impressed.

Clare finally settled down in Hong Kong, where the governor, Lord Murray MacLehose, found her a part-time job at the University of Hong Kong. She rented a two-bedroom apartment with a view of the Foreign Correspondents' Club (FCC). The Club reserved a "Clare's Table" for the 105-year-old *grand dame* of journalism. Traces of her abrasive personality remained: she banged her cane on the floor to catch an inattentive waiter's attention, and talked in a loud, strident voice, a remnant from communicating with her father, who had become almost deaf in his later years. Despite failing eyesight and advanced age, Clare continued to drink bottled beer for breakfast. Not one to see the advantage of retirement, she slept with shoes by her bed and passport in nightstand in case a new scoop beckoned. Queen Elizabeth II bestowed upon her the Order of the British Empire. The human whirlwind can best be understood by her incessant question to editors: "Any foreign trips going? Any wars?"

CHAPTER 16

"Good Enough for Me" (1912)

"I was never afraid. I was too busy to be afraid."

—NANCY WAKE

The expression "quiet as a mouse" conjures up the image of a timid rodent; however, during the dark days of the last world war, a woman known as the White Mouse possessed the roar of a lion.

In the twilight years of the twentieth century, patrons of London's Stafford Hotel could have observed a ninety-something-year-old-woman throwing back the first of her day's several gin-and-tonics. She had a nostalgia for the establishment; in yesteryear it was the bar where she had taken her first "bloody good drink."

An unlikely heroine during the years when the swastika held sway, Nancy Grace Augusta Wake was born in a Wellington, New Zealand, shack, the youngest of six children. The Maori midwife who delivered her pronounced her a *kahu*, one who the gods would watch over.

The words rang hollow during Nancy's childhood, when she shared a guerrilla relationship with her family, with the exception of her adored father Charles. The Wakes moved to the suburb of Neutral Bay in Sydney, Australia; shortly afterwards, Charles went AWOL. At age sixteen, Nancy ran away from home and worked as a nurse near Mudgee, Australia.

A two-hundred-pound inheritance from an aunt enabled Nancy to satisfy her wanderlust, and she traveled to New York, Paris, and London. She made France her home and, following in her journalist father's footsteps, worked for the Hearst newspaper chain who sent her to Vienna. In Austria, she witnessed Nazi gangs beating Jews in the streets. The attacks led her to resolve, "If ever the opportunity arose, I would do everything I could to stop the Nazi involvement. My hatred of the Nazis was very, very deep."

During the day Wake worked as a reporter, and at night she frequented the city's cabarets. Later, Nancy recalled of her younger self that she loved nothing more than "a good drink and handsome men, especially French men." And the French man she fell for was the wealthy, "charming, sexy, and amusing man" Henri Fiocca. Despite his playboy reputation, she married him in 1939. The couple enjoyed a caviar-and-champagne lifestyle until Hitler's army goose-stepped into France. Disgusted at the collaborators, Wake felt she needed to do more than take the role of one of the three proverbial monkeys, and she volunteered to drive an ambulance.

A chance meeting at a bar in the Hôtel du Louvre et de la Paix in Marseille provided a rebel woman with her cause. Nancy met Scotsman Captain Ian Garrow, who enlisted her help with the escapes of downed Allied airmen and desperate Jews. Her mission was to escort her charges to the base of the Pyrenees, from where other guides escorted them to the British Consulate in Barcelona. Henri and Nancy also provided their chalet at Névache, in the Alps, as a safe house in the Resistance's version of the Underground Railway. With her beauty and scarlet lipstick, Nancy was the epitome of a femme fatale, one who was indeed fatal. Nancy said of her covert operation, "It was much easier for us, you know, to travel all over France. A woman could get out of a lot of trouble that a man could not." She was able to elude capture partly because the Germans could not believe their Goliath was a slender, attractive woman.

Inevitably, Wake's exploits came to the attention of the Gestapo, who dubbed her "*la souris blanche*"— "the White Mouse"—as she continuously escaped their traps despite a five-million-franc price on her head. Luck deserted her when the Vichy police arrested her in a random roundup and accused her of blowing up a cinema, an act of sabotage in which she had not participated. After four days of brutal interrogation, Garrow's replacement, Patrick O'Leary, a Belgian doctor whose real name was Albert Guérisse, told her captors Madame Fiocca was his mistress. He added weight to his words with his claim that he was a friend of the Vichy premier, Pierre Laval. O'Leary pleaded with the officer in charge to keep his affair secret because of Nancy's husband. Upon her release, guides hid her in the back of a coal truck with a New Zealander, and two Americans smuggled her into Spain.

Anxiously awaiting a reunion with Henri, Nancy was unaware that the Gestapo had tortured and killed him upon his refusal to divulge information about his wife. Nancy was forever inconsolable at losing the man she deemed the love of her life. His murder intensified her hate, and she said, "In my opinion, the only good German was a dead German, and the deader, the better. I killed a lot of Germans."

Wake joined the British Special Operations Executive (SOE)—one of thirty-nine women and 430 men— created by Prime Minister Winston Churchill to aid the French Resistance. (Tragically, eleven of the female freedom fighters died in concentration camps.) After sixteen weeks of training, Nancy emerged as an expert in explosives and hand-to-hand combat. Despite the horror of the times, Nancy's irrepressible spirit remained undaunted. On one occasion she and her friend Violette Szabo hoisted an SOE instructor's pants up a flagpole.

On a March night in 1943, Nancy parachuted into France in the forests of Auvergne, where approximately seven thousand partisans were gathered. During landing, her parachute became entangled in the branches of a tree. Henri Tardivat, the resistance leader, greeted her with the words "that all the trees in France bear such beautiful fruit this year." In typical Nancy fashion, she retorted, "Don't give me that French shit."

Fellow freedom fighters were reluctant to put their faith in "*une femme*," who was also a foreigner. To change their minds, Wake challenged the leaders to drinking contests, and as she was the "last man standing" at dawn, Nancy garnered newfound respect. What sealed it occurred during an ambush, when Wake slit the throat of an SS sentry to prevent him from raising the alarm. One of the men said, "She is the most feminine woman I know until the fighting starts. Then she is like five men." Nancy also ordered the execution of a French spy. Not one to dwell on guilt, afterwards, Nancy stated that her command "didn't put me off my breakfast. After all, she had an easy death. She didn't suffer." When ten men in her camp refused to perform their water-carrying duties, she persuaded them by pouring a bucket of water over their heads. When not engaged in drinking contests, killing the enemy, or disciplining her fellow fighters, Nancy's mission was to radio London in regard to munitions. Due to the efforts of the woman who went by the code name "Madame Andrée," grenades rained on Nazi helmets.

On D-Day, Wake's activities entailed ambushing Germans, blowing up bridges, and planting explosives on train tracks to reinforce the efforts of the Allies fighting on the beaches of Normandy. Another mission involved a seventy-one-hour ride on a bicycle from Auvergne to Châteauroux, through German-held territory, to replace codes her wireless operator had destroyed to prevent them falling into enemy hands. She recalled of the harrowing journey, "When I got off that damned bike I felt as if I had a fire between my legs. I couldn't stand up. I couldn't sit down. I couldn't walk. When I'm asked what I'm most proud of doing during the war, I say: 'The bike ride.'"

Wake and her fellow freedom fighters were part of the liberation of Vichy from Marshal Philippe Pétain's collaborators, who had made it their capital. In tribute, one of the band of brothers showered praise, saying "Madame Andrée is braver than Jacques, and Jacques is the bravest of us all."

After the war, in honor of Wake's heroism, she received numerous tributes, including the George Medal from Britain, the Congressional Medal of Honor from the United States, and three French awards: the Légion d'Honneur, the Croix de Guerre, the Médaille de la Résistance. The Australian government withheld official recognition on the grounds that she had not fought for any of their country's services. In her final years, the government tried to rectify the oversight, but a still-feisty Wake rebuffed their offer. She groused, "The last time there was a suggestion of giving me an Australian medal I told the government they could stick their medals where the monkey stuck his nuts. They can bugger off!" Ultimately, she accepted the Companion of the Order of Australia in 2004, and two years later received the Royal New Zealand Returned and Services' Association's highest honor, the RSA Badge in Gold. Currently, the Australian War Memorial Museum in Canberra displays these mementos. Nancy Wake became the Allies' most decorated servicewoman.

Dorothy Parker wrote, "They sicken of the calm/who knew the storm," and, in this vein, peace hung heavy as Nancy's *raison d'être* had come to an end. In a newspaper interview in 1983, she mused, "It's all been so exciting...and then it all fizzled out. I had a very happy war." Desirous of finding another cause, she set her eye on the political arena. After two unsuccessful bids for Australian parliament, she bowed out.

She took another walk down the aisle with former Royal Air Force pilot John Forward. The marriage proved happy, as John was able to cope with a wife who oscillated quickly between high spirits and sudden bouts of fury. After her husband's death, the second-time widow relocated to London in 2001 to work for British intelligence, taking up residence in the Stafford Hotel.

The story of the resistance fighter inspired the 1999 novel by Sebastian Faulks, *Charlotte Gray*, that later became a movie starring Australian actress Cate Blanchett as Wake. The wartime heroine said of the movie, "It was well-acted, but in parts it was extremely stupid. At one stage they had me cooking eggs and bacon to feed the men. For goodness sake, did the Allies parachute me into France to fry eggs and bacon for the men? There wasn't an egg to be had for love nor money. Even if there had been, why would I be frying it? I had men to do that sort of thing." Ms. Wake was also angered by a television series that suggested she had been involved in a love affair with a member of the Resistance. She said she had been too busy killing Nazis to be bothered with amorous pursuits. In her old age, she said she regretted not having affairs, but added, "If I had accommodated one man, the word would have spread around, and I would have had to accommodate the whole damn lot!"

Ms. Wake requested cremation and for her ashes "to be scattered over the mountains where I fought with the Resistance. That will be good enough for me."

CHAPTER 17

"Our Lady of Kick-Ass" (1916)

*"If men could get pregnant,
abortion would be a sacrament."*

—FLORYNCE KENNEDY

Badass is the colloquial term for feminists who refuse to march to a patriarchal drummer. And the word is spot-on to describe the woman whose variation of a sit-in proved she was a badass on steroids.

Driving through the streets of New York, a cab driver shared his political views with his passengers. "Those good-for-nothing politicians, including the governor, to hell with 'em. They oughtta be—" After he apologized for his vulgar language, the passenger in the front seat responded, "Ooooooo, honey," she said, "That's just baby talk." She should know, as she greatly enjoyed her reputation as radicalism's rudest mouth.

Florynce Rae was born in Kansas City, Missouri, the second of five daughters of Wiley and Zella Kennedy. Despite the American-royalty connotations of their surname, the family was part of the "pooristocrats" of the Black community. Her father was a Pullman porter and taxi driver; during the Depression, her mother worked as a cleaning lady. Flo, the name used by friend and foe alike, believed radical activism was her birthright. Mr. Kennedy once confronted the Ku Klux Klan with a shotgun when they attempted to drive him from his home in a predominantly white neighborhood. He stood up to the white-robed interlopers, "Now the first foot that hits that step belongs to the man I shoot. And then after that you can decide who is going to shoot me." After a teacher threatened ten-year-old Flo with a whipping for hitting a boy, her father showed the principal his shotgun and threatened to use it if he ever laid a hand on his child. Wiley and Zella rarely criticized their daughters and treated their children as if they could do no wrong. In her autobiography, *Color Me Flo: My Hard Life and Good Times*, she wrote, "Our parents had us so convinced we were precious that by the time I found out I was nothing, it was already too late—I knew I was something." Because of this instilled confidence, even when the Kennedys did not have money to heat their home, Flo wrote letters to people she read about in newspapers as if she were a member of their country clubs. Kennedy later wrote that her mother "epitomized hope;" in an act of optimism, Zella planted rosebushes, even though their yard was too shady for flowers. Her younger sister Joy recalled that Flo was the eternal optimist despite a childhood injury that left her with a fused spine.

In 1934, Flo graduated at the top of her class at Lincoln High School, at which time she engaged in her first tryst with activism when she helped organize a boycott of a local Coca-Cola bottler that did not hire Black truck drivers. As the era dictated that higher education for African Americans was "really kind of unheard of," she ran a hat shop, performed on a radio show, and operated an elevator. After the death of her mother, she and her sister Grayce moved to Harlem. When she announced she was going to go to school despite societal expectations, everyone urged her to take the traditional female route of nursing or teaching. Flo enrolled in pre-law at Columbia University. Adept at the art of the adage, she said, "I find that the higher you aim, the better you shoot."

Despite her A average, Columbia Law School rejected Flo's application, a decision it only reversed when she threatened to sue on the grounds of racial discrimination. She was the only Black person, and one of only eight women, in her class. After graduation, Flo worked briefly for a Manhattan law firm. However, wanting to handle affairs her way, Kennedy established her own practice in 1954. Her career took an upswing when she represented the estates of jazz greats Charlie Parker and Billie Holiday, as well as civil rights leader H. Rap Brown. Another client was Valerie Solanas, the woman who attempted to assassinate Andy Warhol. On one occasion, a judge admonished her for wearing pants. In response, Flo looked at him in his long black robe and retorted, "Judge, if you won't talk about what I'm wearing, I won't talk about what you're wearing."

In 1969, Ms. Kennedy represented twenty-one Black Panthers charged with conspiracy to commit bombings. The trial proved publicity gold for Ms. Kennedy, who seized the opportunity to make a political statement. At the time, Flo and Emily Jane Goodman—who went on to become a justice of the New York State Supreme Court—were renting a house on Fire Island. Never one to miss an opportunity to raise eyebrows and drop jaws, Flo, along with Emily, took the Panthers to dinner at a restaurant that did not serve Blacks or Jews. The appearance of the Black Panthers and the flamboyant Flo created quite the tempest in a teapot, the intended effect. Later, Ms. Goodman asked her friend if their action that night was an appropriate one, considering the life-and-death issues at stake. Kennedy responded, "You have to fight on all the fronts, all the time." Other fronts included the founding of the Feminist Party in 1971, whose first act was to nominate Shirley Chisholm, a Black Democratic Representative from New York, for president.

In a bid to recreate the happy family of her childhood, in 1957, Ms. Kennedy married the ten-years-younger Charles Dudley Dye, a Welsh science fiction writer. He died a few years later from alcoholism, yet she was far from the grieving widow. She said of her non-blissful marriage, "Anyone who marries a drunk Welshman doesn't deserve any sympathy." Thereafter, Flo's views on a husband were, "Why would you lock yourself in the bathroom just because you have to go three times a day?" Flo never remarried or had children.

The catalyst that turned Flo into a human whirlwind of activism occurred in 1965, after she ended up in court—this time as a defendant—for crossing a police barricade near her home. She argued that the reason for her arrest was because, "the cops...

did not believe that I could be a resident in such a nice neighborhood." Her anger led to Flo's eureka moment: she had a self-appointed task to make matters better for her Black brethren. She replaced her conservative clothes with outfits comprised of pink sunglasses, boots, and caps decorated with protest buttons—not typical attire for a Columbia-educated attorney. A 1976 photograph of Kennedy in a cowboy hat and leather vest shows her with an upraised middle finger. Another zinger occurred in the 1970s, when she was a guest on the Phil Donahue Show and sang, "My Country 'tis of thee/Sweet land of Bigotry..."

Her first order of business as a Black female political activist was to establish the Media Workshop to combat racism in journalism. Flo organized a picket line in front of an advertising agency that led to the protestors being invited upstairs to state their case. Flo said, "Ever since, I've been able to say, 'When you want to get to the suites, start in the streets.'" Increasingly, her legal cases became political. Flo often remarked, "Sweetie, if you're not living on the edge, then you're taking up space."

In 1968, Flo sued the Roman Catholic Church for its interference with women's access to abortion. The following year, along with a group of feminist lawyers, she challenged the constitutionality of New York State's abortion law, that helped influence the legislature to liberalize pro-choice. Donning another hat—one that, figuratively, bore her protest buttons—Flo cowrote one of the first books on women's experiences of abortion, *Abortion Rap*. Flo remarked, "It's interesting to speculate how it developed that in two of the most anti-feminist institutions, the church and the law court, the men are wearing the dresses."

In some of the headiest days of the twentieth century, there were many hydra heads to slay, and in addition to fighting sexism and racism, Flo was vocal against America's participation in the war in Southeast Asia. In 1967, Flo took the stage at an anti-Vietnam War convention in Montreal to protest the exclusion of the Black radical Bobby Seale, who wanted to discuss racism. Flo said of the experience, "I went berserk. I took the platform and starting yelling and hollering." Her antics bore unexpected fruit, and an invitation for Ms. Kennedy to speak in Washington followed. Thus began a twenty-year lecturing career that garnered $3,500 per appearance. Flo partnered with fellow when-it-hits-the-fan feminist Gloria Steinem; during one engagement, a man in the audience asked if the two of them were lesbians. Flo looked him in the eye and responded, yes—if he were the alternative. Ms. Steinem called her speaking tour with Ms. Kennedy "the Thelma and Louise of the '70s. I definitely speak first because after Flo I would have been an anticlimax." With her new lucrative career as a college guest speaker, Flo abandoned her law practice. She preferred the role of activist over attorney. "Law was just getting one ass out of the wringer at a time. Now I have one of the best gigs going. I'm a fifty-nine-year-old colored woman. I can afford to be frank and get paid for it." Her bag of tricks included songs such as "Striped Christmas" ("I'm dreaming of a STRIPED Christmas, like Richard Nixon never knew. Where a sheriff's badge glistens and Nixon listens..."). The firebrand also attacked the government for its persecution of prostitutes and stated, "Nobody ever died of performing or receiving fellatio."

The Harvard Pee-In was Flo's brainchild. Although the university had begun admitting female students, the school did not provide restrooms for their use. The situation was unfair as female students took timed exams in Lowell Hall and they were obliged to use a bathroom situated across a street, thereby losing crucial test-taking minutes. Consequently, the male students achieved higher scores. The ladies took their case to their Tom Joad of injustice wherein Flo devised a memorable act of civil disobedience. Female activists went on a protest march carrying signs such as: "To pee or not to pee, that is the question" while holding jars of yellow liquid. Kennedy delivered an impassioned speech stating that the lack of bathrooms was not only an inconvenience but also a sign of institutionalized inequality. On cue, the women took turns pouring the symbolic urine on the steps of Lowell Hall. Afterwards, Kennedy said that the Dean should take note that unless he rectified the situation, next time they would perform the actual act. With the great Harvard Pee-In, she had implemented her motto, "Don't agonize, organize."

Flo was also an advocate for equal opportunity in the job market. She stated, "There are very few jobs that actually require a penis or a vagina. All other jobs should be open to everyone."

As Flo's health deteriorated, her spirit remained steadfast. In her autobiography, she wrote, "I'm just a loud-mouthed, middle-aged colored lady with a fused spine and three feet of intestines missing, and a lot of people think I'm crazy. Maybe you do too, but I never stopped to wonder why I'm not like other people. The mystery to me is why more people aren't like me." There should be no doubt that Flo Kennedy is the patron saint of injustice: Our Lady of Kick-Ass.

CHAPTER 18

"Mother Courage" (1920)

"We are coming down from our pedestals and up from the laundry room."

—BELLA ABZUG

No domestic goddess of today could hold a candle to the 1950s *Happy Days* sitcom mom Mrs. Cunningham, whose advice could slay any crisis. She would have been appalled by the 1980s' Roseanne Barr, who boasted, "As a housewife, I feel that if the kids are still alive when my husband gets home from work, then hey, I've done my job." Bella Abzug was more Roseanne than Mrs. C. as she blazed a luminous trail.

Émile Zola once gave his reason for living as, "I came to live out loud." Bella could have amended his sentiment to, "I came to live out louder." The activist with *chutzpah* started life as Bella Savitzky from the Bronx, the younger sister of Helene, to Jewish immigrants from Russia. Her father Emmanuel, whom his daughter later described as a "humanist butcher," owned the Live and Let Live Meat Market on Ninth Avenue in Manhattan. For Bella, a cherished childhood memory was attending synagogue with her grandfather, Wolf Tanklefsky, though she chafed that women had to sit behind a curtain to separate them from the men. Levi Soshuk, her Hebrew schoolteacher, recruited her to a Zionist group that raised money for a Jewish homeland. Her first speech, at age twelve, was in a New York subway station, where she solicited donations.

Her father's passing when she was thirteen planted the seed from which sprung her fiery feminism. Her earliest act of rebellion concerned the *Kaddish*, the Jewish prayer for the dead, a ritual reserved for males. In her autobiography, *Bella on Bella*, she wrote, "In retrospect, I describe that as one of the early blows for the liberation of Jewish women. But in fact, no one could have stopped me from performing the duty traditionally reserved for a son, from honoring the man who had taught me to love peace, who had educated me in Jewish values. So it was lucky that no one ever tried." Her advice: "Be bold, be brazen."

After graduation from Hunter College, where Bella was the student body president, adept at the art of the argument, she set her sights on becoming a lawyer, her childhood aspiration. Outraged that Harvard rejected her on the basis of her sex, she enrolled at Columbia University on a scholarship, and became editor of the Law Review. During this time, she discovered two passions: poker and romance. While visiting relatives in Miami, she met fellow New Yorker Martin Abzug on a bus, also headed for a Yehudi Menuhin concert for the Russian War Relief. Although they shared a love of music, while politics was an essential part of Bella's DNA, Martin was apolitical. Despite their differences, marriage followed, after Martin assured her she could pursue her career despite the societal stigma against working mothers. They moved to a house in Mount Vernon, New York, where they raised daughters, Liz and Eve. Nanny Alice Williams helped with the girls, as Bella's duties entailed frequent absences. Bella received her degree in 1947; 2 percent of the graduates were women.

In private practice after World War II, Bella fought in defense of the defenseless, such as victims of Joseph McCarthy's anti-Communist witch hunts; she also participated in drafting the 1954 Civil Rights Act and the Voting Rights Act of 1965. A rebel with many causes, she led demonstrations in Washington on behalf of nuclear test bans.

A case that garnered international coverage was her defense of Willie McGee, a young Black man from Mississippi. An all-white jury, after deliberating for three minutes, sentenced him to death for the rape of a white woman. White supremacist groups reacted with hostility to the female Jewish lawyer from the North. The hotel where she had planned to stay refused her accommodation. Bella, eight months pregnant, spent the night on a bench in a bus station. Local newspapers wrote of lynching McGee and his "white, lady lawyer." She pursued the case through two appeals and numerous death threats before Willie's life ended in the electric chair. Martin said of his wife, "That woman has more guts than the whole damn Army."

At age fifty, Bella rose to national prominence when she became the first Jewish Congresswoman. There were only ten female US representatives at the time, and she canvassed with the slogan, "This woman belongs in the House." The era's sexism was apparent when New York Mayor John Lindsay, asked by a TV reporter why there were so few women in his administration, replied, "Honey, whatever women do, they do best after dark." The "mad men" of the time felt no compunctions about discussing a woman's appearance, and Bella's weight served as a target. The all-male New York press club Inner Circle show featured a *zaftig* Abzug impersonator who danced around singing, "I guess I've never been the high-fashion kind/Mother Nature gave me a big behind."

While Bella was often on the receiving end of barbs, due to her outsized personality that made her a human wrecking ball, she was no slouch at lashing out against those who crossed her. One night, a Bella campaign worker left for the Lion's Head bar next door to her Greenwich Village headquarters. As he clutched his side, he swore he would never again work for Abzug, as she had punched him in the side following a disagreement. A remorseful Bella contacted him the day after, "Michael, I called to apologize. How's your kidney?"

Abzug, one of the most outspoken members of Congress, became known as "Battling Bella." She denounced her white male colleagues arguing they were a privileged elite who were out of touch with America. During her tenure, Abzug fought sex discrimination, and she introduced the first gay rights bill.

When people used derogatory terms against Representative Abzug, she responded that if she had been a man, they would have substituted "courageous" for "abrasive," "forceful" for "strident."

In her autobiography, *Bella! Ms. Abzug Goes to Washington*, she wrote, "There are those who say I'm impatient, impetuous, uppity, rude, profane, brash, and overbearing. Whether I'm any of these things, or all of them, you can decide for yourself. But whatever I am—I am a very serious woman."

The desire to be taken seriously was the reason for Bella's trademark floppy hats, which she initially wore so clients would realize she was the attorney, not a secretary. Soon she was collecting hats the way Imelda Marcos would later collect shoes. The fashion statement made her easily recognizable, especially in contrast to the fourteen women in the 435-male-member House dressed as conservatively as possible so as to not draw attention. Her booming Bronx voice was a foghorn that writer Arthur Miller said "could boil the fat off a taxicab driver's neck." Truck drivers and construction workers needed no translation of her oft-used invectives. She upped her style when her purple hat matched her purple suit, a gold-brimmed number coordinated with a gold-checked suit. In her tenure as a congresswoman, she realized fellow politicians disapproved of her flamboyant fashion, which cemented her choice of apparel. The outlandish hats became a foil for comedians; one quipped that one day, Abzug threw one into the air, and it landed on Carl Albert, completely covering the pint-sized representative from Oklahoma. The only man who ever convinced her to go bareheaded was William "Fishbait" Miller, who made the demand when Abzug was about to step out on the House floor for the first time. She told him to perform an impossible sex act, but she removed the offending hat.

Bella also proved a thorn in the side of President Nixon; a visit to the White House prompted her to write in her journal, "Who wants to listen to his pious idiocies?" Never one to mince words, she informed the Chief Executive that her constituents demanded a withdrawal from Vietnam, and demanded the administration surrender the Pentagon Papers. Mrs. Abzug was the first member of Congress to call for impeachment. Gerald Ford, under fire for his pardon of Nixon, agreed to testify before a congressional committee, providing there was a time limit "and no questions from Bella Abzug." A Gallup poll announced she was one of the twenty most influential women in the world. Bella from the Bronx was so high-profile that in 1977, Andy Warhol was on his way to paint a portrait of the congresswoman for *Rolling Stone* to celebrate her run for mayor of New York. Due to Elvis Presley's death, the magazine canceled the cover.

Bella never stopped jousting against windmills. President Jimmy Carter fired her from a voluntary position on a Labor Department advisory committee on women after she criticized his decision to cut funding. The majority of the committee's members resigned in solidarity. She shrugged off her dismissal, saying "I've got to find myself another big, nonpaying job." In 1996, she campaigned for Clinton's reelection "because the Republicans are advancing a pre-fascist state." Among the mountains of hate mail she regularly received, one Democrat wrote, "You have made a Republican out of me." Fellow feminist Betty Friedan threatened to throw a plate of spaghetti at Abzug, who was wearing a white suit. Frances Cash, a former secretary, told *The Washington Post* she quit to become a flagman on a construction site, as she figured it would be easier on her nerves than "listening to Bella screaming." Former President George H. W. Bush, in China during the Beijing Conference where Abzug was a speaker, addressed a meeting of food production executives, saying, "I feel somewhat sorry for the Chinese, having Bella Abzug running around. Bella Abzug is one who has always represented the extremes of the women's movement." Upon hearing Bush's remark, Ms. Abzug, seventy-five and in a wheelchair, retorted, "He was addressing a fertilizer group? That's appropriate."

In contrast, her husband Martin was always in Camp Bella, and weekends were reserved for him. Naturally, being married to a force of nature entailed an existence of shock-and-awe. Bella, empathetic to the gay cause, especially after her daughter Liz came out as a lesbian, locked horns with Baptist singer Anita Bryant, who fought to repeal homosexual nondiscrimination laws. In tribute, four hundred gay men held a candlelit vigil outside the Abzug home.

During Bella's final 1986 campaign, when she ran for a House seat in Westchester County, Martin passed away after forty-two years of conjugal devotion. Nine years later, she admitted, "I haven't been entirely the same since." Her pain was apparent in an article she wrote entitled, "Martin, What Should I Do Now?" During the next decade, Ms. Abzug suffered from breast cancer, but she continued to practice law, to battle for women.

Bella said she was born yelling, and countless realms of ink were employed in describing the force of nature. The most apt of these adjectives: Mother Courage.

CHAPTER 19

"Lions, Not Mice" (1921)

"I paint for myself, basically. If people like it, bravo; if they don't, I don't care."

—FRANÇOISE GILOT

An astute observation is, "Behind every great man there is a great woman." As history can attest, many of these great women were consigned to the dustbin of time, obscured by their "better half" alpha males. Who remembers Mrs. Karl Marx, Mrs. Oscar Wilde, Mrs. Mohandas Gandhi? Yet one feisty wife refused to live under a shadow.

From her vantage point at the top of her grandmother's Parisian staircase, the five-year-old Françoise Gilot stared at the Impressionist painter Emile Mairet, dressed in a flowing black cape. When she asked about the guest, her grandmother replied, *"Ah, mais oui, il est un artiste!"* ("Ah, but yes, he is an artist!"). Françoise responded, *"Ah, moi aussi"* ("Me too").

The woman destined for a dual rendezvous with genius was the only child of Emile, owner of a chemical firm that produced colognes for Christian

Dior, and mother, Madeleine, who encouraged her daughter to have the career she had been denied. Françoise preferred riding horses in the Bois de Boulogne to playing with dolls. In school, Françoise discovered she did not think the same way as the other children, and she said, "I did not submit to rules if I did not see they had any meaning." Nevertheless, under paternal pressure, she enrolled in law at the Sorbonne.

In 1940, in defiance of the Nazi Occupation, the teenage Françoise joined a demonstration at the Arc de Triomphe, where participants placed flowers on the Tomb of the Unknown Soldier. Within days, the authorities had added Gilot to the list of those to be executed if a German met his end at French hands. Every morning, Françoise had to report to the local *kommandantur* (commandant's headquarters) at Neuilly-sur-Seine. As the fascist takeover meant laws no longer existed, Françoise dropped out of law school and pursued her passion for painting. A woman artist was an anomaly that led Françoise to comment, "I have never been stopped by the fact that other people did not like what I was doing. Sometimes the defect of women is that they are used to valuing themselves according to how they believe other people see them."

Three years later, Françoise was at the Left Bank bistro Le Catalan, accompanied by her friend, Genevieve Aliquot, and film actor Alain Cuny. Pablo Picasso and Dora Maar, the mistress he depicted as the weeping woman, were at the same café. When Dora noticed that the girl with the smoky-blue eyes, hair wrapped in a green turban, mesmerized her lover, she was distraught. The possessor of an abundance of *cojones*, Picasso placed a bowl of cherries on Françoise's table and pulled up a chair. Genevieve mentioned that Françoise was also an artist, to which Picasso's scoffed, "That's the funniest thing I've ever heard. Girls who look like you could never be painters." He left, taking the cherries with him.

Genevieve warned her about the man known to be as prolific with his phallus as with his paintbrush, but Françoise decided Picasso was a "catastrophe I didn't want to avoid." Taking up Picasso's offer to give her private lessons in engraving in his studio, Françoise showed up in a black velvet dress. When Picasso said her attire was not suitable for work, she replied that surely he did not mean for them to do any actual engraving. Taken aback, Picasso replied, "What nerve! Couldn't you at least *pretend* to be taken in, the way women generally do?"

Their affair did not take place because Picasso was the master of twentieth-century art, or because younger men were away at war. Françoise said of their relationship, "It was not what we call in French *l'amour fou! Non!*" but was rather "an intellectual love." The meeting of their minds was their shared hatred of fascism. Unlike many of France's other artists, Picasso did not flee during the Occupation, though his "degenerate art" required him to live under the scrutiny of the swastika. Picasso once handed out postcards of his antiwar painting *Guernica* to Nazi officers. When one asked if he had created the painting, Picasso answered, "No. You did."

Similarly, Picasso was drawn to Françoise by her strong sense of social conscience. Picasso had gone to Françoise's art exhibit, one not permitted to display "degenerate" modern art. Her canvases had passed the censors because the Germans did not understand their actual significance. Françoise recalled, "They thought they were just paintings of birds. But the birds were hawks, which symbolized the hated enemy, and the exhibit was a very anti-Nazi statement."

The couple kept their affair under wraps; even her liberal parents would have condemned the relationship. Picasso was sixty-one, their daughter twenty-one. In addition, the Spanish painter was married to the Russian dancer, Olga Khokhlova, with whom he shared son, Paulo. He also had a daughter, Maya, from his former flame, Marie-Thérèse Walter. When her father discovered the truth, he banned her from his house with the words, "You'd better put on some lead-soled shoes and get down to earth. Otherwise you're in for a rude awakening." When she learned "the schoolgirl" had supplanted her, Dora suffered a severe nervous breakdown. She told Françoise her affair with Picasso would not last and that she would be "out on the ash-heap before three months had passed."

Initially, Françoise subjugated her fiery spirit, content to be a mouse-spouse to the great man. One of the perks of being Madame Picasso was she was part of a rarified circle that included Jean-Paul Sartre and Simone de Beauvoir; she caught Matisse in his garden, playing hide-and-seek with his secretary. She refused to visit Gertrude Stein, as she could not tolerate her lover, Alice B. Toklas. After Matisse's comment that he would like to paint Françoise with green hair, Picasso painted *La Femme-fleur*. In the portrait, Françoise is standing because, as he admitted, "she is not at all the passive type."

It was hard being the mistress of a master, as the famed artist proved far from a perfect roommate. She said of her years with Picasso, "it was a permanent *tremblement de terre*—what do you say, earthquake?" His gift of cherries proved an apt metaphor for their relationship; a succulent exterior masked the pit at its core. He kept a goat in their villa and did not mind scorpions in their home as they represented his horoscope sign. At his insistence, "*la Picasotte*" as she was known in the neighborhood, gave birth to son Claude and daughter Paloma, Spanish for "dove." The proud papa doted on the docile Paloma, but was less affectionate with Claude, who he claimed had inherited his mother's willfulness. Eventually, Picasso tired of the domestic bed he had made. For Françoise, the demands of two children—and her third, Picasso—caused her to lose weight, leading to Picasso's reproach that he had a broomstick for a wife. Picasso's wandering eye once more began to wander. No "*paloma*" of the white variety was forthcoming.

Picasso had often remarked, "For me there are only two kinds of women, goddesses and doormats." Françoise tired of being either. After she told him she was leaving, he transformed to an enraged bull, "No woman leaves a man like me." He threatened that, as his common-law wife, she would have no claim to his fortune; he would make sure the art world would never display a Gilot canvas. As the taxi pulled up, Picasso muttered, "*Merde*." Of her escape as a single mother of two, she said, "When I left Picasso, I knew I would have a lot of enemies. They were already there, putting banana peels under my feet all the time." Although Picasso had threatened that without him Francoise would be destroyed, her escape made her the only one of his muses to survive. Olga became a crazed hysteric, Dora went mad, Marie-Thérèse and his last wife, Jacqueline, both committed suicide. Of her ability to escape from her Minotaur, she said, "You always survive if you think you should. I didn't ask permission to be who I am." In 1953, Françoise wed a painter, Luc Simon, from a family that had made cathedral stained-glass windows since the thirteenth century, with whom she had a daughter, Aurelia. After surviving the Occupation and Picasso, Françoise moved to the States and wrote her memoir, *Life with Picasso*. Although he felt entitled to portray Françoise on canvas, Picasso was enraged that she wrote about him in her memoir. Her comparison of Picasso to Bluebeard did not sit well, and he unsuccessfully sued to stop publication.

Picasso had sneered that no one would ever be interested in her except because of a "curiosity they will have about a person whose life has touched mine so intimately." He was wrong. In La Jolla, California, Françoise met Dr. Jonas Salk, inventor of the polio vaccine. Her scientist father would have approved of the match, though the divorced doctor had three adult sons. Françoise stated it was love at third sight: the first meeting was at a business lunch, the second at a dinner party, the third at Salk's oceanfront institute. He pursued her first in Manhattan, then in Paris. After she rejected his proposal, he told her to write down her reasons for her refusal. Her list included, "I can't live more than six months with one person. I have my own children. I have my career as a painter and have to go here and there. I'm not always in the mood to talk." Salk looked at the list and pronounced that they were congenial. They married in 1970 and lived in a wood-framed house overlooking the Pacific. She described Salk as the perfect husband and shared his life until his 1995 passing. Of her two husbands—one common-law, one legal—she wrote, "In Jonas Salk, the man is equal to the artist. Picasso, the man, was not on the same level as Picasso, the artist."

At age ninety-nine, Françoise retains her indomitable spirit. She owns homes in Paris and Manhattan, the latter near Central Park West, an enclave of art-lined walls that belies its proximity to bustling Broadway. When a reporter arrived, armed with a Xerox of her in a Picasso painting, she responded in her thick French accent, "I'm not going to talk about Picasso. I have done my duty to those memories. I have had a great career as an artist myself, you know. I'm not here just because I've spent time with Picasso." What piques her anger is the fear that posterity will only remember her as Picasso's lover, as Matisse's friend. Indeed, Françoise is far more than two great men's significant other; after all, the French Légion d'Honneur inducted her as a member. She also carved out a name for herself in the art world; a large Gilot oil painting fetches $200,000, and four of her works are in the collection of the Metropolitan Museum of Art. In a nod to a life lived her way, she said, "I am not one of those people who say I wish I had done this or that—no, because usually I did what I wanted to do." When a journalist asked her what her plans were, the almost century-old Françoise replied, "I'll paint. What else?"

Intrigued by the woman who had been the lover of two of the men profiled in *Time* magazine's most influential men of the twentieth century, Larry King interviewed Gilot, the possessor of a singular romantic resume. In answer to his question as what it was like to have captured first Picasso and then Salk, Françoise responded, "I'd like to think they had me. Lions mate with lions, not mice."

CHAPTER 20

"More Magical Than a Carriage" (1929)

"I, Kusama, am the modern Alice in Wonderland."

—YAYOI KUSAMA

Artists and eccentricities go together: Vincent van Gogh gave his severed ear to a prostitute as a present; Virginia Woolf heard birds sing in ancient Greek; Ozzy Osbourne bit the head off a bat. And eccentricity on steroids describes the pop-art, polka-dot princess.

Remarkably, Yayoi Kusama, who has spent her life battling the windmill of conventionality, was a product of tradition-bound Japan. Her family lived in rural, mountainous Matsumoto, where her wealthy father owned the region's largest nursery. The Kusama home was a stranger to happiness. Her mother harbored fury against her husband and sent her daughter to spy on him and his current conquest. She vented her rage on Yayoi.

To counteract her misery, Yayoi sketched flowers that transformed into endless dots, and disembodied voices wafted from the nursery. She recalled, "I had thought that only humans could speak, so

I was surprised the violets were using words. I was so terrified, my legs began shaking." These hallucinations haunted her childhood.

To fight her internal horror, Yayoi sketched repetitive patterns. Her work served as therapy, later termed "art-medicine." She continued her passion even though her mother, whom she describes as "an aggressive person," destroyed her canvases. Affirmation arrived at age eleven, when she won first prize for her painting of a pumpkin. After the attack on Pearl Harbor, a factory conscripted her to produce fabrics for parachutes. At night, she painted, sometimes producing seventy watercolors before she slept.

As a teenager, Yayoi and her mother made a deal: Yayoi could attend the Kyoto School of Arts and Crafts provided she also enrolled in etiquette classes. Not one to compromise when it involved her life, Yayoi never attended the school designed to make her a proper Japanese matron. Art classes that focused on Nihonga, a traditional and rule-bound form of painting, did not deliver fulfillment. What did pique her interest was a book by Georgia O'Keeffe, and the fledgling painter sent the American artist a sample of her work that featured surreal vegetables and exploding seed pods. Accompanying her painting was a letter asking for advice on how to break into the New York art scene. Surprised to hear from a woman in rural Japan, O'Keeffe replied that as she lived in New Mexico, she could not offer insight; the correspondence did, however, mark the beginning of a lifelong friendship.

While proper Japanese girls of the 1950s only left home for marriage, Yayoi determined to move to America, although she knew no one there and did not speak English. In order to circumvent postwar currency controls, Yayoi sewed money into her kimono. In her Manhattan apartment, an old door served as a bed; fish heads from dumpsters simmered as a broth; a room without heat led to freezing winters.

Kusama began producing her trademark huge "Infinity Net" canvases—one was thirty-three feet high—covered with seemingly endless, undulating waves of small loops. She described them as, "White nets enveloping the black dots of silent death against a pitch-dark background of nothingness." In her autobiography, *Infinity Net*, she related the occasion when she carried a canvas, far taller than herself, through the streets of Manhattan to submit it to the Whitney. After their rejection, on her forty-block trek home, a strong wind made her feel as if she and the canvas would be airborne. The roadblock she faced was the novel nature of her work; in addition, the New York art world of the era was so male-dominated that even female gallery owners did not want to exhibit paintings that bore a woman's signature.

In 1962, Kusama was overjoyed when she sold her first canvases to artists Frank Stella and Donald Judd for seventy-five dollars. The following year, her avant-garde work and the exotic persona of a kimono-clad Asian drew attention, and she held a solo show at the Gertrude Stein gallery. She displayed a rowboat and oars that she and Judd had covered with plaster phalluses. An art critic dubbed the exhibition "Alice in Willyland." In a decorative touch, she wallpapered the room with innumerable photocopies of the boat. Later, the diminutive powerhouse accused Andy Warhol, whom she had considered her friend, of stealing her idea when he pasted up endless pictures of a cow for his own show. Other objects adorned with a member of the male anatomy were chairs, ladders, mannequins, and baby carriages. Yayoi—who describes herself as asexual—claimed she made the phallic ornaments as a way of overcoming her phobia of penises, a souvenir from watching her father having intercourse with his geisha. Yayoi said, "I am terrified of just the thought of something long and ugly like a phallus entering me, and that is why I make so many of them."

The only romance of Yayoi's life was with the sculptor Joseph Cornell who, obsessed with Kusama, sent her a dozen poems a day. She told an interviewer of her decade-long relationship, "I disliked sex and he was impotent, so we suited each other well." Nonetheless, the couple drew each other in the nude; she described his penis as "a big, desiccated calzone." One afternoon, she was sitting on his lawn when his mother dumped a large bucket of water over their heads. In a nod to Norman Bates, Joseph clung to his mother and begged for forgiveness. The incident cooled Yayoi's ardor, though not her love.

As the hippie movement gained momentum, Kusama came into her own, and she staged "happenings" in which she enticed onlookers to strip naked in Central Park, at the Statue of Liberty, and on the Brooklyn Bridge, then painted their nude bodies with polka dots as they cavorted to the beat of bongo drums. Predating the Occupy Wall Street Movement, Kusama organized an event in Manhattan's financial district to "Obliterate Wall Street men with polka dots."

Yayoi became increasingly known for her outlandish behavior; she offered to sleep with President Richard M. Nixon in exchange for his ending the war in Vietnam. She wrote him, "Let's paint each other with polka dots." The Quaker president declined. During the 1968 Summer of Love, she staged—half a century ahead of its time—New York's first homosexual wedding. Branching out into fashion, Yayoi sold polka-dot designs with holes to reveal buttocks and breasts. Not desirous of being the archetypal starving artist, she worked rigorously at self-promotion because "the garret life of Van Gogh and Modigliani is not where it's at." Her publicity ploys worked, and she proudly declared that she made the news as much as her polar opposites: Jackie O, Andy Warhol, and President Nixon. Her notoriety made it back to Japan and her mother said she wished her daughter had died during a childhood illness.

After Nixon's reelection in 1972, the pendulum swung to conservatism, and society turned its back on the boundary breakers. Falling out of vogue, coupled with the deaths of Joseph and her father, in homing-bird fashion, Yayoi returned home despite her label, the "shame of Matsumoto City." There was no warm welcome for the return of the Prodigal Daughter; her high school had erased her name from its alumni list. Her tenth-floor apartment was in a tower block in Shinjuku, Tokyo, overlooking a cemetery, where she worked on surreal collages as an elegy to Joseph. The artist turned author with her novel *The Hustler's Grotto of Christopher Street,* in which she compared the world of art to the world of pimping. The hallucinations and panic attacks of her youth returned, and she sought relief in suicide. However, her desire to paint superseded her desire to die, and she checked herself into a psychiatric hospital. For more than twenty years, she remained a forgotten footnote.

A change in fortune occurred in 1989, when the Center for International Contemporary Arts in Manhattan put on a display of Kusama's works that ushered in her revival. When the city held an exhibit at the David Zwirner Galley, people waited in line for forty-five seconds of viewing time. For the exhibition at the Venice Biennale, she filled a mirrored room with pumpkins. Several years later, the Museum of Modern Art in New York, a venue where she had once held a "happening," arranged a retrospective.

Currently, the ninety-one-year-old Yayoi is a global phenomenon; more than five million visitors have lined up for viewings of her solo shows in Rio de Janeiro, Seoul, and Taiwan, while traveling exhibits made their way to the United States and Europe. Kusama's signature polka dots—her clothes mimic the themes of her canvases, such as one outfit covered with yellow tentacles—are globally recognized. In 2017, the artist opened her own five-story gallery in Tokyo; in a nod to irony, Japan also has the Yayoi Kusama Museum. In Los Angeles, the Broad Museum sold ninety thousand twenty-five-dollar tickets in one afternoon for her exhibit, that led *The Los Angeles Times* to ask if the artist was now "Hotter than *Hamilton*?" The different drummer dame had her own balloon in a Macy's Thanksgiving Day Parade alongside Pikachu, SpongeBob, and the Elf on the Shelf.

The woman who had survived on fish-head broth achieved not only fame, but also a wealth beyond the wildest dreams of a child who once saw hallucinations in a field of flowers. Her trademark polka dots cover everything from Louis Vuitton dresses to buses in her hometown. In 2014, a canvas sold for $7.1 million, a record for a female artist. Fans have hashtagged her more than three hundred thousand times, and Adele used one of her famous Infinity Mirrored Rooms as the setting for a 2016 performance. The backdrop displayed mirrored walls adorned with paper lanterns that rotated and shimmered with splashes of color.

After forty years, Yayoi remains a volunteer resident at the psychiatric hospital that lies in proximity to her three-story studio. Her official hours are from nine to six, but she often arrives at three in the morning in the desperate attempt to silence the voices in her head. Despite the ninety-one-year-old's reliance on her blue polka-dotted wheelchair, she is able to stand for periods of time in front of her easel. Although Yayoi has an international reputation and is in possession of a many-splendored bank account, she still seeks validation, an echo of the girl who lurks in a septuagenarian body.

Any interviewer who asks the Grande Dame of pop art what she feels has been the highlight of her career is likely to receive a glaring expression under eyes framed by red anime bangs of a color not found in nature. Yayoi feels her greatest work lies in the possibility of tomorrow. However, given her age and her brushes with the Grim Reaper, Kusama is planning her final resting place in Matsumoto—though not in the family plot. The artist's thoughts on her mortality shine a light on her indomitable spirit. "But I'm not dying yet. I think I can live another twenty years." The polka-dot princess's life proves that sometimes a pumpkin can prove more magical than a carriage.

CHAPTER 21

"Santa's Female Counterpart" (1931)

"Wouldn't it be better to die doing something interesting than to drop dead in an office and the last thing you see is someone you don't like?"

—BARBARA HILLARY

In 1953, Edmund Hillary stood on the summit of the world, the first man to scale Mount Everest. Fifty-four years later, a woman who shared his surname also achieved a historical first, all the more remarkable as she did so in her seventh decade. Her life serves as a resounding slap to the stereotypes regarding old age.

A remarkable life began in Harlem during the Great Depression. Barbara Hillary's father passed away when she was two, leaving her mother Viola to raise Barbara and her sister Dorothy on her income as a maid. Barbara reminisced, "We were sub-depression poor but there was no such thing as mental poverty in our home...no such thing as woe is me." Escape came from books, and Barbara preferred ones that dealt with surviving in extreme circumstances. Her favorite was Daniel Defoe's *Robinson Crusoe*.

Hillary received her bachelor's degree at New York's Bellevue School of Nursing and earned her master's in gerontology at New School University. Post-graduation, she worked in nursing homes, founded the *Peninsula Magazine*, a multi-racial publication based in Queens, and drove a taxi. Her hobbies included archery, guns, big trucks, and big dogs. Her garden was a study in scarlet, where she grew tomatoes and red roses. Her tips for life were, "One, mind your own business; two, maintain a sense of humor; and three, tell an individual to go to hell when it's needed." Having survived breast cancer in her twenties, she came down with lung cancer in her sixties, requiring an operation that reduced her lung capacity by a quarter.

Many long for retirement and dream of mornings free of the tyranny of alarm clocks, meals not served on trays, binge-watching Netflix. In marked contrast, after working as a nurse for fifty-five years, Barbara retired, and in celebration she left for a dog-sledding vacation in Québec. However, her rendezvous with the road less traveled began when Barbara saw a picture in a catalogue of a polar bear and decided to be the one to take the photograph. At age seventy-one, as her visit to the Central Park Zoo failed to do the trick, she flew to Churchill in northern Manitoba, Canada. Besotted with what she called the "stark beauty and pristine cleanliness" of her surroundings, she took dozens of snapshots to commit the landscape to memory. When she discovered that no African American woman had ever reached the North Pole, she resolved to change that paradigm. She exclaimed, "What's wrong with this picture?" After all, Ms. Hillary's roadmap to life was WWRCD? (What would Robinson Crusoe do?) The aspiration would be daunting for most twenty-somethings, let alone a septuagenarian, but the tenacious bulldog did not countenance the mindset of *I can't.*

In her aspiration, Barbara was walking in lofty, snow-covered footsteps. In 1909, a *New York Times* headline proclaimed, "Robert Peary Discovers the North Pole after Eight Trials in 23 Years." The news ricocheted around the world, as the virgin territory had remained one of the last uncharted territories. The photograph of Peary planting a tattered American flag on the icy surface is iconic. Seventy-seven years later, Ann Bancroft, a physical education teacher and explorer from Minnesota, became the first woman to set foot on the snowy wonderland. Barbara Hillary, of Harlem, deemed it time for another historical first.

Her goal seemed in keeping with the *Man from La Mancha's* lyric, "To dream the impossible dream." The intrepid spirit was in her seventies, had only 75 percent breathing capacity from her cancer surgery, and did not possess the requisite funds. Moreover, as she had never married or had children, and with contemporaries who did not dream of embarking on her endeavor, she had no traveling companion. These factors did not derail her quest.

As Barbara's proposed journey predated Kickstarter and GoFundMe, she turned to Mayor Michael Bloomberg, who suggested she contact the Department for the Aging. She received a form letter listing all the activities she could participate in at the local center. Barbara retorted, "Mister, don't you get it? If I'm going to the North Pole, why the hell do

I need a senior center?" Hillary raised $25,000 for equipment and transportation with the support of several private donors.

Part of her trek would involve skiing, something Barbara had never attempted. As she explained, "It wasn't a popular sport in Harlem." In preparation, she took cross-country skiing lessons and hired a personal trainer in her gym in Rockaway Park, Queens, New York. Her new regimen included a quantity of vegetables, vitamins, and workouts with weights and the treadmill.

There are only a limited number of ways to reach the North Pole, located in the middle of the Arctic Ocean, where the waters are covered with shifting slices of ice. Ms. Hillary signed on for her expedition with Eagle's Cry Adventure, who deposited her by helicopter at Longyearbyen, Norway, approximately thirty miles from her destination. Thereupon, she and her guide—a contemporary Sir Edmund and his Sherpa, Tenzing Norgay—struggling under the weight of heavy gear, set off on the thirty-mile trip on skis.

When Sir Edmund Hillary stared out from the summit of the world, the panorama of the Himalayas lay before him: Tibet to the north, endless jagged mountain peaks, the glittering Kangshung Glacier ten thousand feet below. The scene was one he would recollect all the days of his life, "The whole world around us lay spread out like a giant relief map. I am a lucky man. I have had a dream and it has come true, and that is not a thing that happens often to men."

In the same vein, Ms. Hillary told a reporter from the *New Yorker*, of the moment her skis came to a standstill on the white frost of the North Pole, "I have never experienced such sheer joy and excitement. I was screaming, jumping up and down, for the first few minutes." In her euphoria, she forgot the cold and removed her gloves to fist-pump the air, leaving her fingers frostbitten. Barbara dedicated the expedition to her mother.

A few years later, months shy of her eightieth birthday, the adventurer was determined to tackle another groundbreaking journey. Feeling as she had conquered one pole and therefore why not another, she set out to raise the $40,000 required to reach the South Pole, a feat she accomplished in 2011. The trek was not without creature comforts, and on the ends of the earth, Barbara indulged—actually, as she admitted, over-indulged—her love of milk chocolate. As she told *The New York Times* upon her return, "If I had frozen to death down there, wouldn't it be sad if I'd gone to hell without getting what I want?" While Barbara consumed quantities of her favorite treat, Norgay, a devout Buddhist, had buried chocolate and biscuits as an offering to the gods of Everest.

A further similarity between the New Zealand mountaineer and the Harlem explorer was that both their journeys made them into environmental activists. Edmund was appalled at the commercialization and circus atmosphere surrounding expeditions of Mount Everest. In 2003, as a crowd converged in Katmandu, Nepal, for the fiftieth anniversary of his singular accomplishment, he groused, "I'm not very happy about the future of Everest. Yesterday there were a thousand people there and some five hundred tents. There was a booze place for drinks. Sitting around in a big base camp and knocking back cans of beer. I do not particularly view that as mountaineering."

Upon her return to New York, Ms. Hillary embarked upon a second career as a climate change activist. From her experiences at the North and South Poles, Barbara understood that climate change was wreaking havoc on the planet, especially in the polar extremities. Her concerns led her to lecture on the topic, one near and dear to her heart. She told an interviewer for the *New Yorker*, "I think we're hell-bent on blowing ourselves up into hydrogen particles." An additional hat that Hillary wore was that of a motivational speaker. In 2017, Barbara delivered the commencement address at the New School, formerly the New School for Social Research, her alma mater. She shared with the graduates her life's guiding philosophy: "At every phase in your life, look at your options. Please, do not select the boring ones."

Hillary continued to spread her message into her eighties, but that did not mean her traveling days receded in the rearview mirror. Despite failing health, in 2019, at age eighty-seven, Barbara traveled to Outer Magnolia, where she spent time with nomadic tribes and discussed their concern about the climate crisis eroding their way of life. In the rugged terrain, she met a female falconer—someone who hunts using birds of prey—a custom extremely rare among the women of the region. The encounter of the two women from worlds away was a nod to serendipity.

For her next destination, Barbara had set her sights on Russia. However, given her poor health, she understood the journey might not materialize. She told a reporter, "Dreams, even if they don't come true, are important." Unsurprisingly, Ms. Hillary poured gold into her golden years.

The two Hillarys shared another commonality, besides their names and reaching the highest and lowest places on the planet. In 1985, Edmund, along with astronaut Neil Armstrong, flew a twin-engine ski plane over the Arctic and landed at the North Pole. The feat made him the first to stand at both Poles. The intrepid trailblazers both passed away at the age of eighty-eight. However, the world lavished laurels on Edmund, and his name has a secure niche in history. Upon his return from Mount Everest, the newly crowned Queen Elizabeth II conferred upon him the title of Knight Commander of the Order of the British Empire and a Knight of the Order of the Garter. In 2003, Nepal presented him with honorary citizenship, making him the first foreign national to receive the distinction. Although not crowned with such lofty laurels, Barbara achieved a measure of renown and a realm of self-satisfaction.

Barbara had a tradition of celebrating each of her birthdays by giving gifts to people in her neighborhood, such as the mechanic or the butcher, to show her appreciation for their services. In that regard, she shared another connection with the North Pole: she was Santa's female counterpart.

CHAPTER 22

"Touch, Touch" (1932)

"I do not sing politics. I merely sing the truth."

—MIRIAM MAKEBA

Nelson Mandela, who endured twenty-seven years in South Africa's brutal Robben Island, was instrumental in shaking off the yoke of apartheid. For his lifelong arm-wrestle against the Afrikaner regime, he became a beloved icon, the father of his people. Another freedom fighter against colonialism was the woman known by the epithet "Mama Africa."

Destined to travel long and far from her ancestral home, Zenzile Miriam Makeba's given name originated from the Xhosa language and translates to "You have no one to blame but yourself." Miriam was the youngest of six children, raised in the Black shantytown of Johannesburg to a Xhosa father, Caswell, and Swazi mother, Christina, both tribes hailing from the Eastern Cape region. When Miriam was eighteen days old, local authorities arrested Christina—accompanied by her baby—for a six-month jail term for brewing and selling homemade beer, an illegal activity for Africans. The family later relocated to Transvaal, where Caswell worked as a clerk for

Shell; Christina was an *Isangoma* (a healer and diviner possessed by spirits) who doubled as a maid for white families. Despite the racism and poverty, the Makeba home resonated with music: Christina played traditional instruments, and Caswell was a member of a band, the Mississippi Twelve. After sneaking into church choirs where her sister Mizpha sang, Miriam became a member. Her brother Joseph introduced her to American great Ella Fitzgerald. Caswell passed away when Miriam was six, and as a teen she followed in her mother's domestic footsteps.

Music, which Miriam described as "a type of magic," provided solace, "Who can keep us down as long as we have our music?" The teachers at her Methodist Training School in Pretoria praised her talent, and she performed "What a Sad Life for a Black Man" with fellow students for King George VI's visit. After Miriam and the other classmates waited in the rain for the royal, he drove by without stopping. After apartheid became the law of the land, life was even more oppressive for South Africa's indigenous population.

At age seventeen, Miriam began a relationship with James Kubay, with whom she had her only child, Sibongile (Bongi). After the birth, her doctor advised her to undergo a breast removal after he detected a cancerous growth. Miriam credited her recovery to her mother, who treated her with tribal medicine. The couple married, but the union was short-lived: Kubay beat her senseless and slept with her sister.

What helped combat her illness and broken marriage was Miriam's artistic success. Since the turn of the century, American jazz and ragtime had blended with Anglican Church hymns in a new genre termed "*mbube*," one for which her voice was well suited. Makeba's big break arrived in 1954, when she joined the country's 1950s superstar band, the Manhattan Brothers. On tour with her new group, she visited Rhodesia (Zimbabwe) and Congo, where her powerful vocals earned her the nickname "The Nightingale." In 1957, Miriam became a soloist in the African Jazz and Variety Review, which toured Africa for eighteen months. Afterwards, she landed the female lead role in *King Kong*, a South African musical about the life of a legendary boxer. The show spread her reputation with both Black and white audiences. The feisty township singer was already a celebrity when she had a cameo in a controversial film, *Come Back, Africa*, covertly filmed by the American director Lionel Rogosin, which he smuggled abroad to broadcast the angst of apartheid. In 1959, Miriam married African Indian balladeer Sony Pillay; the marriage ended the same year. Rogosin brought Miriam to the movie's screening at the Venice film festival; this appearance earned her international acclaim. Her signature song was "Pata Pata"—that, she explained, was "the name of a dance we do down Johannesburg way." The exotic performer in leopard-skin dresses, hair fashioned into cornrows decorated with large white beads, enthralled fans.

While Miriam's songs made her famous, her politics made her infamous to the Afrikaner regime. After making plans to return home upon her mother's 1960 passing, she reported to the South African Consulate in Chicago, where an official stamped her passport "invalid." Angered at Makebo's resistance, her homeland blocked her reentry, making her a stateless individual. In solidarity, other countries, such as Cuba, Guinea, and Tanzania. issued her honorary passports. She became a wandering symbol of her nation's brutality, but it failed to silence their songbird: after the Sharpeville massacre, she recorded "Soweto Blues." When she sang "Pata Pata," audiences swayed to her music and swayed against the regime she consistently denounced. Of her exile, she said, "No pain matches the pain of not having a country." She said her agony would never end until she could return to the land that formed the bedrock of her soul.

Calypso singer Harry Belafonte—whom she called Big Brother—had been her fan since viewing *Come Back, Africa*, and he arranged bookings in the United States. Their album, *An Evening with Belafonte/Makeba*, garnered a Grammy Award. Through Belafonte's connections, Makeba was a guest on *The Steve Allen Show* and *The Ed Sullivan Show*, where the latter introduced her as "magnificent." Other performances were at the Village Vanguard jazz club, Manhattan's hottest nightclub; in the audience were celebrities Sidney Poitier, Miles Davis, and Bing Crosby—as well as detractors. As Miriam recalled, "At the end of one show, two men come to see me. I can tell right away by their Dutch looks, and by the way they look at me as if they own me, that they are Afrikaners. One of them says, 'We came here because we thought we'd hear music from home. Why don't you sing any *lietjies*?' 'When you start singing in my language,' I tell them, ' I will start singing in yours.' " On a positive note, *Time* magazine ran a feature on Makeba, and she met her idol, Ella Fitzgerald. The African nightingale also appeared at Carnegie Hall and the Newport Jazz Festival. The mind boggles at the juxtaposition of two women entertainers who performed at President Kennedy's forty-fifth birthday celebration at Madison Square Garden. One was Marilyn Monroe, in a figure-hugging sequined gown, who purred, "Happy burrthay, Mr. President"; another was Miriam Makeba, dressed in a tribal-themed dress, who belted out "Pata Pata." Suffering from a fever, Miriam did not go to the after-show party; however, as President Kennedy insisted on meeting her, Belafonte arranged transportation, and she shook the leader of the free world's hand. She said of the encounter, "I was very happy to have met a president of the United States—little me!"

Unlike other entertainers, Miriam did not concern herself with royalties or fame; her mission was to rid the world of the stench of racism. Makeba had first arrived in America during its civil rights struggle, and to further its cause, Miriam performed at the Reverend Dr. Martin Luther King Jr.'s marches. At the United Nations General Assembly, she followed Belafonte's advice to not be a tornado, but to be a submarine, when she denounced apartheid; in retaliation, South Africa banned her records. In contrast, Emperor Haile Selassie chose her as the only singer to participate in the inauguration of the Organization of African Unity in Addis Ababa.

Makeba made a third walk down the aisle with Hugh Masekela, a South African trumpet player; his addictions and her cervical cancer contributed to the demise of their two-year relationship. Her most scandalous marriage took place in 1967, when Miriam wed the militant Stokely Carmichael, despite her manager's warning that people would not feed the hand that was going to slap them. Carmichael was responsible for designing the Blank Panther logo and the slogan Black Power. Stokely—who went by his adopted name of Kwame Touré—and Miriam moved to Guinea, where the leader of the African Marxist state, Sékou Touré, offered sanctuary to enemies of the capitalist West. The couple lived in a seaside villa, where Stokely greeted visitors in the green uniform of a Guinean soldier, replete with a pistol. Eschewing anything as prosaic as "Hello," he answered their phone, "Ready for the revolution!" As the wife of Carmichael, Miriam became a double exile: unable to return to the land of her birth, and unwelcome in America, which turned against her for her association with the Black Power radical. Promoters canceled her concerts; her record company did not call when it was time to release her new album. She became persona non grata in the United States, where the FBI harassed her, and Jamaica, the Bahamas, and others removed their welcome mats. Her unabashed response to the ending of her American career was, "I didn't care about that. He was somebody I loved, who loved me, and it was my life."

Life in Guinea was far from peaceful; in 1970, Portuguese mercenaries launched an invasion, and in 1974, Miriam and Stokely parted ways. What helped with the hurt of her fourth divorce was singing at the festival that accompanied "The Rumble in the Jungle" in Zaire, between Muhammad Ali and George Foreman. Her love of being on stage was made obvious when she said, "that is the one place where I am most at home, where there is no exile." The greatest heartache of her life was the loss of her beloved Bongi, who died after a miscarriage that caused her to succumb to a "spiritual madness." Her fifth bid for marital happiness was with Belgian airline executive Bageot Bah, which also came with an expiration date. Miriam said of her peaks-and-valleys days, "My life has been like a yo-yo. One minute I'm dining with presidents and emperors, the next I'm hitchhiking. I've accepted it. I say, 'Hey, maybe that's the way it was written, and it has to be.' "

After two decades of obscurity, Miriam returned to the spotlight, joining Paul Simon's Graceland World Tour. The event thrust her into the eye of a storm, as it defied the United Nations' cultural boycott of South Africa, a ruling she, ironically, had instigated. Nevertheless, the tour offered a universal message of brotherhood that transcended politics.

When Nelson Mandela left prison in 1990 and apartheid was in its death throes, Mama Africa could at last end her thirty-one-year exile. She told a crowd of well-wishers who had gathered at the airport, "My umbilical cord is buried in this soil." South Africa reinstated her citizenship. In her ancestral home, she did what she had always done: use music as a balm for healing. Two years later, along with actress Whoopi Goldberg, she starred in the film *Sarafina!* set against the backdrop of the Soweto youth uprisings.

Ever the activist, in 2008, Miriam performed in Italy at a benefit concert for Roberto Saviano, an author who had received death threats after exposing organized crime. As she was exiting the stage, she collapsed, and passed away as a result of cardiac arrest. Mandela said of her passing, "Her music inspired a powerful sense of hope in all of us. She was South Africa's first lady of song." While apartheid translates to "apart-ness," the last song she performed was a plea for unification: "Pata, Pata" ("Touch, Touch").

CHAPTER 23

"Keep the Beat" (1934)

"You can have what you ask for,
ask for everything."

—DIANE DI PRIMA

In 1955, Allen Ginsberg introduced his poem "Howl" at San Francisco's Six Gallery. The café had advertised the event with a postcard: "Remarkable collection of angels all gathered at once in the same spot. Wine, music, dancing girls, serious poetry, free satori." The term "satori" meant a deep understanding in the Zen sense; the words "dancing girls" displayed the Beatniks as a band of brothers who viewed females as accessories. The most egregious instance of a woman wronged was when William S. Burroughs, author of *Naked Lunch*, killed his wife in a drunken game of William Tell. Yet, a sister made her niche in their ranks, one who put the heartbeat in the Beat Generation.

Diane Rose di Prima read two of her poems at the Last Waltz, the famous final concert by the Band, filmed as a documentary by Martin Scorsese; she served as the bridge between the Beat Movement and the emergent hippies; and became Poet Laureate of San Francisco, all just the tip of the di Prima iceberg. She lived a life far afield from the suburban-housewife world of the 1950s that extolled a culture of conformity: white picket fence, docile wife, two children who looked like Dick and Jane from the basal reader.

She was born in the Italian-American neighborhood of Red Hook, Brooklyn, to Emma, a reading teacher, and Francis, a lawyer. Her mother, and grandmother Antoinette, shared an oft-repeated proverb, "Women had to learn to bear more pain than men. That's just how they were made." In her 2002 memoir, *Recollections of My Life as a Woman: The New York Years*, di Prima wrote, "It was at my grandmother's side, in that scrubbed and waxed apartment, that I received my first communications about the specialness and the relative uselessness of men." What counteracted the message was her grandfather, Domenico Mallozzi, a tailor and anarchist, a champion of Emma Goldman, who introduced her to the poetry of Dante. Diane decided she was going to be a pirate when she grew up; Emma insisted she take typing classes. At one point, Diane changed her surname from DiPrima to di Prima to correct a misspelling made when her grandparents arrived at Ellis Island.

Instead of attending the local high school, Diane transferred to Hunter, the Manhattan magnet school for gifted children. Away from her suburban Italian neighborhood, Diane fell in with a crowd who called themselves the Branded. Together they explored Greenwich Village, the haunt of the Beatniks, the addicts, the fringe figures of society. Diane also began corresponding with the incarcerated poet Ezra Pound, and paid him a visit at St. Elizabeth's Hospital for the Criminally Insane in Washington, DC.

A scholarship led to Swarthmore College in Pennsylvania; to her parents' horror, Diane dropped out after three semesters and moved to Greenwich Village, where the Brooklyn moth morphed into a bohemian butterfly. She determined, "No matter what I will be a poet. Be great, whatever that means. I can taste the struggles. The things I now leave behind...the quiet unquestioned living and dying, the simple one-love-and-marriage, children, material pleasures, easy securities. I am leaving the house I never will own. Dishwashers. Carpets. Dull respect of dull neighbors. None of this matters, really. I have seen it all for the prison it is."

Diane rented cheap Manhattan apartments and opened her door to freeloading acquaintances that consisted of gay artists, at a time when homosexuality was illegal. Allen Ginsburg and Jack Kerouac crashed for a time at her second apartment in Hell's Kitchen. Di Prima found her niche in the city's labyrinth of jazz clubs and dyke bars, happenings and protests. She also tuned in, turned on, and dropped out with Timothy Leary at his commune in Millbrook, New York.

At age twenty-two, Diane decided to have a baby and chose a father, Stefan Baumrin, based on his willingness to stay out of her life. She explained her decision thus: "To my mind, 'father' was a mythic, insubstantial relationship" that did little to inspire responsible behavior. Convinced pregnancy was a natural state rather than an illness, she refused to see a doctor for prenatal care. In her poem, "Song for Baby-O, Unborn," she wrote, "I won't promise you'll never go hungry or that you won't be sad on this gutted breaking globe but I can show you baby enough to love to break your heart forever." Jeanne di Prima's delivery was in a hellish New York City Hospital.

Motherhood did not always mesh with the Beat lifestyle. One evening, Diane left a Beat party at eleven thirty, as she had to return home to relieve the babysitter. In response, Kerouac told her that, if she was going to concern herself with domesticity, she would never make it as a writer. Diane proved Jack wrong; her poem "Loba" is considered the female equivalent of Ginsberg's "Howl." Years later, Ms. Di Prima said that she did not attribute Kerouac's comment to sexism. As she told *The Washington Post* in 2017, "Jack wanted me to hang out because everyone was gay and I was straight. He was probably hoping to get laid later."

In 1961, along with her lover, the African American poet Le Roi Jones (who later adopted the name Amiri Baraka), Diane produced a mail-order literary newspaper, *The Floating Bear*. The FBI arrested Jones and di Prima for distributing obscenity, a case a grand jury threw out. Conflict arose between the couple when Baraka insisted Diane have an abortion, as his wife, Hettie Jones, would have raised hell. Unaccompanied by her lover, she boarded a bus bound for an underground clinic, a decision for which she harbored lifelong remorse. The next time she became pregnant, against Baraka's wishes, she gave birth to her second daughter, Dominique di Prima. The two grew apart when Jones traded the

Village for Harlem and its Black Arts Movement. After innumerable lovers, Diane married Alan Marlowe, with whom she had children Tara and Alexander Marlowe.

In 1968, Diane headed west to California, the epicenter of hippie hedonism. Although she had missed the Summer of Love, she created her own variation. The di Prima household included fourteen adults, their children, pets, and typewriters, her door a revolving one for those passing through. One person who was not present was Alan, who was on an extended stay in India. The task of keeping everyone supplied with miso soup, oatmeal, and pot fell to Diane, as most of her guests were not gainfully employed. She scrambled for work in offices and bookstores and kept a "Free Bank" on the top of her refrigerator—just "a shoebox full of money" for anyone in need. A source of income arrived when the French publisher Maurice Girodias (infamously responsible for *Lolita*) hired di Prima to write sex scenes to spice up his writers' novels, a job she compared to "adding oregano to tomato sauce." He also persuaded her to write a book based on her fictionalized memoir of her 1950s Manhattan years. She sent drafts of her work to Girodias, who returned them with a note to add more sex. She obliged with passages of erotic acrobatics. For verisimilitude, in order to observe what angles and positions were anatomically accurate, Diane arranged for her guests to act out sex scenes, though they did so while fully clothed. The result was *Memoirs of a Beatnik*, published by Olympia Press, in 1969. Diane revealed that the book was based on actual events, "except for the sex parts." The *NOLA Express* wrote of *Memoirs*, "Probably the most forthright and true-to-life book ever written by a woman. If you read it, you'll probably wonder if most of the members of the Women's Liberation Movement would really be as uninhibited as Diane di Prima." A harrowing event occurred in her home when her friend, the twenty-eight-year-old dancer Fred Herko, high on speed, committed suicide by jumping out the window.

The lure of Haight-Ashbury had drawn Diane to San Francisco, and a further lure was the opportunity to work with the Diggers, a group of artists and activists who provided food to the homeless teens who flooded the city in the late 1960s. In her adopted state, Diane studied Sanskrit, Buddhism, and alchemy. Armed with her newfound beliefs, di Prima cofounded the San Francisco Institute of Magical and Healing Arts, where she spread the word about Western spiritual traditions. Her California experiences culminated in her 1971 book *Revolutionary Letters*. Lawrence Ferlinghetti, the founder of City Lights, the legendary San Francisco bookstore, described her collection as "a series of poems composed of a potent blend of utopian anarchism and ecological awareness, projected through a Zen-tinged feminist lens." The volume offered tidbits such as in "Revolutionary Letter #5" where she wrote to "take vitamin B along with amphetamines." The book caused ripples in the male-dominated Beat poetry world, as her erotic depictions were far more explicit than any they had penned. Her compilation of letters was a paean to hope for a better world—one without capitalism, consumerism, or incarceration. The keys to the utopia were sex, art, and love. By 1970, di Prima and Marlowe were estranged, and she embarked on an affair that led to her second marriage with Grant Fisher, a conscientious objector to the Vietnam War. Their relationship resulted in her fifth child, Rudi di Prima, and ended in a 1972 divorce.

In the late 1970s, Diane met Sheppard Powell, an energy healer and meditation teacher. After ten years of living together, they moved to the Excelsior neighborhood of San Francisco, where di Palma became a first-time homeowner. The coupled took their vows at City Hall where Diane gushed, "We were like teenagers. We just kept falling in love over and over again."

In her later years, Diane taught at the California Institute of Integral Studies and Naropa University's Jack Kerouac School of Disembodied Poetics. The rebel with many causes fought for gay rights, environmental protection, and the fat acceptance movements.

Diane remained indefatigable even when battling Parkinson's disease, failing vision due to glaucoma, and arthritis. In 2017, her deteriorating health necessitated a move to a nursing home. Despite illness, she continued to write poetry every day and pursued several book projects, even after her transfer to San Francisco General Hospital. She remarked of her persistence in keeping pen in arthritic fingers, "I'm more concerned with the fact that I have about fifty more books I have to get out." Sheppard, her partner of forty-two years, was at her bedside when she passed away at age eighty-six. In her obituary, her family described her as a devout Buddhist. However, Diane's own words describe her best. In her final poem, she wrote, "Keep the Beat."

CHAPTER 24

"Worth Fighting For" (1934)

"The greatest danger to our future is apathy."

—JANE GOODALL

From the trenches of France in 1920, Hugh Lofting wrote to his sons about a British physician, John Doolittle. Despite the apathetic-sounding surname, the doctor possessed the most remarkable gift: he could talk to animals. The letters transformed into a beloved children's classic and inspired one of the greatest scientific discoveries of the twentieth century.

An extraordinary woman with an extra-ordinary life, Valerie Jane Morris-Goodall was born in London and grew up in "The Birches," her home in Bournemouth. Jane's first encounter with the animal that would dominate her life was a first birthday present from her father, Mortimer. The toy was a plush chimpanzee whose manufacturer named it Jubilee, after a chimp at the London Zoo, christened after King George V's Silver Jubilee. Her non-stuffed canine companion was a collie named Rusty. Jane's favorite storybook characters were Dr. Doolittle, who left for Africa to save its monkeys, and Tarzan, a feral boy raised by apes. Goodall was so smitten with Tarzan that she joked, "He married the wrong Jane. The wretched man." When Jane mentioned that she was going to go to Africa, people said she was dreaming men's dreams.

One who did not laugh was Jane's mother Myfanwe, known as Vanne, who advised her daughter that she would find a way. One evening, Vanne spied dozens of earthworms in Jane's bed. Rather than a knee-jerk shriek, Vanne explained that Jane's little friends needed soil to live, and together they returned them to the garden. Her mother's devotion helped compensate for her absentee father, who had shipped out to France during World War II and obtained a divorce in 1950.

Jane's uncle, Sir Michael Spens, arranged for Jane to be a debutante for the 1955 season. He hired a refugee from Vienna to teach her how to curtsey, and instructed her that when she met the royals, to lower her eyes. Wearing a dress with red lace and long black gloves, Jane observed the other women, the start of her behavioral studies. When fellow debs asked if it were her dream to become a lady-in-waiting, Jane replied, "Absolutely not." During the presentation, Jane held the gaze of Queen Elizabeth II and Prince Philip. After the ceremony, Jane learned that there were three girls who had especially caught the attention of the Prince's wandering eye, one of whom had been the attractive Ms. Goodall.

Without the means to attend university, and with no desire to snag a wealthy husband, Jane ended up in secretarial school. Escape appeared in 1957, when her school friend Marie-Claude Mange, who had relocated to Nairobi, invited her for a visit. Jane returned to Bournemouth and worked as a waitress for two years until she had saved enough money for the trip. While waiting to board her ship, *Kenya Castle*, Jane realized her passport was missing. A stranger found the document, with an itinerary from Cooks Travel Agency. After delivering it to the agency, a Cook employee rushed to the dock, and Africa was once again on the horizon. Because war had closed the Suez Canal, the ship had to take the longer passage around the Cape of Good Hope.

In Africa, Jane drew on her innate chutzpah and called Dr. Louis Leakey, the famed paleoanthropologist. Her opening gambit was on the pathetic side: "I'd love to come and talk to you about animals." His wife, Mary, was likewise no slouch in the scientific arena. In 1957, she had unearthed a 1.8-million-year-old fossil she named "the Nut-cracker" due to its huge jaws and molars. Leakey took Jane on a trip to Kenya, where she scaled a gorge to escape a lion, and came to face with an angry rhinoceros, quite the experience for the twenty-three-year-old British woman. She passed muster, and three years later Leakey proposed she take a position observing chimpanzees in the wild, to support his theory of a shared human primate ancestor. He felt that the fact Jane did not have a university degree was a bonus, as her mind would be free of preconceived theories. Though worried his wife could prove to be what she had named her fossil, Leakey made sexual advances to the beautiful hazel-eyed blonde. Not viewing his marital status, three children, or the thirty-six-year age gap as problematic, he bombarded Jane with declarations of love. Although the eminent doctor had her future in his hands, Jane's response was, "No, thanks." Mrs. Leakey drowned her jealousy with brandy.

Leakey backed off on the romantic front and sent off his Trimates, the name given to his three female researchers: Goodall to study chimpanzees, Dian Fossey to observe gorillas, and Birutė Galdikas to report on orangutans. Goodall remembers Dian as extremely tall and a dedicated husband-hunter known to ask, "Do you know a man who is six foot five and loves gorillas?" Poachers murdered Fossey in 1985 when she went after them for hunting her beloved gorillas. Her burial site is in a cemetery she had built for gorillas slain by poachers.

Jane's lodging was in the Gombe Stream Chimpanzee Reserve in the British colony of Tanganyika, now Tanzania, terrain not for the faint of heart. No one else lived there, although the locals believed it was where they would be reborn, after death, as primates. Her first dwelling, before she set out for the reserve, was a lodging in a prison camp. She had arrived accompanied by her mother because the authorities believed that a young British girl could not survive in the bush without an escort. The region was a hotbed of unrest as the Belgian Congo had just erupted into civil war, and the area was overrun with refugees. While Jane departed in search of chimps, Vanne and a slightly inebriated African cook opened the windows to let in air; what also came in included spiders, snakes, and baboons.

While Vanne was learning survival in her new home, Jane was staking out the chimpanzees, who fled from the interloper. She also endured other phenomena in her army tent, including thunderstorms, extreme heat, scorpions, and loneliness. Even more pressing, she understood that the Royal Geographical Society had only funded her expedition for six months and would withdraw patronage if results were not forthcoming.

The ever-patient observer christened each of her subjects, as they were possessed of unique personalities and appearances. She named her furry children Leakey, Mr. McGregor, and Frodo. After four months, the power of persistence paid off when the apes began to accept Jane's presence as nonthreatening, partly because of the occasional gift of bananas. An adult male, called David Greybeard because of his silver goatee, proved the friendliest. Jane watched in fascination as David Greybeard and his primate pal, Goliath, stripped leaves from twigs before pushing them into a dirt mound to forage for their favorite snack of termites. Through him, in an African rainforest, Jane made a revolutionary discovery: that chimpanzees both made and used tools, something previously believed only the provenance of man. Elated, Goodall telegraphed Leakey with the news that amounted to the greatest scientific breakthrough of the twentieth century. Her boss responded, "Now we must redefine man, redefine tools, or accept chimpanzees as humans."

When Goodall's discovery made headlines, the story of the beauty and her beasts created a media sensation. However, Jane had her detractors, who said she had only become the *National Geographic* cover girl because she had nice legs. Unperturbed, Jane responded that yes, her legs were actually very nice.

The *National Geographic* article and documentary on Goodall and her Gombe chimpanzees lifted a veil to reveal an unknown world.

To generate publicity, Leakey sent out the Dutch photographer Baron Hugo Van Lawick, and the scientist doubled as a matchmaker: he dashed off a letter to Vanne saying he had found a husband for Jane. Initially, Jane was put out by Hugo's arrival in her sanctuary, and by the trail of his cigarette butts, although they soon bonded over their shared love of animals. When they left for their respective homes for Christmas, a telegram arrived in Bournemouth: WILL YOU MARRY ME STOP LOVE HUGO. Her response: YES STOP JANE. No doubt her former fellow debutantes would have been astounded that Jane ended up a baroness. Jane felt as if she had found her own cape of good hope. Three years later, they had son Hugo Eric Louis, nicknamed Grub. Hugo spent his early years in a protective cage, which was painted blue and hung with mobiles, staring out at the wild creatures of the jungle. The toddler's first sentence was, "That big lion out there eat me." Their home was a corrugated tin shack, where a table held an assortment of animal skulls. Sadly, Van Lawick also married the wrong Jane. Their marriage collapsed when he left to shoot nature films across Africa, and she declined to follow in the role of assistant. Grub ended up in a boarding school in England, as his mother felt that was best for him, and it allowed her time to devote herself to the chimps. Her second husband was Derek Bryceson, a Royal Air Force veteran who had helped Tanzania win its independence. Six years later, his death from cancer left Jane devastated.

Leakey, anxious for his protégée to gain academic credibility, arranged for Goodall's acceptance to Cambridge University, where she became only the eighth person in its history to study in a PhD program without a BA. Elation was short-lived, as the professors informed her that her research was flawed. The academics scoffed because she had given the chimps names rather than numbers. Moreover, they did not give credence to her claims that the chimps were akin to humans on a biological and behavioral level. However, Rusty had taught Jane that animals possessed distinct personalities, and she remained defiant of the Cambridge academics. After receiving her doctorate, a position as professor held little appeal, and she was happy to exchange the halls of ivy for the jungles of Africa.

In spirit and appearance, Jane remains an older version of the young woman who, five decades ago, had dared to dream men's dreams. Her long hair, now silver, is still tied back in a ponytail. At age eighty-seven, Goodall remains a rolling stone as she travels the globe, promoting the principles of the Jane Goodall Institute, which she founded in 1977. A legendary figure, her fans include Angelina Jolie and Colin Firth. After meeting Muhammad Ali, Jane declared that he "did indeed float like a butterfly." Goodall revealed that Michael Jackson wrote "Heal the World" with her in mind. The scientist and a roll call of celebrities attended a screening of the film *Jane* which featured a live orchestra at the Hollywood Bowl, the first time a documentary sold out the venue's 17,500 seats. Jane never did become a lady-in-waiting; however, she did become a Commander of the British Empire.

While Jane was demanding animal protection, her contemporary Gloria Steinem campaigned on the feminist forefront. However, these words of Ms. Goodall's are also a nod to gender equality: "There are indigenous people in Latin America who have a saying that their tribe is like an eagle: one wing is male, and one wing is female. And only when the wings are equally strong will their tribe fly high. And this, indeed, is worth fighting for."

CHAPTER 25

"Loved Not Wisely" (1941)

*"You cannot defeat us ever.
The tyrant will be brought down."*

—DR. BRIDGET ROSE DUGDALE

In his seventeenth-century home in Delft, Holland, Johan van der Meer captured on canvas scenes of domestic tranquility: *Lady Writing a Letter with her Maid, The Guitar Player, Girl with a Pearl Earring.* While immortal works of art end up adorning the walls of palaces, mansions, and museums, van der Meer's masterpieces spent time in the trunk of a car and an Irish cemetery due to a rebel with a religious-like passion.

In 2016, in the upstairs room of a Dublin bar, Bridget Rose Dugdale and Liam Sutcliffe sat downing their drinks. What set them apart from the other patrons was that the man and woman were radical legends. Sutcliffe's claim to infamy was that he had orchestrated the 1966 Operation Humpty Dumpty, which resulted in the destruction of the 1809 Nelson's Pillar, a statue featuring the British Nelson's likeness peering down from his 121-foot column. And yet Sutcliffe's deed paled in comparison to that of his female companion.

Bridget Rose's middle name is an apt metaphor, as her life encompassed many a thorn. She was the daughter of multi-millionaire James Frederic Compton Dugdale, a large shareholder in Lloyd's of London, and his wife Caroline, whose family fortune had originated from slavery. The trappings of their wealth were a six-hundred-acre estate, Yarty Farm, in Devon, an estate in Chelsea, and a mansion in Scotland. Along with her elder sister Caroline and younger brother James, Rose spent Sunday morning services at Chelsea Pensioners Chapel, and watched Margot Fonteyn starring as Cinderella from the Dugdale family box in the Royal Opera House.

From an early age, Rose butted heads with her authoritarian mother. When Caroline had Rose's ears pierced without her permission, the child became enraged and claimed she was "disfigured." As an adult, Rose never wore earrings. Not being allowed to talk to the "common" local children in Devon also did not sit well. Rose related more to her elderly French governess, whom she called "Mam'zelle." The sisters attended the exclusive Miss Ironside's School for Girls in Kensington, where Rose and Caroline wore identical white dresses for piano duets. Her classes never satiated Rose's intellectual thirst, as they focused on skills such as learning how to curtsey. At age fourteen, her parents sent Rose on a grand tour of Europe, where she visited Italy, Greece, and Austria. There was also a stay at the home of a well-heeled French family, and four months as a guest in

Germany in the home of the former Nazi secretary of propaganda, Joseph Goebbels.

Her 1958 return to England coincided with the social season, where Elizabeth II welcomed 1,200 debutantes to Buckingham Palace. Afterwards, the upper-class women embarked upon a four-month season of glittering gowns and lavish balls in the hope of meeting eligible bachelors. Rose remarked that the ritual brought on her eureka moment, "I loathed the season. I think it is probably from that date that some kind of awareness or understanding of the limitations of the way in which people of my parents' class lived came in on me. My coming-out ball was one of those pornographic affairs which cost about what sixty old-age pensioners receive in six months."

In exchange for agreeing to be a debutante—in what she referred to as a "marriage market"—Rose had extracted a promise from her parents that she would be allowed to attend St. Anne's College, Oxford, where she studied politics, philosophy, and economics. In the process she became, as she put it, "an intellectual of the worst sort." Despite her trust fund, Rose lived, even by student standards, in squalor. Along with her studies, she had imbibed the seeds of rebellion, and crashed the Oxford Union Debating Society dressed as a man to protest their male-only membership policy. In the United States, at Mount Holyoke in Massachusetts, she scored interviews with Dr. Martin Luther King, Jr. and John F. Kennedy for the school newspaper.

Over the next decade, Rose earned a PhD in philosophy at London University, visited Cuba while it was in the throes of revolution, and was also part of the sit-ins at universities protesting the war in Vietnam. In a more conservative vein, Rose worked for the United Nations in their offices in England, New York, Rome, and Geneva. What tarnished the silver spoon of her birthright was the activism of the 1960s. Throwing her lot in with the downtrodden, Rose turned to social causes and worked to better the lives of the poor in Tottenham, North London. In order to fit in with the working class she championed, Rose learned to camouflage her posh accent that outed her as a member of the upper crust. She gave away thousands of pounds from the trust fund that furnished her with $200,000 annually, millions in today's currency. Her reasoning was, "For years my family have been taking money from the poor. I am just trying to restore the balance by giving some of it back."

The 1972 Bloody Sunday protest, where British paratroopers gunned down unarmed protestors in Derry, led to Rose's twin crusades: a free Ireland and the end of capitalism. Her comrade in arms and in bed was the petty criminal Walter Heaton. In a mea culpa to his wife and children, she gifted them $50,000. Walter was a product of a Leeds slum and had become a self-described "revolutionary socialist." Although the Irish Republican Army (IRA) never officially recognized her as a member, Dugdale embarked on a number of missions for the militant organization. Aware that her parents were at the Epsom Derby, Dugdale, along with Walter, raided their Devon estate, making off with paintings, silverware, and antiques worth 82,000 pounds, which they used to finance their cause. At her trial, she shouted at her father, "I love you—but I hate everything you stand for." No doubt Mrs. Dugdale bought a lifetime supply of smelling salts; however, in the words of Al Jolson, "You ain't seen nothing yet, folks." As the theft had been Rose's first brush with the law, the judge, Sir Hugh Park, considered the risk of her committing any further criminal acts "extremely remote." While the judge gave Rose a two-year suspended sentence, Walter received a six-year jail term. Dugdale denounced the disproportionate sentences as a blatant example of capitalist injustice. The defiant defendant told the jury, "In finding me guilty, you have turned me from an intellectual recalcitrant into a freedom fighter. I know no finer title." Rose's subsequent actions proved the judge wrong in his assumption that her earlier crime had been the result of a youthful act of rebellion against her parents. Along with her new lover Eddie Gallagher, as part of an IRA mission, she was involved in hijacking a helicopter in Donegal they used to drop milk churns filled with explosives on an Ulster police station. The homemade bombs failed to detonate, and the radicals became Ireland's and Britain's most wanted. Making her life on the run even more precarious, Rose was pregnant with Gallagher's child.

While some expectant mothers knit booties, Dugdale turned her attention to the eighteenth-century Kenwood House, situated on 112 acres in North London, a property deeded to Britain by Lord Iveagh, the Guinness brewery magnate. In 1974, thieves broke into the museum and made off with the multi-million-dollar Vermeer painting *The Guitar Player*. A substantial ransom note demanded the transfer of IRA bombers, Dolours and Marian Price, engaged in a hunger strike, from their prison in England to one in Northern Ireland. Three months later, the police discovered the portrait hidden in a London cemetery. Although the perpetrators were never apprehended, the theft bore the hallmark of Rose Dugdale.

Two months after the heist, a woman mimicking a French accent knocked on the door of Russborough House, a baronial Irish manor, explaining that her car had broken down. Moments later, she and three armed men forced their way in. At the time, Sir Alfred, heir to a South African diamond-mine fortune, and his wife, Lady Clementine Beit, were in their living room, listening to classical records. Brandishing revolvers, the intruders shouted slogans such as "capitalist pigs" and "exploiters" and used nylon stockings to restrain the aristocratic couple. After pistol-whipping the seventy-one-year-old baronet, they dragged Lady Clementine down a flight of stone steps to the cellar. She later remarked, "I was convinced that, like the unfortunate Romanovs, I was to be shot in the cellar." The female ringleader calmly ordered the removal of masterpieces by Goya, Rubens, and Gainsborough. Another theft was of the only privately held Vermeer in the world, *Lady Writing a Letter with her Maid*. A ransom note offered to return the paintings in exchange for the release of the Price sisters.

All nineteen masterpieces were eventually discovered in Rose's rented cottage in County Cork and in the trunk of her car. Dr. Bridget Rose Dugdale's trial in the Special Criminal Court was pure theater. The defendant described herself as "the perpetrator of a calm political act to change the corporate conscience of the Cabinet." Far from contrite, Rose accused the Irish government of collaborating with the British, who had tortured six brave Irish prisoners who were still languishing in jail. Putting speaking her truth over self-preservation, Rose kept interrupting Judge Andrew O'Keefe during the two-hour trial. In a lengthy speech, she declared that the court had no right "to deprive us of our freedom to fight for Ireland and the freedom of the Irish people." The judge disagreed and ordered her to serve nine years in prison. Upon hearing the sentence, Dugdale gave a clenched-fist salute. The case garnered global headlines; *Time* magazine called her the Renegade Debutante. Gallagher, who had received a twenty-year sentence, and Rose became the first convicted prisoners in Irish history to wed behind bars. The British Bonnie and Clyde married in the chapel of Limerick Prison; in attendance was their three-year-old son, Ruairi. At his prison birth, the doting mother declared, "He's going to be a guerilla." After the ceremony, guards returned the groom to his maximum-security prison sixty miles away.

Upon her 1980 release—she served six years—Dugdale was active in the campaign in support of republican prisoners during the Irish hunger strike. Currently, Rose appears no different than the other pensioners living in a drab Irish housing project. The only clue is her upper-class accent, revealing a world where she had curtsied before the queen. Over the years, she used her well-modulated tone to tell journalists, "Clear off, right. I'm not answering any questions." As a speaker at the 2007 Sinn Fein political party conference, in a slip of the tongue, Rose said, "I'm here in support of the revolution—I mean the resolution." Three years later, Rose revealed she had no regrets and reminisced of her 1960s joyride when she played the part of a contemporary Robin Hood, "You mustn't forget it was very exciting times...the world looked as if it could change and was likely to be changed and, whoever you were, you could play a part in that." The Renegade Debutante remains a rebel at heart.

In a fit of misguided jealousy, Shakespeare's Othello strangled his beloved wife, Desdemona. His parting words could well describe Rose's life: "Then you must speak of one that loved not wisely, but too well."

CHAPTER 26

"Binding with Briars" (1942)

"I don't see why the walls of Jericho didn't fall down after I said that."

—SHERE HITE

A character in South African Doris Lessing's *The Golden Notebook* remarked, "Women of any sense know better, after all these centuries, than to interrupt when men start telling them how they feel about sex." Fourteen years later, an American writer did just that when she had the chutzpah to announce "the great thrust" was not the be-all and end-all, thereby taking the female orgasm out of the closet.

The woman who dared to challenge Freud was Shirley (Shere), the daughter of sixteen-year-old-Shirley and her serviceman husband, Paul Gregory, born in Saint Joseph, Missouri. The marriage ended at the same time as World War II; Shere never saw her father again after the age of nine. With her mother's remarriage, Shere took the name of her stepfather Raymond Hite, a truck driver, with whom she butted heads. After confiding that she wanted to be a composer, he informed her that no woman could succeed in that profession. Later, Shere remarked,

"I think he resented me as a sign of my mother's former sexuality." After her second divorce, Shirley, who told her daughter that she was her "cross to bear," sent Shere to live with her grandparents. Shere recalled these years as a happy time and likened the experience to Dorothy's midwestern childhood. Oz ended after her grandparents broke up, and her aunt in Florida became the teenager's guardian.

Ms. Hite received her bachelor's and master's degrees in history from the University of Florida at Gainesville in the mid-1960s and enrolled at the University of Columbia to pursue her doctorate. Faced with astronomical tuition, down to her last subway token, the blonde beauty posed nude for *Playboy*, yet it was another modeling assignment that altered the trajectory of her life.

The Italian-owned company Olivetti hired Shere for a television commercial, and only later did she discover they used it in their advertising campaign with the slogan "The Typewriter So Smart, She Doesn't Have to Be." Repulsed by its misogynistic message, Shere joined a feminist group picketing the Olivetti office in protest of the ad. The New York chapter of the National Organization for Women (NOW), founded by Betty Friedan, author of *The Feminine Mystique*, recognized Shere as the model and invited her to become a member. In consciousness-raising groups, the feminists disclosed that they were not fulfilled during heterosexual sex. Their remarks led to Shere's eureka moment: sexual liberation was the missing component in the struggle for women's liberation. Her introduction to sex had occurred as a teen when she was necking with her boyfriend on her front porch. Her grandmother told her, "You know, they only marry the nice ones."

Columbia proved too conservative to allow her to pursue a doctorate on female sexuality, and Shere dropped out to embark on independent research. Her investigation revealed that a society obsessed with sex is one that has a lack of satisfying erotic encounters. Shere determined to write a thesis centered on a questionnaire concerning women's ability to orgasm. In 1972, Hite distributed the questionnaire through NOW, women's magazines, church newsletters, universities, abortion rights groups, and university centers. Subsisting on an annual income of $10,000, for the next five years, Shere analyzed that data that she referred to as a "giant rap session on paper."

Although Hite's reports were sensational for the era, she had not been the first to conduct research in the field of human sexuality. The original pioneers had been Alfred C. Kinsey, followed by the team of William H. Masters and Virginia E. Johnson. However, while these scientists wrote of their findings in clinical terms, Shere's approach was hands-on: "Researchers should stop telling women what they *should* feel sexually and start asking them what they *do* feel sexually." Despite the swinging sixties having given an open-sesame for women to have no-strings sex with whomever they chose, it had done little to change the male-dominated bedroom. Erica Jong, author of *Fear of Flying*, zeroed in on the situation, "Most of the respondents to Hite's questionnaires thought that the sexual revolution was a myth, that it had left them free to say yes (but not to say no).

These respondents felt that the double standard was alive and well, that the quantity of sex had gone up, not the quality."

In 1976, Shere published *The Hite Report: A Nationwide Study of Female Sexuality*, that sparked a sexual revolution. She based her findings on three thousand responses from subjects ranging in age from fourteen to seventy-eight. A sample answer: "Yes, I always fake orgasms. It just seemed polite." The book challenged Freud's theory that female intercourse would result in orgasm unless a woman was frigid. She contended that penetration was not the only show in town, and that the Viennese doctor was responsible for countless women faking it in bed. *The Hite Report* became a bestseller; forty-eight million copies were sold and led to a dozen translations.

Men took the information as an attack declaring them obsolete on a horizontal plane, and they looked upon Shere as the males of Salem did their witches. Her detractors sent Hite death threats by post and phone, and the paparazzi pounced from bushes. The Christian right preached that she was destroying traditional family values, and the media portrayed Shere as a man-hater. A comment that made the rounds was "Shere Hype"; *Playboy* jumped into the fray and labeled *The Hite Report* "The Hate Report." Naysayers argued that her research involved "methodological mayhem," as she had no method of verifying the truth of what her anonymous respondents wrote. In rebuttal to the claim that she did not access all demographics, Shere retorted that Freud had only interviewed three Viennese women. She also commented, "When people say 'It's not scientific,' what they really mean is 'You're not a man, you're not wearing a white coat. It's just women talking, that's nowhere, not Important with a capital I.' " Feminist Gloria Steinem issued a statement condemning the media hostility as a "feminist backlash and against the rights of women everywhere."

Disregarding the hostility, Shere followed *The Hite Report* with *The Hite Report on Men and Male Sexuality* that examined questionnaires from more than seven thousand men. Based on the responses, Shere concluded that most males had deep fears of sexual inadequacy and of intimacy. The trilogy ended with *Women and Love: A Cultural Revolution in Progress*, in which questionnaires from 4,500 women led the "sexpert" to assert that women regarded their relationships with men with "increasing emotional frustration and gradual disillusionment." Hite's books painted a bleak erotic landscape in which females were flies caught in a spiderweb of marriage that did not fulfill their emotional or physical needs. Susie Homemaker was ready for action outside her home. A journalist for the *London Daily Mail* wrote, "These implausible majorities read like the old-style Albanian elections results, where 99.9 percent of the electorate voted for the dictator." The uproar was such that Hite appeared on the cover of *Time* magazine and the accompanying article claimed *Women and Love* was simply an excuse for "male-bashing." Many radical feminists of the 1970s were also antagonistic, as they felt Shere's seductive clothes, red lipstick, and bleached blonde hair went against the precepts of the sisterhood by aiming to look like a male fantasy.

The pressure of attacks on both fronts got to Shere, and rumors ran rife of Hite's increasingly erratic behavior. One was that she attacked a limousine driver because he committed the cardinal sin of calling her "dear." Infuriated at a negative review of her book, she allegedly phoned the critic at two thirty in the morning to share what she thought of it and did not mince words. The antithesis of scientific detachment, Shere stormed out of television interviews. Fearing his star client had become a liability, Sterling Lord, her prominent literary agent, dropped her from his roster.

Both revered as a feminist icon and reviled as a pillager of propriety, Ms. Hite remained a media sensation who offered a peephole into American bedrooms. Oprah Winfrey invited her on her talk show, and the next day she spoke at Oxford University. Her platform: women needed to be half of the sexual equation.

However, a positive was that Shere's runaway success meant a well-padded bank account. As she told *The Washington Post* in 1977, "now I can eat regularly and I know I'll be able to eat regularly for a number of years. And I don't have that horrible lurking feeling whenever I go out of my apartment, the fear that I'll run into the landlord." With the money from her books, Shere moved to a four-bedroom, $1.5 million Fifth Avenue apartment opposite the Central Park children's zoo. She shared the palatial digs with the German concert pianist Fred Horicke, nineteen years her junior, whom she had wed in 1985.

Fred often introduced himself with the words, "I'm Shere's husband."

In 1989, seeking a more accepting society, the first couple of nonconformity moved to Europe. Six years later, Hite applied for German citizenship, which required her to relinquish her American citizenship. For two days, before receiving her new passport, she was stateless. After her divorce, Shere settled in North London with Paul Sullivan, whom she married in 2012.

In 2000, Shere wrote *The Hite Report on Hite: A Sexual and Political Autobiography*. In the review of the memoir, the British newspaper *The Guardian* supported the American expat, "Strip away the sneers and what really scares people about Hite is the fact that she is a beautiful, clever, sexy, self-made woman." In the same year, Shere released an updated version of the sex lives of women, *The New Hite Report*. In classic Shere fashion, she wrote that British women were the most sexually confident and liberated in the English-speaking world, although British men were a disappointment in bed.

When asked if feminism had progressed since the publication of *The Hite Report*, the author responded that it had, "But we have to ask why men are still saying, 'She's a bitch,' 'she's a whore,' 'she's neurotic,' 'she's abnormal.' " On a note that revealed her vulnerability, Shere confessed, "Because I have sold a lot of books I think that women think that I'm fine, but I'm not fine. I hope they realize that." The trailblazer, suffering from Alzheimer's and Parkinson's, passed away from a rare neurological disorder at age seventy-seven.

Ms. Hite wanted sex to be fun and fulfilling, her beliefs aligned with those expressed by William Blake in his poem "The Garden of Love," where he wrote, "And Priests in black gowns, were walking their rounds/And binding with briars, my joys and desires."

CHAPTER 27

"The Pink Pussycat Club" (1943)

"Racism and sexism in America were equal parts in my oppression."

—ELAINE BROWN

In 1968 the Beatles sang, "You say you want a revolution..." A fist-raised woman was in agreement with the British boy band's lyric. The Black activists of the 1960s civil rights era were male; their wives were expected to serve as handmaidens—or widows—to their cause. Thus, it was all the more shocking when a female rebel-rouser assumed control.

The word that defined Elaine Brown's childhood was nothingness. Her father, Dr. Horace Scott, a prominent physician from Philadelphia's Black middle class, was married, with an adopted daughter, and he never acknowledged Elaine as his child. Her mother, Dorothy Brown, was miserable with her lot as a single mother, stuck in a dead-end clothing factory job from which she sometimes stole a dress for her child. Elaine recounted of her childhood, "In the silence of our nights my mother would summarize her days: 'They treated me like I was nothing. They must think I'm nothing.' In our room was complete darkness, and the recognition of nothingness, accompanied by the magnified sounds of mice scurrying and hearts beating in fear." Determined that her gifted daughter deserved more than local education, with the help of donations, she enrolled Elaine in a private school. The illegitimate Black student from the wrong side of the tracks was far different from her wealthy Jewish classmates. After high school, her self-esteem went even further south as the result of a failed interracial love affair. An additional trauma was her narrow escape from a gang rape.

Desperately desiring escape, Elaine took off for California in 1965, hopeful a record company would buy her songs. Street-savvy but politically naïve, Elaine was unaware that the Watts riot had recently erupted, and that President Lyndon Johnson had just signed the Voting Rights Act. With her three hundred dollars depleted, Elaine found work in Hollywood's Pink Pussycat Club, a strip joint where she was the only Black cocktail waitress.

One evening, Frank Sinatra, a Pink Pussycat patron, invited her to a party to be the date for his friend, Jay Kennedy, a screenwriter and Harry Belafonte's former manager. The following night, Elaine and Kennedy had their first date at the Beverly Hills Hotel, where he asked if she had attended the March on Washington two years earlier. Apolitical, she replied that she could not fathom why anyone would willingly expose themselves to police hosing and bites from vicious dogs. By the end of the meal, Elaine understood the civil rights movement; she also understood she was in love with Kennedy. They embarked on an affair where Sinatra's lavish estate served as the setting for their rendezvous. Kennedy never invited her to his home on the East Coast, as he shared it with his wife and daughter. After two years of empty promises to end his marriage, Elaine mustered the courage to tell him that, if there was no place for her in his world, then he did not belong in hers.

During Elaine's time as the other woman, the radicals Huey Newton and Bobby Seale cofounded the Oakland-based Black Panther Party, which they described as focused on "self-defense against the police." The group—who popularized the slogan, "Black is Beautiful"—with their berets and black leather coats and raised fists, shaped by childhood ghettoes and the jungles of Vietnam, sent chills down the spine of conservative America. The militants came onto the radar of J. Edgar Hoover, the dreaded FBI director, who warned, "The Black Panther Party, without question, represents the greatest threat to the internal security of the United States." Enveloped by the familiar sense of nothingness after parting from Kennedy, and with her newly awakened political consciousness, Elaine joined the revolutionaries. The Black Panthers provided Elaine with purpose, guiding principles, and a surrogate family. They also provided Elaine with sexual partners; she was hypnotically attracted to dangerous men, something never in short supply within the Party's members. With the Panthers, sex was just another way of saying hello. One of those to whom Elaine said hello was Newton, who had first heard her songs while doing time. He had landed in prison after his conviction for killing an Oakland police officer in a traffic-stop confrontation, a charge later overturned. In a stand-by-your-man gesture, to rent a penthouse for Newton after his release, she turned to producer Bert Schneider for money. After he gave her $12,000, Elaine recalled, "I brashly brushed my hand along the front of his pants. 'Let's just say that you defy the cherished myths about black men.' " The fly in their romantic ointment was Newton's cocaine and cognac addiction. Life in the movement was never dull: she was at UCLA when a shootout between the Panthers and Ron Karenga's US organization resulted in the deaths of Panthers Bunchy Carter and John Huggins. Jail was also added to Elaine's resume when 150 cops descended on her communal house.

Although women had been a pivotal force in the civil rights movement, men had always overshadowed their efforts. No female had ever been at the helm of the Southern Christian Leadership Conference, the National Association for the Advancement of Colored People, or the Student Non-Violent Coordinating Committee. The paradigm shifted in 1974, when Newton fled to Cuba after the accusation he had killed a seventeen-year-old Oakland prostitute and designated his lover Elaine the new leader. Brown became the first and only female to head the Black Panthers. Her initial speech opened with the same words she would use in the beginning of her autobiography, *A Taste of Power*, "I have all the guns and all the money. I can withstand challenge from without and from within. Together we're going to take this city. We will make it a base of revolution." Larry, a bodyguard who held a .45 automatic pistol under his jacket, was instrumental in silencing resistance.

In order to solidify her position, the rebel with a cause chose members whose staunch loyalty to Newton would protect her position. Her agenda entailed increasing free-breakfast programs, and she created the Oakland Community Learning Center, which became an oasis in one of California's poorest neighborhoods. Ms. Brown also ran twice (unsuccessfully) for the Oakland City Council, and she collaborated with state officials on the construction of the Grove-Shafter Freeway extension that helped revitalize the city's downtown and created hundreds of jobs. With Elaine's leadership that prioritized activism over arms, the party registered nearly a hundred thousand new voters for the 1977 election that made Lionel Wilson the first Black mayor of Oakland. Brown stood by his side during his victory speech. One of her many hats was that of the party's minister of information, a post formerly held by Eldridge Cleaver, who had jumped bail and fled to Algeria. Channeling her musical talent, Elaine created the album "Until We're Free," wrote the Panther national anthem, and edited its newspaper. The Black Forum label, a short-lived subsidiary of Motown Records, picked up one of her records. Through her recordings, Suzanne de Passe, a Motown vice president, became a lifelong friend. Although it aroused outrage, Brown chose several women for key positions, an act viewed as eroding Black manhood. One member groused at a Brown rule, "I hear we can't call them bitches no more." Stokely Carmichael commented, "The only position for women is prone." In her book, Elaine wrote, "A woman asserting herself was a pariah. A woman attempting the role of leadership was, to my proud Black brothers, making an alliance with the "counterrevolutionary, man-hating, lesbian, feminist white bitches." Unlike the girls from her neighborhood, who rarely ventured forth from their Philadelphia tenements, as a representative of the pro-Marxist foundation, Elaine traveled to North Korea, China, Cuba, Russia, and Vietnam. Brown became the new black, a woman at the pinnacle of a male-dominated hierarchy. With her myriad duties, she did not have much time for her daughter, Erika, the product of an affair with Panther Raymond (Masai) Hewitt. Hewitt later became a pawn in an FBI plot to target actress Jean Seberg, a prominent supporter of the Party. Federal agents planted rumors that Seberg was pregnant with his baby, an accusation aimed at destroying her reputation. Hewitt's neglect of Erika was a sad echo of her own father's abandonment. Erika's childhood consisted of men who carried loaded guns and a bodyguard who trailed her even when she went to buy a treat from an ice cream truck.

The old feeling of nothingness returned when Newton returned from Cuba and resumed leadership of the Panthers. During her tenure, Elaine had struggled to curb the criminal impulses of the Party, a trend Newton did not emulate. In 1977, after he authorized the beating of Regina Davis (she suffered a broken jaw), a woman Elaine had appointed to a key position, Brown knew it was time to escape with seven-year-old Erika.

For a time, Elaine lived with her mother, who had relocated to Los Angeles, then couch-surfed in Suzanne's apartment. As a single mother without alimony, money was in short supply. After all, "Black Panther head honcho" on a resume would have served as an impediment for employment. When she did find a job selling advertisements for newspapers, it ended after she threw a beeper at her boss. Another position as a paralegal did not pan out; during a confrontation at her office, she swept everything off her desk onto the floor. Jay Kennedy came to her rescue by introducing her to therapist Kay Levatter, who helped her overcome her crippling depression and rage. Therapy helped exorcise her demons and, with her newfound equanimity, Elaine enrolled in law school at night. However, fellow students included police officers who remembered her past and never missed an opportunity to harass the former Panther. Brown also experienced prejudice from a professor, a former FBI agent, who purposely gave her poor grades. She dropped out after two years, a decision she felt at peace with as she realized she would never be able to honor the laws of a racist country.

In 1990, with her autobiography almost completed, and with Erika studying at Spelman College in Atlanta, Elaine found herself without direction. At this juncture, Suzanne invited Brown to a Hollywood party, where she met Pierre Elby, who, she said, was the only interesting man in the room. When he told her about his youth in France, living in a chateau with 132 rooms, Elaine responded that there weren't even 132 rooms in York Street, her childhood address in Philadelphia. Despite their vastly divergent backgrounds, sparks flew. His friends told him he was out of his mind; how could he considering dating a former leader of the Black Panthers? Elby did not see her past as a barrier. The couple moved to Paris, where Elaine said she enjoyed an "oasis of happiness." She felt she deserved it after a tempestuous life.

Until she wrote *A Taste of Power*, Elaine never realized how much she had loved Huey Newton, who she only saw once after her escape. In 1989, after she received a call saying Newton had been murdered during a suspected drug deal in Oakland, Elaine attended his funeral. Brown said she planned to contribute a third of the money she made from her book to build a school in South-Central Los Angeles, where the Southern California Panther headquarters had once stood. Elaine's life was an extraordinary one, bookended by the Panthers and the Pink Pussycat Club.

CHAPTER 28

"Goin' Home Alone" (1943)

"I'm saving the bass player for Omaha."

—JANIS JOPLIN

"Freedom's just another word for nothing left to lose..." The song lyric, the paean to anguish, serves as the existential cry of Janis Joplin, the poster child for angst. The singer blazed across the sky, a comet whose brightness illuminated the darkness before disappearing into the night.

The spotlight of notoriety rested on Janis Lyn Joplin, eldest of three children, born in the conservative Texas oil town of Port Arthur. Her mother's aspiration for her two daughters was for them to become Miss Suzie Homemakers. Janis's pariah status partly stemmed from her appearance, which was the antithesis of her era's prom-queen ideal. As a teen, she was self-conscious over her weight, acne, hooknose, and bushy hair. Alienation intensified when she started hanging out with what Port Arthur considered a bohemian crowd. In a town that viewed xenophobia as a virtue, and had a Ku Klux Klan chapter, Janis had the gumption to speak out against racial segregation. Her differences made her a target amongst her classmates, many of whom were card-carrying rednecks. Later the legend recalled, "They laughed me out of class, out of town, out of the state." As a celebrity with superstar status, she reminisced about her years in the Lone Star state, "Texas is okay if you want to settle down and do your own thing quietly, but it's not for outrageous people, and I was always outrageous." Janice crossed over the Louisiana border to drink and listen to bands with a group of boys, which led her town to brand her a harlot. A school football player nicknamed her "Beat Weeds," a reference to her pubic hair. One of the jocks was Jimmy Johnson, future coach of the Dallas Cowboys, who later mentioned in a *Sports Illustrated* interview, "Beat Weeds...never wore any panties." When the magazine pressed for details, Johnson admitted the information was not based on primary research. No one asked Janis to prom, although she would have accepted a date with a male or female, as she was democratic in her choice of sexual partner. She took to heart her song "Get It While You Can" and had sex with musicians, fans, sailors, and members of the Hell's Angels.

To appease her parents, Janis enrolled at the University of Texas, socially high school all over again. A fraternity pronounced her the "ugliest man on campus." Bullies profiled her in the student newspaper with the damning headline "She Dares to Be Different!" The article read, "She goes barefooted when she feels like it, wears Levi's to class because they're more comfortable and carries her Autoharp with her everywhere." In mockery, the mean kids plastered posters of her around the school.

Janis spent her teenage years on the road, following in the footsteps of her literary hero, Jack Kerouac. Hitchhiking from one Beat haven to another—Venice Beach, Palo Alto, Greenwich Village—she hooked up with assorted male and female lovers, autoharp or pool cue in hand. To get by, she performed at coffee houses and hootenannies, worked as a waitress in a bowling alley, panhandled, and turned tricks. Her sojourn came with a price: an arrest for shoplifting, a street fight, an abortion in Mexico. Always a heavy drinker, she also began using methamphetamine. Her drug addiction led to her return to Texas, where she dried out and promised to stay clean. In a bid at different lifestyle, Janice took sociology classes at Lamar University, avoided illegal substances, and sported a beehive hairdo. However, she rebelled against the straitjacket of conformity. Looking back, she described herself as "a plain overweight chick. I wanted something more than bowling alleys and drive-ins. I'd've f—ed anything, taken anything. I did. I'd take it, suck it, lick it, smoke it, shoot it, drop it, fall in love with it."

Music served as an antidote to pain, and Janis spent endless hours listening to performers like Leadbelly and Bessie Smith. Her dream of dreams was to become a professional singer, and it turned into a reality when Travis Rivers formed the San Francisco band Big Brother and the Holding Company and asked her to be its lead singer. Janis left Port Arthur in the rearview mirror as she headed for the Haight-Ashbury, the 1960s Mecca. Of the city where she finally felt at home, she said, "I couldn't believe it, all that rhythm and power. I got stoned just feeling it, like it was the best dope in the world." She said she was in nirvana, "getting laid, getting stoned."

The ultimate hippie's powerhouse vocals became the soundtrack to San Francisco's Summer of Love. Suddenly the hottest singer of the era, Janice had concerts at the Whiskey A Go Go in Los Angeles, the Kinetic Playground in Chicago, and the Psychedelic Supermarket in Boston. Her big break arrived when her band performed in front of tens of thousands at the iconic Monterey Pop Festival, a show that turned her into a star. "Mama" Cass Elliot, watching from the audience, mouthed "wow" as Joplin electrified the crowd with her primal, wailing vocals. In 1969, Janis said in a *New York Times* interview, "You better not compromise yourself, it's all you got... I'm a goddam living example of that... People aren't supposed to be like me, sing like me, make out like me, drink like me, live like me, but now they're paying me $50,000 a year for me to be like me." Being like her meant cursing, dispensing with undergarments, and prowling for sexual conquests. Her bed was a revolving door where Kris Kristofferson, Joe Namath, Jim Morrison, Jimi Hendrix, and Dick Cavett spent time. When Bruce Springsteen's band opened for Joplin in Jersey, he told his guitarist, "Help! She's after me!" Leonard Cohen used her as his muse in "Chelsea Hotel No. 2." The flip side of fame was that it was not easy living up to Janis Joplin. Her surging popularity was all the more remarkable as she made it big at a time when the expected norm for female performers was to look feminine. While Janis wailed into the microphone, face pouring sweat, dancing as if she were a rainmaker, the Supremes were wearing sleek sequined gowns, crooning love songs to Mr. Right. The girl from small-town USA made her niche in the male domain of dope and drink, guitars and groupies.

Janis invited her parents and two siblings to San Francisco to watch her perform in the hope the black sheep would at last be redeemed. The Joplins were more upset by the hippie scene than impressed by their daughter's onstage gyrations. Her letters home made it achingly clear that, despite her breakout popularity, Janis craved parental approval. Always susceptible to the depression she referred to as the "kozmic blues," she remained anguished by her family's condemnation of her lifestyle. To anesthetize her pain, she turned to her old stand-bys, alcohol and drugs. A failure to form a lasting relationship exacerbated her dizzyingly downward spiral.

Though far from a conventional beauty, Janis's unabashed sexuality transformed the ugly duckling of Port Arthur to the peacock of Haight-Ashbury. Her album *Cheap Thrills* sold more than a million copies, and Big Brother and the Holding Company gave fellow Bay Area bands the Grateful Dead and Jefferson Airplane a run for their money. Ms. Joplin belting out, "Take another piece of my heart, baby" became the auditory equivalent of the painting *The Scream* for a disenfranchised generation. Her signature style consisted of colorful boas in untamed hair, oversized granny glasses, endless bracelets. Thrilled that Joplin always clutched a bottle of Southern Comfort during her concerts, the distillery gifted her a fur coat. With the same élan she took from songs, sex, and illicit substances, Janis drove her Porsche, decorated with psychedelic butterflies, through the hills of San Francisco.

As outrageous offstage as she was on, Janis decorated her San Francisco home as a madam would a bordello, a space she shared with her dog George and a Siamese fighting fish, Charley, whose aquarium was a wine bottle. Her behavior—fueled by alcohol, drugs, and inner demons—was explosive. In 1996, after a concert in Florida, she screamed obscenities at a policeman who tried to stop audience members from dancing, an act that that led to her arrest.

Due to tensions, Janis split from the Holding Company, started the Janis Joplin Full Tilt Boogie Band and adopted the name Pearl. The first year she struck out on her own, Joplin appeared at Woodstock, performing for an hour until her voice gave out. Cashing in on the Joplin craze, Ed Sullivan and Dick Cavett had her as a guest on their television shows. The Port Arthur girl knew she had succeeded in drawing the sword from the stone when *Newsweek* featured her on its cover. At London's Royal Albert Hall, with the force of her supersized personality, she was able to bring a normally staid audience to its feet. When friends warned her that her voice and health could not withstand her demands, she replied, "Man, I'd rather have ten years of super-hype than live to be seventy by sitting in some goddam chair watching TV."

Janis Joplin's last public sighting occurred when she showed up in Port Arthur for the 1960 Thomas Jefferson High School class's tenth annual reunion. The town's Prodigal Daughter wore pink and blue and feathers in her frizzy hair, an outfit of purple and white satin and velvet with gold trim, sandals that revealed her painted toes, and an abundance of rings and bracelets. No doubt, the most used expressions that night: "a spectacle of herself." The pop princess said of returning to the blue-collar town that had made her life hell, "It makes me happy to know I'm making it and they're back there, plumbers just like they were."

Janis gave a little piece of her heart to her fans, friends, and lovers, until there was nothing left. In 1970, she wrote to her parents, "I guess that's what ambition is—it's not all a depraved quest for position or money, maybe it's for love. Lots of love!" Most of Janice's life entailed a deep loneliness that even astronomical success could not alleviate.

In 1970, after a night of drinking with her band, Joplin returned to her room at the Landmark Hotel, a popular hangout for visiting musicians. The walls sported psychedelic designs, but its greatest draw was the management. One night a guest called to complain about the noise coming from the rooms where members of the Jefferson Airplane were hosting a party. The person who complained was asked to leave—definitely Janis's type of place.

John Cooke, a manager for the Full Tilt Boogie Band, went to check on Janis when she did not answer her phone, and he became concerned when, though her car was in the parking lot, she did not come to the door. The management agreed to let him into the room where they discovered Janis had joined the 27 Club of famous musicians who had passed away at that age. The rock star was lying on the floor with fresh heroin needle marks on her arm. She was never again to enjoy nights of bliss with "Bobby McGee." The core of Janis's despair can be traced to a proposed title for a song she was composing shortly before her death, "I Just Made Love to 25,000 People, But I'm Goin' Home Alone."

CHAPTER 29

"Wears Vegan" (1949)

"When it comes to pain, love, joy, loneliness, and fear, a rat is a pig is a dog is a boy."

—INGRID NEWKIRK

Finding our grand passion gives direction to our lives; it is a Holy Grail that turns the black and white of everyday to Technicolor. Some who determined to pursue their callings: Saint Joan perished in flames, Madame Curie died of radium poisoning, Susan B. Anthony ended up under arrest. One activist was British by birth, raised in India, and discovered her mission in America: to provide a voice for the voiceless.

The woman who always threw her lot in with the four-footed started life in Surrey with a menagerie of pets, and the one who set her on the path of Fur Mama was her dog, Shawney, who convinced her that he shared the same emotions as humans. Although devoted to animals, Ingrid nevertheless ate meat—her favorite dish being liver awash with onions—and was the proud owner of a fur coat and rhino-skin boots. Her early years were an odyssey, when the Wards moved to Hertfordshire, the Orkney Islands,

France, and India, where she attended a convent school in the Himalayas which she recalled as "all cold showers and abusive nuns." During vacations, Ingrid helped her mother—alongside Mother Teresa—in caring for lepers, unmarried mothers, and orphans. An incident that left an indelible stamp occurred in New Delhi, after nine-year-old Ingrid spied an emaciated bullock struggling to pull a cart up a hill, urged on by its owner lashing it with a stick. The child wrested the stick from the man's hands.

With the Vietnam War raging, when Ingrid was eighteen, the Wards relocated to Florida where her father took a position with the United States Air Force, designing bombing systems for aircraft. In the Sunshine State, Ingrid met her husband, Steve Newkirk, a racecar driver. He introduced her to Formula One racing, for which, along with sumo wrestling, she developed a lifelong passion. Ingrid told the *New Yorker* about her hobby, "It's sex. The first time you hear them rev their engines, my God! That noise goes straight up my spine!"

The couple moved to Maryland where Ingrid set her sights on becoming a stockbroker. When a neighbor abandoned nineteen kittens, Ingrid took them to the local animal shelter. A woman took the animals and mentioned that she would put them down. Raised in England and India, and unfamiliar with the euphemism, Ingrid interpreted her words on a literal level. After discovering the cats had been euthanized, Newkirk abandoned her career aspirations and took a position at the pound. The nascent activist blew the whistle on the shelter and took a position as an animal protection officer for the District of Columbia.

Unorthodox, she crashed through fences to reach dogs in distress. ("She's not big on gates," explained an acquaintance.) Ward became DC's first female pound master, and her initial order of business was to halt the sale of animals to labs. The state awarded her the honorific "Washingtonian of the Year," and in her acceptance speech, she said, "as children we are taught to be kind to the dog and eat the pig, an irrational concept." In solidarity with her fellow creatures—from crustaceans to chimpanzees—Ms. Newkirk adopted the mantra, "My test is, if it screams and runs away when you go after it, don't eat it." Although she no longer eats meat, Ingrid said she would eat roadkill if it were not morally unjust.

The trajectory of Newkirk's life changed at an animal shelter where she met Alex Pacheco who gave her the book *Animal Liberation* by the Australian philosopher Peter Singer. The author argued that animals' capacity for suffering exempted them from being used for man's benefit. In 1980, Alex, Ingrid, and five friends founded People for the Ethical Treatment of Animals (PETA) in the basement of her Maryland home. The mission statement of their fledging movement: "Animals are not ours to eat, wear, experiment on, or use for entertainment."

Ingrid's crusade came with collateral damage. Steve Newkirk had married a woman who loved racecar driving, sumo wrestling, and liver, and found himself the husband of a vegetarian animal activist who cared more about the four-footed. Because of her acts of civil disobedience, Ingrid spent as much time at the local jail as she did at home, further widening their marital rift. Another reason Steve second-guessed his marital vows was that the couple regularly received bloody carcasses in their mailbox, compliments of those who used animals for livelihood or sport. The couple divorced in 1980; there was no custody battle, as Ingrid had undergone sterilization at age twenty-two because she felt there was something wrong with bringing a baby into a world filled with orphans. Alex and Ingrid began living together; however, as their sexual chemistry did not equate to the excitement of Formula One racing, their partnership dissolved.

Newkirk started off small, but her vision was great. Not content to fight for her cause by handing out petitions, PETA adopted a Barnum-like approach to attract attention. At President Reagan's inauguration, PETA held a demonstration—an event carried on national news—to protest First Lady Nancy Reagan's love of fur coats.

The following year, the animal activist's target was a Maryland laboratory that experimented on monkeys housed in filthy cages and subjected to agonizingly painful procedures. Ingrid's efforts resulted in the first police raid of any US research laboratory on the grounds of animal cruelty. The Silver Spring Monkeys—as the case became known—led to an amendment of the Animal Welfare Act. Newkirk—a self-described press slut—loved the adrenalin rush of notoriety that gave her the same chills as watching sumo wrestlers.

Milking the media became a tenet of PETA, and their stunts were pure theater that also carried a moralistic message. Knowing nudity garners attention—a truth first established by Lady Godiva and her horse—the organization created a campaign where celebrities would shed their clothes for the sake of animals. The activists photographed five supermodels, including Naomi Campbell, sans garments, with the caption, "We'd rather go naked than wear fur." Ever the principled idealist, Naomi donned a fur coat a few days later, and an infuriated Ingrid banned her from future billboards. Another foray into nudity took place in London when sixty-six-year-old Ingrid created a photo op of her hanging naked on a meat hook alongside the carcasses of pigs. The accompanying caption: "We're All the Same: Go Vegan in 2016."

A few years later, two formidable British women, on opposite ends of the fur controversy spectrum, had an encounter. Anna Wintour, the editor of *Vogue*, was at the Four Seasons Hotel in Manhattan when a well-dressed woman, a PETA plant, placed a dead raccoon on Anna's plate. After the woman screamed, "Anna wears fur hats!" a deadly calm descended on the upscale eatery. Ms. Wintour remained calm, covered the carcass with a napkin, and ordered coffee. Other terrorist souvenirs: bloody paw prints and the words "Fur Hag" on the steps in front of the fashion doyenne's residence. If one were to ask Ms. Newkirk how many times she has been arrested, her answer would be in the neighborhood of fifty, and counting. One of these arrests occurred when Ingrid invaded the *Vogue* offices, and for her efforts, two of New York's finest dragged her away. However, before the men in blue arrived, she managed to grab a ringing telephone and answered, "I'm awfully sorry, we're closed today due to cruelty to animals." On another crusade, Ingrid entered a Pennsylvania field where a group of men, some in Ku Klux Klan robes, were shooting pigeons for sport. PETA stopped their entertainment, and Ingrid's view for the next fifteen days was of bars.

Another of General Newkirk's campaigns took place at a Victoria's Secret fashion show, where the models wore nothing but stilettos and lingerie. The audience members had paid five hundred dollars, including Donald Trump, Woody Harrelson, and eleven million who watched at home. As Brazilian supermodel Gisele Bündchen sashayed down the catwalk, dressed in a beaded bra and black panties, despite state-of-the-art security, four PETA members leapt onto the stage, holding signs that read, "Gisele Fur Scum." PETA took umbrage with Gisele for wearing a black mink coat for a Blackglama fur ad—"What becomes a legend most?"—where she followed in the footsteps of Marlene Dietrich, Maria Callas, and Bette Davis. Fur coats that PETA manages to extract from their owners are distributed to homeless shelters, such as a shipment of mink and ermine that Newkirk dispatched to the poor of Afghanistan.

Now, in her seventies, the evangelist's zeal is as strong as ever. The organization that began in a Maryland basement is currently the largest animal rights group in the world, with 360 employees, thousands of volunteers, and a thirty-million-dollar annual budget. Furry companions (PETA employees despise the word pet) roam the corridors because they feel it is not right to leave them on their own. Staff members receive bereavement days when companions pass away, and they need time to mourn and arrange funerals. The international organization has offices in London, Rome, and Bombay.

When an interviewer asked Ingrid if she had plans to retire, she looked at him as if he had asked her if she wanted a veal cutlet. A nonfictional Tom Joad, as long as an injustice exists, she will be there. As indefatigable as ever, Ward still engages in shock-and-awe tactics. A poster campaign compared people who eat chicken to Nazis, slaughterhouses to the Holocaust, the Westminster Dog Shows to the Ku Klux Klan, and dog breeders to slave traders. Ingrid is proof positive that unabashed tactics work.

PETA victories include a ban on using animals in crash tests, and convincing major US cosmetic companies to stop using animal ingredients in make-up. A further PETA push was to draw attention to the inhumane living conditions of livestock destined to end up as fast food. They pushed their agenda through campaigns, such as kentuckyfriedcruelty.com, murderking.com, and wickedwendys.com, that obliged corporations to adopt animal-welfare regulations. Many people despise Newkirk for her terrorist tactics, something that does not faze her in the slightest. She stated, "I'm tough. I have been called every name in the book. Personally, it's inconsequential if people hate me."

In her will, Ingrid directed that the meat of her body be used for a barbecue, her feet be used as an umbrella stand (as was a practice with elephant's feet in India), and her liver be shipped to France, pointing to the nation's consumption of foie gras. In a softer vein, she requested that "a little piece of her heart" be interred beside the Ferrari pits where Formula One racer Michael Schumacher won the German Grand Prix.

What becomes a legend most is dedication to one's passion. Hence, while "The Devil Wears Prada," an angel activist wears vegan.

CHAPTER 30

"Can the Bird Fly?" (1978)

"We are our sisters' keepers."

—MALALAI JOYA

A girl with haunted, sea-green eyes peered from a 1985 *National Geographic* cover. The iconic photograph made the twelve-year-old the poster child for the Afghani refugees who fled in the wake of the Soviet Union invasion. Another such victim is the poster woman for hope.

Activist Malalai Joya began her memoir, *A Woman Among Warlords: The Extraordinary Story of an Afghan Who Dared to Raise Her Voice*, with the sentence, "I come from a land of tragedy called Afghanistan." The source of the sorrow is her homeland's strategic location at the crossroads of central Asia that has long caused foreign interests to eye the country with the lascivious licking of lips.

Malalai was born in Farah, Afghanistan, one of ten children. Her namesake was Malalai of Maiwand, a famous freedom fighter who, in 1880, rallied against the imperialism of the British Empire at Maiwand. When the soldiers were facing defeat, she marched to the front line and hoisted the Afghan flag. Although she died for her bravery, the English suffered a defeat, thus ridding Afghanistan of a hated overlord. Malalai's father abandoned his medical studies to join the warlords committed to the fight against the Soviet occupiers. A landmine resulted in the amputation of his leg; no longer able to fight, with a price on his head, he headed for the mountains. Malalai remarked, "Since then, all we have known is war."

When Malalai was four years old, the family, reunited with the exiled patriarch, ended up in an Iranian internment camp where eighty-five thousand Afghans were packed together in the desert of the Birjand district. While the rest of the world knew the region for its Persian carpets and its storied association with the ancient Silk Road, the refugees survived in filthy tents, sweltered in the heat of the day, shivered in the freezing nights. As schools were nonexistent, the family departed for Pakistan. After learning how to read, Malalai devoured books—from Persian poetry to the plays of Bertolt Brecht, to the speeches of Dr. Martin Luther King, Jr. Malalai did her utmost to educate the women in her camp, including her mother.

When she was sixteen, an underground charity, Organization for Promoting Afghan Women's Capabilities, presented her with a daunting offer: to return to Afghanistan to help establish a clandestine school for girls, one that needed to escape the Taliban radar. At the time, the Islamic militants had driven out the Soviets; tragically, under the new regime, females became the victims of unimaginable abuse. Girls were denied education after the age of eight, were unable to obtain employment, and were not allowed to leave the house without a burqa, a garment that shrouded even their eyes. Domestic abuse, rape, forced marriage, and suicide by way of self-immolation made their conditions "worse than hell." The Taliban, not known for their power of patience, meted out punishments such as lashings, chopping off noses and ears, and beheadings. Ironically, the burqa, the hated symbol of oppression that Malalai refers to as "a shroud for the living," allowed her to camouflage her identity. As a further precaution, she had to assume a different surname. She chose Joya after Sarwar Joya, an Afghan who spent twenty-four years in jail; his enemies murdered him when he refused to denounce his democratic ideals. Despite the deaths of untold martyrs for freedom, Malalai takes comfort from her country's proverb, "The truth is like the sun. When it comes up, nobody can block it out or hide it."

After World War II, the democratic nations of the world were aghast that countries such as Hungary, after freeing itself of the swastika, had fallen prey to the hammer and sickle. A similar situation occurred in Afghanistan that came under the yoke of the Soviet Union, the Taliban, followed by a third torturous takeoever. After the defeat of the Taliban, the fundamentalist mujahedin, warlords, seized power, backed by the United States. Unimaginably, the fate of females in the beleaguered land went even farther south: rape was a tactic used to punish enemies and reward soldiers. To camouflage their barbarism, the warlords created a puppet parliament. Malalai experienced their brand of rule when she set up her illicit school, outlawed by the warlords, as she was a female and a critic of fundamentalism.

In 2003, the world's media descended on Kabul to watch the delegates who would determine the future of Afghanistan. The representative from Farah was twenty-five-year-old Malalai Joya, who had become a member of the Loya Jirga, "meeting of the elders," whose task it was to draft a new constitution fashioned on democratic principles. The nascent politician says, "It turned out my mission would be to expose the true nature of the Jirga from within." When Joya first entered the parliament, her eyes met a most unwelcome sight: "a long row with some of the worst abusers of human rights that our country had ever known—warlords and war criminals and fascists." Her take on the new "democratic" government invoked an old Afghan proverb: "It's the same donkey, with a new saddle."

As the men delivered lengthy speeches congratulating themselves on the transition to a government of the people, Joya was a bundle of nerves. What gave her strength was the oppression of her sisters, and anxiety transformed to anger. Allowed to speak for three minutes, Malalai, in an impassioned voice, asked, "Why are we allowing criminals to be present here? They should instead be prosecuted in the national and international courts." After nineteen seconds, her detractors turned off her microphone, infuriated at their exposure by a young woman. Outraged, they shouted that Joya was a whore, a Communist, and an infidel. While the Jirga descended into a riot, the United Nations representatives whisked Malalai away in a car with dark tinted windows to a hiding place. She later said her greatest fear was reprisal by rape.

After the episode at the Loya Jirga, bodyguards in camouflage uniforms with AK-47 assault rifles helped foil four attempts on Malalai's life. Threats came by way of the telephone and in leaflets: "We will kidnap you, then kill you. You stand to benefit if you stop your struggle." In 2004, two men plotted to shoot her after she gave a speech for International Women's Day; security spirited her out through a back door. In her home province of Farah, her enemies detonated a bomb to disperse the crowd. Enemies called her a "dead woman walking." Of her life as a fugitive, hiding out with bodyguards and a burqa, Malalai said, "I don't fear death. I fear remaining silent in the face of injustice. They will kill me, but they will not kill my voice. Because it will be the voice of all Afghan women. You can cut the flower, but you cannot stop the coming of the spring."

Any semblance of a stable life was impossible. The walking poster of protest traveled from one safe house to another, never sleeping in the same location for more than a night. In response to her friends' pleas that she escape the country referred to as "Warlord-istan," Joya responded, "I can never leave when all the poor people that I love are living in danger and poverty. I am not going to search for a better and safer place, and leave them burning in hell." Again, quoting Brecht, she continued, "Those who do struggle often fail, but those who do not struggle have already failed."

In equal measure to the hate Joya engenders is the fierce loyalty of her followers. When Malalai visited a maternity hospital in Kabul, the expectant mothers waiting in the heat became delirious upon learning the identity of the veiled stranger. "It's Joya, Joya is here!" spread through the crowd. Women have walked for miles to touch her in the belief that she is the only hope for their future, for the future of their daughters.

Men of the tempest-tossed nation also turn to the five-foot dynamo. Abdul Halim told Joya how, after he spoke out against a Jihadi commander—who had become a member of parliament—retaliated by having his two young sons shoved in a sack and thrown into the river. Halim secured an interview with President Karzai, showed him the photographs of the children, and related the heinous crime. The president responded, "You are young, have more babies."

Amidst the horror, in 2004, Malalai was at a press conference where she met a Kabul University student who shared her passion for social justice. When their relationship deepened, Malalai made sure he understood that their marriage would be far from traditional. She outlined that her political agenda would come first, their meetings would be in secret, and that she could be killed at any time. Another stipulation was that any child would have to be adopted, as persecution had left countless orphans. When he said that her conditions would be met, Malalai responded, "Mubarak!" the Persian version of "congratulations." On the day of their engagement party, Joya was a no-show, as she had to attend a meeting in Kabul.

Their wedding took place in 2005 in a tent; the bridal party consisted of Malalai's bodyguards, who checked each bouquet of flowers and all presents for explosives. The bride gave away any expensive presents to fund those in need. Her wedding wish (to placate her elders, she did not deliver a speech, as that would be unbecoming for a female) was that Afghan fathers stop selling their daughters, to give them an education. The response from many was laughter. Because of Malalai's commitments, there was no time for a honeymoon. For security, Malalai is steadfast in her refusal to disclose her husband's name.

With her popularity surging among ordinary Afghans, in 2005, Joya again ran for office, though she was skeptical of the outcome. As she said, "What matters is not who is voting, it's who is counting." Her bid proved successful, and she became the country's youngest official elected to the national parliament, the Wolesa Jirga, as a representative of Farah. The newly minted member began her first speech, "My condolences to the people of Afghanistan." A fierce critic of her fellow members of parliament, Malalai scoffed that "though they now wore suits and ties, they were still the same murdering warlords and religious fundamentalists who had contributed to their country's scars." In a television interview, the firebrand claimed the legislature was "worse than a zoo." In retaliation, her enemies found Joya guilty of violating Article 70 of the Rules of Procedure, which forbids lawmakers to criticize each other. Joya pointed out their hypocrisy: fellow members of parliament had thrown bottles and sandals at her and made death threats. In solidarity, a month after her expulsion, her supporters, from locales ranging from Rome to Vancouver, observed an international day of action and vainly demanded her reinstatement.

Ms. Joya made her plea for gender equality couched in a literary analogy, "Society in my opinion is like a bird. One wing is man, one wing is woman. When one wing is injured, can the bird fly?"

CHAPTER 31

"We Are the Champions" (1985)

"Being a gay American, I know what it means to look at the flag and not have it protect all your liberties."

—MEGAN RAPINOE

In a bid to dispel February blues—a situation that arose from wintry weather and a lull in sports—André Laguerre, the editor of *Sports Illustrated*, willed into existence "The Swimsuit Edition." Soon a burst of Malibu tropical winds arrived in mailboxes across the nation, featuring bodacious babes in Barbie-sized bikinis, frolicking against a backdrop of white sand and azure seas. Then came Megan Rapinoe.

The woman with pink pixie hair blazed like a fiery comet over the sporting world's skies, leaving a trail of controversy in her wake. Her story began in Redding, a small, conservative, working-class city in Northern California. Her father, Jim, worked as a construction contractor while her mother, Denise, worked nights as a waitress at Jack's Grill. The household included seven children, including three the couple had together: son Brian and twins Megan and Rachael. Brian, five years older than his sisters,

set up cones to teach them how to dribble, thereby
sowing the seeds of fame. As female athletes were
invisible at this time, Megan plastered posters of
Michael Jordan on her bedroom walls. A devoted
mother, Denise drove her daughters two and a half
hours each way for practice in Sacramento.

As a senior at Foothill High, her classmates voted
Megan Most Likely to be Famous. Concerned that
her daughter's head would swell as her school's
shining star, Denise told her, "You're not the shit just
because you're good at sports." When the twins were
in second grade, Brian started using drugs; they were
ten when they heard on the radio the chilling words,
"Brian Rapinoe has been arrested for burglary."

Though the possessor of a close-knit family and
athletic prowess that assured her popularity, as a
teen, Megan felt lost and alone. However, with the
realization that she was gay, she understood what
had been nibbling at her soul, and she was ready
to move on. Megan came out at the University of
Portland in Oregon and recalled, "I didn't struggle
to come out. I thought: 'Well, yeah, obviously, I'm
gay.' Everyone should have told me: it was obvious
for my whole childhood—hello?" Indeed, she
reveled in sidestepping the mainstream and felt
that conservatism was highly overrated. Her parents
worried about what people would say, but Megan's
attitude was Jimmy-crack-corn—she did not care.
When her mother confided to friends that both her
teens were gay, the response was that their own kids
were dropping out of high school, high on drugs;
perspective served as a salve.

Upon graduation, the girl with the pastel-hued hair enjoyed a meteoric rise. Megan's professional career began in 2009 when she played with the Chicago Red Stars. During the next ten years, she moved between clubs in Seattle, Sydney, Boca Raton, and Philadelphia, until Megan found her niche with France's Olympique Lyon, considered one of the strongest teams in women's soccer. Upon her return to the United States, Megan signed up with Reign, her current team, based near Seattle. Her big breakout occurred during the 2011 World Cup, after the US defeated Colombia. Ecstatic at their victory, Rapinoe grabbed an on-field microphone and belted out Bruce Springsteen's song "Born in the USA."

Although the athlete and performance star basks in the limelight, she does not depend on crowd approval for self-affirmation. She expressed this when she said, "Of course I like the attention. Who doesn't want 50,000 people going: 'You're awesome!' But, in the same sense, I'm not a slave to it; it's not the reason why I do or say those things." Affirmation comes not from the fans, but rather from those closest to Megan: her mother, her twin, her best friends, and Sue. Sue Bird, an Israeli American WNBA basketball star and four-time Olympic champion, is Megan's girlfriend; sparks ignited at the Rio Olympics where Megan also garnered a gold medal. The power couple became the first same-sex couple to pose nude for ESPN's Body Issue. Asked how it felt to lead the US soccer team, Rapinoe cried out, "Go gays!"

The athlete-turned-activist felt the stadium to be a powerful platform. In 2016, Megan took the knee during the national anthem, a gesture introduced by

National Football League star Colin Kaepernick in protest of police brutality against African Americans. Rapinoe became the first high-profile female athlete to undertake the gesture of civil disobedience. Clearly unimpressed, the owner of Jack's, with the approval of customers, took down Megan's photos, which a bartender had hung in the restaurant. Her father, an army vet, though upset at what he considered his daughter's lack of patriotism, was nevertheless incensed by the hate mail that arrived at the Rapinoe home. In response to what they considered unsportsmanlike behavior, the US Soccer Federation amended its rules and required all its players to "stand respectfully." Ms. Rapinoe agreed, although she refuses to sing, to place her hand over her heart. Instead, she silently replays the names of Blacks who have lost their lives as victims of hatred: Trayvon Martin, Michael Brown, Tamir Rice... At a *Glamour Magazine* event, Megan pointed out that, while she and Kaepernick had engaged in the same act of civil disobedience, because of white privilege, fans feted her as a World Cup champion while he remained unemployed. Ms. Rapinoe told *The New York Times Magazine* that her involvement in social issues reflected the work of movements like LGBTQ advocacy, #MeToo, and Black Lives Matter. When she received FIFA's award for the greatest soccer player, she mentioned "Blue-Girl," an Iranian woman who disguised herself as a man to go to a soccer game. Afterwards, the woman set herself on fire to avoid charges for violating a ban on women in stadiums.

In recognition of her advocacy work helping societal underdogs, Michelle Obama recruited her to join a voter-participation initiative, Congresswoman

Alexandria Ocasio-Cortez invited her to Washington, and Gloria Steinem thanked Rapinoe for carrying her torch. The activist turned angel when Victoria's Secret ditched their male fantasy models for Ms. Rapinoe, in a move calculated to prioritize acheievement over curves. Megan acknowledged that Brian's struggles with drugs had awakened her social conscience. One of the hydra heads she is working to slay involves getting society to view drug addiction as an illness, rather than a moral failing.

A rebel with many causes, Rapinoe spearheaded a lawsuit against the US Soccer Federation, alleging "institutionalized gender discrimination" in a bid to achieve pay for female players equal to their male counterparts'. In protest, in Dallas to face off against Japan, the Women's Soccer Team wore their royal blue warm-up shirts turned inside-out, leaving a blank space where their crest would normally be displayed. One of the financial inequities is that, while the Men's World Cup players receive four hundred million dollars in prize money, the Women's World Cup Players receive thirty million.

Always a media magnet, in 2019, Megan launched a blitz of coverage before the World Cup Final against the Netherlands in Lyons, France. Prior to the tournament, President Trump had told the team that, if they returned victorious, their reward would be a visit to the White House. Although the soccer team had been the guests of President Barack Obama, Megan, a self-proclaimed "walking protest" against the POTUS, responded in a video that went viral, "I'm not going to the fucking White House." President

Trump tweeted, "Megan should WIN first before she TALKS! Finish the job." And she did.

The woman from Redding, although performing on the international stage while under attack by a world leader, proved triumphant. To the accompaniment of fans chanting "Equal pay!" Rapinoe made a score that brought the American team a record fourth title. She was tempted to flash double middle fingers, but she resisted, saying that even she had limits. After her victory, she struck the pose that became the sporting image of 2019: pink head tipped back, arms outstretched, eyes closed as if in prayer to the soccer gods. In the sea of spectators were her parents and twin sister. Brian had watched his kid sister's first two World Cups from prison. On this occasion, he cheered her on from a San Diego transitional facility.

Although the US Women's Soccer Team were no-shows at 1600 Pennsylvania Avenue, they did make it to New York, where the city honored them with a ticker-tape parade. Thousands of diehard fans clad in red, white, and blue, many of whom had arrived as early as five o'clock in the morning for prime viewing spots, lined the stretch of Broadway known as the Canyon of Heroes. A caravan of floats carried the twenty-three-member squad to City Hall, where Mayor Bill de Blasio presented them with keys to the city. Construction workers blared air horns from buildings high above; confetti rained down from skyscrapers in Manhattan's financial district. The soccer stars wore black T-shirts that read "World Champions"; co-captain Rapinoe also sported oversized bright red sunglasses. Post-parade, DK Khaled's "All I do Is Win" played from loudspeakers.

Rapinoe addressed her fans, "This group is just so badass. There is nothing that can faze this group. We're chilling. We have pink hair and purple hair, we have tattoos and dreadlocks. We got white girls and everything in between. Straight girls and gay girls." She concluded with a plea to love more, to hate less, to make this world a better place. As the crowd roared its approval and her teammates rose to their feet, Rapinoe adopted The Pose and shouted, "New York City, you're the mother-fucking best!"

The ticker-tape parade planted another laurel on Megan's pink hair, and her reception was far different from another female soccer player's historic moment. Norwegian athlete Ada Hegerberg was the first recipient of the prestigious women's Ballon d'Or award. Until then, the prize had only been presented to men for more than sixty years. In the Grand Palais in Paris, Ada raised a golden soccer ball over her head before kissing it. After she delivered a moving speech in which she told girls to "please believe in yourselves," the event's host, French disc jockey Martin Solveig, incongruously asked, "Do you know how to twerk?" Hegerberg shook her head. Had he posed the question to Megan, her response would have been more along the line of a foot-to-groin movement.

The year ended with another singular honor when *Sports Illustrated* named Megan Rapinoe Sportsperson of the Year, joining Mary Decker, Chris Evert, and Serena Williams as the only women in the sixty-six-year history of the award. Megan had the unique distinction of being the only gay honoree. The cover showcased Megan holding a sledgehammer.

The model wore shoes designed by Maison Margiela, a gown created by Valentino, but the pink hair and sass were classic Megan.

Ms. Rapinoe, touted as her generation's Muhammad Ali, points out that any wind beneath her wings is provided by her teammates, who can be described by the lyric they sang as they disembarked from their plane from France: "We are the Champions."

CHAPTER 32

"The Good Old Days" (2001)

"Nothing really scares me, to be honest."

—BILLIE EILISH

In 1955, Frank Sinatra crooned that "love and marriage/they go together like a horse and carriage." Fast-forward three decades: what currently goes together are pop princesses and sexualized attire. Madonna's black bustier is bondage-and-discipline costume; Britney Spears' Catholic school uniform is the stuff of future confessionals; Miley Cyrus's flesh-colored bikini smacks of a conjugal visit. In contrast, a current pop star bares her soul, rather than her body.

Anyone with internet connectivity was privy to the image of a teenager in an outlandish outfit holding a handful of megaphone-shaped trophies at the 2020 Grammy Awards Ceremony. Billie Eilish, who won five Grammys, became the first woman, and the youngest person, ever to accomplish this feat. While the other female vocalists seemed dressed for a prom, Ms. Eilish seemed dressed for a rave. Her hair and sleeves were of a slime green hue; her green oversized coffin-shaped nails resembled a dragon's talons. Before the announcement for winner of Album of the Year, the camera caught her whispering, "Please don't be me, please."

While the Prince of Wales has four given names—Charles Philip Arthur George—the American pop princess sports five: Billie Eilish Pirate Baird O'Connell. Her parents, Maggie and Frank, self-described as mainly unemployed actors, christened her Billie after her maternal grandfather, William, who died a few months before she was born; Eilish, after an Irish conjoined twin who had been the subject of a television documentary; Pirate, what the four-year-old Finneas called his newborn sister; and her parents' surnames, Baird and O'Connell. However, a difference between the British and American royal is that, while Charles grew up in the 775-room Buckingham Palace in London, Billie has lived her whole life in a two-bedroom home in Highland Park, an East Los Angeles neighborhood yet to be gentrified.

Finneas's birth coincided with the Hanson Brothers' smash hit "MMMBop," and Maggie and Frank decided to homeschool, as did the religious Oklahoma parents of the boy band. In addition, Maggie—who was born in Colorado, where the Columbine massacre had taken place when Finneas was two—cited the horror as another reason to avoid public education. Their decision may have prevented schoolyard bullies from teasing Billie, who has Tourette syndrome, which causes tics; mathematics triggers her symptoms. Billie's perspective on her parents' decision is: "I'm so glad I didn't go to school, because if I had, I would never have the life I have now. The only times I ever wished I could go were so

I could fuck around. At times I just wanted to have, like, a locker, and get to not listen to the teacher and laugh in class." At age fifteen, Billie passed her high school equivalency exam. Her vernacular is in keeping with her wardrobe sense, and she talks like a human Instagram caption: everything is "fire," "trash," "bro," "deadass."

Like the von Trapp family (as to their love of music, not their lifestyle), music dominated the O'Connell household. Patrick found an ancient piano that someone was giving away on the internet, and a parental rule was that the kids did not have to observe a bedtime routine if they were involved in a creative activity. At age seven, Billie composed her first song on the ukulele, and she learned how to play the guitar and the piano from YouTube videos. Maggie enrolled Billie in a songwriting class that included an introduction to the Beatles. College was never an O'Connell priority, as Frank said, "If we modeled anything, it was being broke and artsy." The family is vegetarian—Billie never ate meat, with the exception of an ant she once accidentally swallowed in a glass of soy milk. The O'Connell clan all shared one bed until Finneas turned ten; for two of those years, he insisted on wearing his cowboy boots while sleeping. Frank and Maggie moved cots into the living room when their son and daughter were older, to give them their own space. In typical tween fashion, Billie covered her bedroom walls with her idol, Justin Bieber. In 2020, Billie was over the moon when she met Bieber at the Coachella Music Festival. While most photographs of Bieber show him with scantily-clad beauties, on this night he hugged Billie, who was dressed in oversized denim bootleg Louis Vuitton.

Finneas altered the trajectory of his family's lives when he wrote "Ocean Eyes" for his band and enlisted his thirteen-year-old sister as its singer. The siblings uploaded the song to the music-sharing website SoundCloud for Billie's dance teacher, who wanted to use it for choreography. The music industry beat a path to her door, and the siblings had a billion streams on Spotify even before her album debuted. The success cemented Billie's dream of fame that she had aspired to since she was twelve, after a trip to Manhattan where she watched a Broadway crowd applaud the young star of *Mathilda*.

While Britney had crooned, "Baby do it one more time..." Billie's lyrics are somber, and their accompanying videos a nod to the macabre: cigarettes being put out on her cheeks, black tears streaming from her pale blue eyes, tarantulas crawling from her mouth. Despite the grimness of the post 9/11 world, in her song that doubles as a public service announcement, "When the Party's Over," she sends the message never to camouflage pain with benzos and opioids. "I don't need a xanny to feel better/Don't give me a xanny now or ever." Billie never takes drugs, though she loves the scent of marijuana, making her a moral antihero.

Despite Billie's happy version of the Partridge Family and her startling success, she has battled debilitating depression and crippling panic attacks. She traces the cause to various sources: a severe injury she sustained during a dance class, a failed romantic relationship, the murder of her friend, the rapper XXXXTentacion. The series of events led to a self-harming phase, and she felt she deserved the pain. Ages thirteen through sixteen proved dark phase; as she put it, "I have to be in this bitch all the time." While on tour in Berlin, alone in a hotel, she saw the window as an avenue of escape; thoughts of her mother prevented her from taking a fateful final step. With the help of therapy, a close-knit family, and music, she has been able to ride out the interior storm.

Billie's appearance attracts as much attention as her music, and her uber-baggy clothes are far different from other pop princesses' attire that screams couture by Hefner. Her first act of following her own fashion was at age four, when she wore her onesie with her underwear on the outside. Her silhouette-obscuring apparel had its genesis when she was thirteen and enrolled in dance classes where the skin-tight bodysuit exacerbated her body dysmorphia, so much so that she could not look in a mirror. At thirteen, rather than scouring the malls for the latest trends, she shopped at Target, cut up her purchases, and sewed them into unique shapes; similarly, she fashioned a shirt from an IKEA shopping bag. Now that Finneas has bought his own home (four miles away), Billie, in Scarlett O'Hara fashion, is eyeing her brother's dragon-print curtains as a potential clothing fabric. Her message to fans and fellow pop princesses is that you can have a stage presence minus the push-up bra.

Success has surpassed even the teen idol's wildest expectations, yet she remains unpretentious. She has played to sold-out concerts of delirious young fans, many dressed in homage to the musician's garish aesthetic. Their style serves as a collective thumbing of the nose at the stereotypical teen pop star's sexual objectification. The emperor's new fashion is not one for which they lust. In an Instagram post to her forty-six million followers, Billie stood in the doorway of a trailer, wearing a graffiti-printed T-shirt with the caption, "if only i dressed normal id be so much hotter yea yea come up with a better comment im tired of that one."

If reigning at the Grammy Awards was not heady enough fare, Hollywood chose the eighteen-year-old Billie to perform at the Oscars. After Steven Spielberg introduced the singer-songwriter superstar, Eilish sang the 1965 classic "Yesterday" for the In Memoriam segment, proof positive that Hollywood has embraced its rebellious daughter. On the giant screen behind her played a montage of the illustrious icons who had recently passed away: Kirk Douglas, Doris Day, Kobe Bryant. While the legends were a nostalgic nod to yesterday, Eilish was a symbol of today.

In a 2020 trifecta, Billie became the youngest person ever to record a theme song for the twenty-fifth James Bond film release, another in a string of achievements that made the teen Guinness-Records-worthy. As with all her other music, she wrote and produced "No Time to Die" with her big brother partner. One of its lyrics is, "The blood you bleed is just the blood you owe." The song could potentially earn Ms. Eilish another trophy: the last two Bond ballads, Sam Smith's "Writing's on the Wall" and Adele's "Skyfall," both garnered Oscars. Perhaps there is another "Please don't be me" moment on the entertainment horizon.

The fashion industry was not slow to pick up the new diva of the dark. Her appearance in "I Speak My Truth in #MyCalvins" is worlds away from the 1980 Calvin Klein jeans ad featuring a fifteen-year-old Brooke Shields—in skin-tight denim with bare midriff—with the insinuating caption, "What gets between me and my Calvins? Nothing." Another feather in Billie's green hair is her appearance on the cover of the American edition of *Vogue Magazine* with the caption, "THE OUTSIDER How Billie Eilish Reinvented Pop Stardom." Anna Wintour, *Vogue's* editor-in-chief, praised Eilish's style and activism regarding body positivity. *Rolling Stone* featured Billie on its cover, which described her story as "The Triumph of the Weird."

The O'Connells, who almost lost their 1,200-square-foot home because, as Billie puts it, "we were as poor as fuck," have no financial woes, as Billie is the possessor of a multi-million-dollar fortune. Unlike the Beverly Hillbillies, who moved to a mansion when they struck oil, the family has no plans to relocate. However, on her seventeenth birthday, her recording company presented her with the car she had dreamt about since age thirteen: a black—not green—Dodge Challenger she nicknamed the Dragon. In Billie-speak she said, "Look at her fine ass. I love this car so much." Her newly minted driver's license reads "Name: Billie Eilish O'Connell. Eyes: Blue. Hair: Other."

Despite Billie's youth, she understands a truth that even those far older do not grasp, "I'm realizing the place I'm in right now is kind of my time, my moment. These are the good old days."

CHAPTER 33

"Shall Lead Them" (2003)

"I want you to panic."

—GRETA THUNBERG

A Victorian adage states that "Children should be seen and not heard." The nineteenth-century standard does not apply to a Swedish teen who has made it her mission to both be seen and heard, not for self-aggrandizement, but the well-being of the planet.

While females are mostly associated with pink, one associated with green is Greta, born in Stockholm to mother Malena Ernman, Sweden's leading opera singer, and father Svante Thunberg. After dating Svante for six months, Malena became pregnant with Greta; as she made more money, Svante became a self-described "housewife" who raised Greta and later, her sister, Beata. Their life was a nomadic odyssey across Europe for opera concerts.

As a child, Greta had memorized the capitals of every country and the names of cities—both forward and backward. Over her bed hung a periodic table of the elements which she likewise committed to memory.

Although home was a happy place, at school, bullies made life miserable, and recesses were spent hiding in the bathroom. She never received invitations to parties, and she was always the outsider.

At age eight, Greta first discovered the problem of climate change when a teacher showed the documentary *The Great Pacific Garbage Patch* about the melting Arctic, marine animals bloated with plastic. Thunberg wept as she watched. The other students brushed off the film, something Greta could not do. In solidarity, the family became vegan, though Greta has caught her mother sneaking cheese in the middle of the night.

As a preteen, Greta suffered from interminable crying jags, stopped speaking with anyone other than her family, and barely ate, a self-starvation that stunted her growth. The first panic attack occurred when Greta refused to eat freshly-baked cinnamon buns; concerned about her loss of appetite, her parents' knee-jerk reaction was anger. The response from their daughter was "an abysmal howl that lasted for over forty minutes." The doctors finally came up with a diagnosis: obsessive-compulsive disorder, high-functioning autism, and Asperger syndrome.

The Thunbergs wrote a memoir of their family crisis, *Our House is on Fire: Scenes of a Family and a Planet in Crisis*. The book was a chronicle of the challenges of raising Greta and Beata, who had her own issues. Beata went through a stage where every attempt at conversation ending with her screaming, "Shut up, you fucking idiot!" Doctors also diagnosed her with elements of Asperger syndrome and obsessive-compulsive disorder.

In 2018, the fifteen-year-old realized something that many with gray hair never do: action succeeds more than grousing. She wrote an essay denouncing climate change, picked up by a Swedish newspaper. Encouraged, Greta urged local activists to take the same path as the students from Marjory Stoneman Douglas High School in Parkland, Florida, who had organized school strikes to protest gun violence after their school suffered a mass shooting. They declined the suggestion as too radical, which made her realize she had to become a solitary conscientious objector. Greta informed her parents that she was going to go on strike to urge the government to meet the goals of the Paris Agreement, and she would return to her classes after the election. Malena and Svante were not on board with her plan, and this did not have to do with their daughter being AWOL from her classes. Their concern stemmed from Greta becoming a target of attention when she had finally put her life on track. Her parents suggested she come up with an alternative; the five-foot dynamo was immovable.

Thunberg's first order of business was a flyer that read, "My name is Greta. I am in ninth grade, and I am school-striking for the climate." Wearing a blue hoodie, the teenager stood in front of the parliament building holding a sign painted in black letters: *Skolstrejk for kimatet* ("School Strike for Climate"). The following day a stranger joined her; a few days later, a few more activists came on board, including a member of Greenpeace. As their daughter's grassroots movement spread, tension escalated in the Thunberg household. Svante and Malena were condemned as conspiracy theorists who agreed to their child's truancy to further their own agenda.

Detractors contended the Thunbergs were subjecting their child to brainwashing. Locals shoved excrement into the family mailbox. Her parents grew increasingly anxious that the authorities would remove Greta from their home. Malena wrote, "The price of being heard is hate. The price of being seen is hate."

The protest that had started off with a lone figure grew to include hundreds. After the election, the teen titian of climate activism announced she would continue with her strike every Friday—this initiated the Fridays for Future. Consequently, thousands of students across the world began skipping school on Fridays. The newspapers carried the images of strikers in New York City marching in Battery Park, in London in the shadow of Big Ben, and in Germany, congregating at the Brandenburg Gate. The rallying cry for environmentalism was "Make the World Greta Again." Crowds chanted, "Greta, Greta, Greta..." much to her chagrin. Her focus is on the cause, not on self. Hundreds of thousands of "Gretas" have been truant due to global climate strikes. Actress-activist Jane Fonda, another Greta convert, was so inspired by Thunberg's actions that she hosted her own Fire Drill Fridays. Regarding the diminutive dynamo, Fonda said, "I was just filled with depression and hopelessness, and then I started reading about Greta. She inspired me to get out there and do more." In contrast, Prime Minister Theresa May's cabinet condemned school walkouts as it "wastes lessons time." Greta—who has almost five million Twitter followers, retaliated with "But, then again, political leaders have wasted thirty years of inaction. And that is slightly worse." Signature Greta: sarcastic; unabashed.

Despite her one-girl crusade, Greta retains aspects of a typical teen. She shares matching bracelets with her sister, and dotes on Moses, her golden retriever, Roxy, her black Labrador, and Freyja, her Icelandic horse. While learning about the specter of climate change had triggered her depression, fighting against it alleviated its symptoms. As she put it, "I don't have time to be depressed anymore." With her limited amount of time, she published a book, a collection of her lectures, *No One Is Too Small to Make a Difference*. A positive aspect of 2020 was that filmmakers, intrigued by the teen who transformed angst into action, released *I am Greta*, a ninety-seven-minute documentary that trailed the crusader on her journeys around the world, raising awareness of earth's fragility.

Thunberg's time is a scarce commodity as she is an international speaker who has had audiences with heads of state and the Pope. At the Vatican, swelling crowds chanted, "Go Greta, save the planet!" At the World Economic Forum in Switzerland, she said, "I want you to feel the fear I feel every day. And then I want you to act." Although Greta told the adults that "they are fools and their plans are lame and short-sighted," they nevertheless awarded her with a standing ovation. Afterwards, they retreated to luxury cars and private planes that belched diesel, leaving dark streaks against the blue of the Alpine sky.

Thunberg, who only travels on solar-powered boats, eschews air travel and helped Sweden coin the phrase *flygskam*, "flight shame." She sailed to the United States from England to testify before Congress and garnered praise from former President

Barack Obama, who praised her as "one of our planet's greatest advocates." At the United Nations Climate Change Conference in Poland, she told the spectators, "You say you love your children above all else. And yet you are stealing their future in front of their very eyes." The address went viral. When speaking to the heads of state during the UN General Assembly, the world's most powerful body, the pint-sized teen with the gargantuan commitment pulled no punches, "We are in the beginning of a mass extinction, and all you can talk about is money and fairy tales of eternal economic growth. How dare you? How dare you!" David had taken on Goliath.

The image of Greta in her trademark braids proliferated on the internet, in Halloween costumes, and on the covers of *Rolling Stone* and *Time* magazine. In 2019, the latter publication made her the youngest Person of the Year; the photograph shows her on the shores of Lisbon, Portugal, with the caption "GRETA THUNBERG The Power of Youth." The Nobel Peace Prize nominated her for the award, though she did not make the cut.

In contrast, Greta's opponents wanted to drive a stake into the heart of the rebel-rouser who threatens big business. In Alberta, the heart of Canada's oil industry, a sticker distributed by an oil company depicted her as the victim of a sexual assault. After broadcaster Michael Knowles referred to Greta as "a mentally ill Swiss child," Fox News issued an apology. An article in the *Melbourne Herald Sun* carried the words, "I have never seen a girl so young and with so many mental disorders treated by so many adults as a guru." President Trump tweeted, "Greta Thunberg needs to work on her anger management. Chill! Greta, Chill!" Eleven months later, when Trump was lashing out against "voter fraud," Greta tweeted, "Donald needs to work on his anger management problem. Chill! Donald, chill!" Brazilian President Jair Bolsonaro described her with an adjective that translates to "little brat" after Greta tweeted about the slaughter of indigenous people in his country. In a very below-the-belt comment, the day before Greta spoke at the UN, Dinesh D'Souza, a conservative commentator, compared her image to those in Nazi propaganda campaigns. He continued his vitriol when he posted a picture of Thunberg on Twitter next to an illustration of a young woman standing in front of a flag emblazoned with a swastika. The accompanying caption: "An old Goebbels technique!" Another Fox News host, Laura Ingraham, ran a segment on her show with an excerpt from *Children of the Corn*, the 1984 Stephen King movie about a farming community where children murdered adults. Due to death threats, the Thunbergs need police protection when they travel.

While most teen media darlings wear attire reminiscent of the emperor's new clothes, Greta frequents secondhand stores. Although some have mocked Greta for her Velcro running shoes and oversized clothing, she has become a fashion icon. During a Pitti Bimbo fashion show—the semi-annual children's trade show in Italy—a recording of Thunberg's voice served as a backdrop, "How dare you? How dare you!" Munchkin models paraded down the runway holding posters reading "Cool Kids Saving a Hot Planet" and "There is no planet B." The show concluded in a shower of green confetti.

Greta Thunberg is a contemporary Joan of Arc, though she wears hand-me-downs instead of white armor, and her voice comes from the earth rather than the saints. Given her impact on making the environment sustainable, an applicable biblical quotation would be "And a little child shall lead them."

"Harrumph"

Bashful, in Disney's 1937 animated feature film *Snow White*, was prone to embarrassment, his cheeks often red from blushing. The movie's heroine is likewise unassuming. Aside from her credential as a diligent housekeeper, she exists only to be victimized by her evil stepmother—a far more interesting character— and to wait for Mr. Right. The lyrics of her theme song reflect her damsel-in-distress persona: "Someday my prince will come." Generations of girls sang along, convinced a prince would arrive to deliver a happily ever after. (Yes, I was one of their number.)

The reason why the feisty females portrayed in my book are so invigorating is that they sidestepped what has been traditionally held as a female code of ethics: let men win at tennis, snare an impressive number of karats, be the chatelaine of a picture-perfect home. In the days of yore, face and figure paved the road to success. And what courage it took to rise above time-honored constraints against retaining custody of children in a divorce, the inability to vote, the right to prevent pregnancy. They refused to kowtow to the concept of decorum: obedience to spouse, sexual restraint, not speaking one's mind. Remarkably, each generation had fearless femmes who thumbed their noses at societal norms, although the rejection of being a happy homemaker often came at considerable cost. In 1913, Rebecca West wrote of the difficulty of speaking up, "I myself have never been able to find out precisely what feminism is. I only know that people call me a feminist whenever I express sentiments that differentiate me from a doormat, or a prostitute."

According to the Oxford English Dictionary, "ladylike" means "having the distinctive manner and appearance of a lady," thereby implying possession of a sense of propriety and abiding by socially acceptable means of feminine behavior. In other words, women were consigned to living in a social straitjacket. In the 1964 movie *My Fair Lady*, Professor Higgins deemed it his greatest accomplishment to turn a Cockney flower girl into a class act by teaching Eliza Doolittle to speak and dress properly. Yet she was much more colorful when, showing her true personality, while attending a society-sanctioned horserace, she screamed, "Come on, Dover! Move your bloomin' arse!" How much more refreshing than when she appeared at the ball, where she only repeated, in an upper-crust tone, "How do you do?" The professor preferred to keep his Pygmalion in check, as evidenced in "A Hymn to Him": "Why is thinking something women never do? Why is logic ever tried/Straightening up their hair is all they ever do/Why don't they straighten up the mess that's inside?" Shame on you, 'enry 'iggins!

To be called ladylike was once a compliment; however, for unabashed women, it is a term of approbation. They prefer adjectives such as badass, opinionated, offbeat. The brash individuals revealed in this volume would not, in the vein of Ms. Doolittle, docilely bring the professor his slippers; instead, they would use the slippers to slap him silly.

Growing up in the mid-1950s, etiquette imposed a net of always being nice, of always caring about others before self. The Talmudic injunction, "If I am not for myself, who is for me?" was not part of the equation. While people think of midcentury suburbia as a place of green lawns and cookie-cutter houses, it was also an era where misogyny ruled. When I told my father I was dumb in math, he said girls were supposed to be. He steered my brothers to law school; his expectation was that I would marry a lawyer. In the same vein, when I announced my intention to go to university, my parents' friends snickered that I was out to get my "MRS."

In my teens, I grew a pair of feisty wings. I determined that, if I ever did become a Mrs., I would keep my maiden name. My decision was not out of fealty to my surname; rather, it was my way of defying the double standard of women taking their spouses' name while men kept their own. In addition, I would be a Ms., never a Mrs. Sexism in language, like all gender inequity, needs to go the way of the rotary phone.

Alas, I did fall prey to the tyranny of beauty, and spent countless hours of the first half of my life transforming my hair color to a shade nature never intended. Indeed, by my early thirties, I was at a loss to remember its virginal hue. Not a fan of my natural waves, in those pre-straightening-iron days I slept in a tight ponytail with my hair wrapped around a Tab can. Yes, my hair was straight, but it was devoid of what lies under my neck. However, I had my limits. I am a lifelong abstainer from any form of shaving of body hair, and refuse to wear heels, though the latter means I can never be one of the royal women who rarely stray outside their castle walls in flats.

Every generation takes a step further in leveling the playing field. While my mother was Mrs. Harry Wagman, I am Ms. Wagman-Geller; while my father did not allow my mother to work outside the house, I am a high school teacher. As a child, I admired Snow White; now I appreciate Mae West's remark, "I used to be Snow White, but I drifted."

For those who admire the progress of women from the suffragettes to Vice President Kamala Harris, we appreciate your well-wishes. For those who do not, in the expression Grumpy used in relationship to Bashful, "Harrumph."

THE ROAD NOT TAKEN

By Robert Frost

Two roads diverged in a yellow wood,
And sorry I could not travel both
And be one traveler, long I stood
And looked down one as far as I could
To where it bent in the undergrowth;

Then took the other, as just as fair,
And having perhaps the better claim,
Because it was grassy and wanted wear;
Though as for that the passing there
Had worn them really about the same,

And both that morning equally lay
In leaves no step had trodden black.
Oh, I kept the first for another day!
Yet knowing how way leads on to way,
I doubted if I should ever come back.

I shall be telling this with a sigh
Somewhere ages and ages hence:
Two roads diverged in a wood, and I—
I took the one less traveled by,
And that has made all the difference.

Acknowledgements

The most heartfelt part of writing is the Acknowledgement Page, where the author thanks those who helped turn what began as a gleam in the eye to the finished book. Creating is a lonely pursuit, and those who made it less so deserve my eternal gratitude.

While diamonds were Ms. Monroe's best friends, for a writer it is a literary agent, and mine is Roger Williams. Together we have birthed seven books; your belief in me always led to a belief in myself. My editor, Brenda Knight, is a sterling example of an unabashed woman; her enthusiasm, insight, and knowledge have been of incalculable assistance. Jamie Lovett, my dearest friend and first reader, has left her DNA on *Unabashed Women*. Her editorial eagle eye has served as my personal Sherlock, finding errors invisible to my eye. Thank you, Jamie, for being my nonbiological sister.

I also want to thank my husband, Joel, and daughter, Jordanna. My job as a high school English teacher, coupled with my writing career, has made me the antithesis of Martha Stewart. They understand that I am dancing as fast as I can and do not mind meals that come from cans, from Styrofoam.

Lastly, I want to mention the unabashed women who form the bedrock of my book. These feisty femmes trod difficult roads that made the path smoother for those who followed. Traditionally, society has given approbation to the shrinking violets, the wallflowers: a nice girl did not cause ripples. The ladies included here not only made waves, they made tidal waves that helped sweep away archaic mindsets that put women in intellectual and societal corsets. Discovering their stories was endlessly enlightening.

One of the unexpected but delightful consequences of publishing is meeting wonderful individuals whose path and mine would never have otherwise crossed. A heartfelt hug to those who contacted me to say they enjoyed my books. Their kind words always put a spring in my step. Having back-to-back full-time jobs means giving up what had once been taken for granted—watching television, enjoying movies, going out for lunch. However, in order to get something, one has to give up something else, and my readers have made any sacrifice worth taking.

Completing a manuscript is a bittersweet experience. The bitter as I have to let go of a project that long consumed my life, the sweet as I send it out with the hope that it will find favor. Now is that time.

Hearing from readers means so much. Please reach out through the following:

- Website: marlenewagmangeller.com
- Email: wagmangeller@hotmail.com
- Facebook: www.facebook.com/ marlene.wagman.5/

If the spirit moves you, reviews on Amazon and Goodreads would be most appreciated.

Marlene Wagman-Geller
San Diego, California 2020

Bibliography

CHAPTER 1—SARAH BERNHARDT

Blume, Mary. "Sarah Bernhardt and the Divine Lie." *The New York Times*, October 7, 2000. www. nytimes.com/2000/10/07/style/IHT-sarah-bernhardt-and-the-divine-lie.html.

FitzHerbert, Claudia. "Sarah: The Life of Sarah Bernhardt by Robert Gottlieb: Review." *The Telegraph*, October 22, 2010. www.telegraph. co.uk/culture/books/bookreviews/8080312/ Sarah-the-Life-of-Sarah-Bernhardt-by-Robert-Gottlieb-review.html.

Gottlieb, Robert. *Sarah: The Life of Sarah Bernhardt*. New Haven, CT: Yale University Press, 2013.

Laing, Olivia. "Sarah: The Life of Sarah Bernhardt by Robert Gottlieb." *The Guardian*, October 23, 2010. www.theguardian.com/books/2010/oct/24/ sarah-bernhardt-robert-gottlieb-review.

Martin, Julie. "She Loved Playing Sarah Bernhardt." *The New York Times*, September 22, 1991. www. nytimes.com/1991/09/22/books/she-loved-playing-sarah-bernhardt.html.

Rothstein, Edward. "Celebrity So Extraordinaire She Rivaled the Eiffel Tower." *The New York Times*, December 2, 2005. www.nytimes. com/2005/12/02/arts/design/celebrity-so-extraordinaire-she-rivaled-the-eiffel-tower.html.

Trimboli, Isabella. "Desperately Seeking Susan and She-Devil: Absurd 80s Comedies Ripe for Redemption." *The Guardian*, April 28, 2020. www.theguardian.com/culture/2020/apr/28/ desperately-seeking-susan-and-she-devil-absurd-80s-comedies-ripe-for-redemption.

CHAPTER 2— ELIZABETH COCHRANE

Bernard, Diane. "She Went Undercover to Expose an Insane Asylum's Horrors. Now Nellie Bly Is Getting Her Due." *The Washington Post*, July 28, 2019. www.washingtonpost.com/history/2019/07/28/ she-went-undercover-expose-an-insane-asylums-horrors-now-nellie-bly-is-getting-her-due/.

Gregory, Alice. "Nellie Bly's Lessons in Writing What You Want To." *The New Yorker*, May 14, 2014. www. newyorker.com/books/page-turner/nellie-blys-lessons-in-writing-what-you-want-to.

Lichtenstein, Grace. "AROUND THE WORLD IN 72 DAYS." *The Washington Post*, March 13, 1994. www.washingtonpost.com/archive/ entertainment/books/1994/03/13/around-the-world-in-72-days/fe964a0f-e224-45c8-a8cc-3a9b03756a5a/.

Rosenfeld, Megan. "Echoes of 'Nellie Bly.' " *The Washington Post*, April 3, 1982. www.washingtonpost.com/archive/ lifestyle/1982/04/03/echoes-of-nellie-bly/ d842c83e-af90-4f60-9cfc-ac0a94391d36/.

Sims, Patsy. "Her Place Was in the News." *The New York Times*, March 6, 1994. www.nytimes.com/1994/03/06/books/her-place-was-in-the-news.html.

CHAPTER 3—PRINCESS SOPHIA DULEEP SINGH

Anand, Anita. *Sophia: Princess, Suffragette, Revolutionary*. London, UK: Bloomsbury, 2015.

---. "The Incredible Suffragette Princess Lost to History...until Now." *The Telegraph*, January 15, 2015. www.telegraph.co.uk/women/womens-life/11345857/Incredible-suffragette-princess-was-lost-to-history...until-now.html.

Bakshian Jr., Aram. "The Little Princess Who Could." *The Washington Times*, April 13, 2015. www.washingtontimes.com/news/2015/apr/13/book-review-sophia-princess-suffragette-revolution/.

Berne, Suzanne. " 'Sophia: Princess, Suffragette, Revolutionary,' by Anita Anand." *The New York Times*, January 23, 2015. www.nytimes.com/2015/01/25/books/review/sophia-princess-suffragette-revolutionary-by-anita-anand.html.

Kampfner, John. "Sophia: Princess, Suffragette, Revolutionary Review—a Radical Indian Royal in the Heart of Empire." *The Guardian*, January 11, 2015. www.theguardian.com/books/2015/jan/11/sophia-princess-suffragette-revolutionary-anita-anand-review-radical-indian-royal.

Parker, Peter. "Sophia Duleep Singh: from Socialite to Socialist." *The Spectator*, January 24, 2015. www.spectator.co.uk/article/sophia-duleep-singh-from-socialite-to-socialist.

Scutts, Joanna. "Book Review: 'Sophia: Princess, Suffragette, Revolutionary,' by Anita Anand." *The Washington Post*, January 23, 2015. www.washingtonpost.com/opinions/book-review-sophia-princess-suffragette-revolutionary-by-anita-anand/2015/01/23/10da40c2-86ff-11e4-9534-f79a23c40e6c_story.html.

CHAPTER 4—MAE WEST

Adair, Gilbert. "THE GUILLOTINE: Twentieth-Century Classics That Won't Last No 9: MAE." *The Independent*, October 23, 2011. www.independent.co.uk/arts-entertainment/the-guillotine-twentieth-century-classics-that-wont-last-no-9-mae-west-1080597.html.

French, Philip. "Observer Review: Mae West by Simon Louvish." *The Guardian*, October 29, 2005. www.theguardian.com/books/2005/oct/30/biography.features.

Louvish, Simon. *Mae West: It Ain't No Sin*. Northampton, MA: Interlink Books, 2018.

"Mae West, Hollywood's Sex Symbol, Dies." *The Washington Post*, November 23, 1980. www.washingtonpost.com/archive/local/1980/11/23/mae-west-hollywoods-sex-symbol-dies/21d91e47-e6af-466a-8d4f-58506de45a65/.

"Mae West, Stage and Movie Star Who Burlesqued Sex, Dies at 87." *The New York Times*, November 23, 1980. movies2.nytimes.com/books/97/07/27/reviews/west-obit.html.

Sigal, Clancy. "Mae West's Obituary." *The Guardian*, November 24, 1980. www.theguardian.com/theguardian/1980/nov/24/greatinterviews.

Weales, Gerald. "MAE WEST, DIAMOND' IN THE ROUGH." *The Washington Post*, January 11, 1996. www.washingtonpost.com/archive/lifestyle/1996/01/11/mae-west-diamond-in-the-rough/d6bcb120-79ba-4d59-9053-cd2e7d974950/.

CHAPTER 5—DOROTHY PARKER

Gottlieb, Robert. "Brilliant, Troubled Dorothy Parker." *The New York Review of Books*, July 19, 2020. www.nybooks.com/articles/2016/04/07/brilliant-troubled-dorothy-parker/.

Parker, Dorothy. *The Portable Dorothy Parker*. New York: Penguin Books, 2006.

Spurrier, Christian. "Now, Seriously..." *The Guardian*, July 30, 2005. www.theguardian.com/books/2005/jul/30/edinburghfestival2005.classics.

Whitman, Aiden. "New York Times Obituary." Dorothy Parker Society. Accessed August 6, 2020. dorothyparker.com/gallery/new-york-times-obituary.

CHAPTER 6—P. L. TRAVERS

Cain, Chelsea. "The Nanny Diarist." *The New York Times*, October 22, 2006. www.nytimes.com/2006/10/22/books/review/the-nanny-diarist.html.

Fox, Margalit. "P. L. Travers, Creator of the Magical and Beloved Nanny Mary Poppins, Is Dead at 96." *The New York Times*, April 25, 1996. www.nytimes.com/1996/04/25/arts/p-l-travers-creator-of-the-magical-and-beloved-nanny-mary-poppins-is-dead-at-96.html.

Griswold, Jerry. " 'Mary Poppins' Creator P.L. Travers Is Even More Fascinating than Her Fiction." *The Washington Post*, December 17, 2018. www.washingtonpost.com/entertainment/books/disney-tried-to-erase-mary-poppins-creator-pl-travers-shes-still-more-fascinating-than-fiction/2018/12/13/7e77b6c6-f89f-11e8-863c-9e2f864d47e7_story.html.

Guppy, Shusha, and Tom Vallance. "Obituary: P. L. Travers." *The Independent*, October 23, 2011. www.independent.co.uk/news/people/obituary-p-l-travers-1306698.html.

Hughes, Kathryn. "Review: Mary Poppins She Wrote by Valerie Lawson." *The Guardian*, December 3, 2005. www.theguardian.com/books/2005/dec/03/featuresreviews.guardianreview7.

Jones, David. "How Mary Poppins' Creator P L Travers Wrecked the Lives of Two Innocent Boys." *Daily Mail Online*. Associated Newspapers, October 25, 2013. www.dailymail.co.uk/news/article-2477111/How-Mary-Poppins-creator-P-L-Travers-wrecked-lives-innocent-boys.html.

Picardie, Justine. "Was P L Travers the Real Mary Poppins?" *The Telegraph*, October 28, 2008. www.telegraph.co.uk/culture/donotmigrate/3562643/Was-P-L-Travers-the-real-Mary-Poppins.html.

Singh, Anita. "Story of How Mary Poppins Author Regretted Selling Rights to Disney to Be Turned into Film." *The Telegraph*, April 10, 2012. www.telegraph.co.uk/culture/film/film-news/9195930/Story-of-how-Mary-Poppins-author-regretted-selling-rights-to-Disney-to-be-turned-into-film.html.

Zipp, Yvonne. "Trapped inside Mary Poppins." *The Christian Science Monitor*, October 10, 2006. www.csmonitor.com/2006/1010/p14s02-bogn.html.

CHAPTER 7—ELLA MAILLART

Anderson, Sarah. "Obituary: Ella Maillart." *The Independent*, October 22, 2011. www.independent.co.uk/news/people/obituary-ella-maillart-1266265.html.

Johnstone, Richard. "More Necessary than Life." *Inside Story*, August 4, 2017. insidestory.org.au/more-necessary-than-life/.

Miville, Graf. "Ella Maillart." Accessed October 7, 2020. www.ellamaillart.ch/bio_en.php.

Murray, Jean. "Ella Maillart—A Life-long Adventurer—Unconventional and Multi-Talented." Accessed October 7, 2020. www.jeanwilsonmurray. com/ella-maillart-a-life-long-adventurer-unconventional-and-multi-talented/.

Schreyer, Simon. "Ella Maillart: Voyage, Voyage." Accessed October 7, 2020. simonside.net/ ella-maillart/.

Snaije, Olivia. "Arts: Afghanistan; the Land That Time Forgot." *The Guardian*, October 10, 2001. www.theguardian.com/culture/2001/oct/10/ artsfeatures.

Thomas Jr., Robert Mcg. "Ella Maillart, a Swiss Writer and Adventurer, Is Dead at 94." *The New York Times*, March 31, 1997. www.nytimes. com/1997/03/31/world/ella-maillart-a-swiss-writer-and-adventurer-is-dead-at-94.html.

Wittmeyer, Alice P.q. "Overlooked No More: Annemarie Schwarzenbach, Author, Photographer and 'Ravaged Angel.' " *The New York Times*, October 10, 2018. www.nytimes.com/2018/10/10/ obituaries/annemarie-schwarzenbach-overlooked.html.

CHAPTER 8—ANAÏS NIN

Arana-Ward, Marie. "PLAYGIRL OF THE WESTERN WORLD." *The Washington Post*, April 16, 1995. www.washingtonpost.com/archive/entertainment/books/1995/04/16/playgirl-of-the-western-world/b469e177-c2b4-46fc-9d85-cd52a091d7f8/.

Bawer, Bruce. " 'I Gave So Much to Others?' " *The New York Times*, March 5, 1995. www.nytimes.com/1995/03/05/books/i-gave-so-much-to-others.html.

Corbett, Sara. "The Lover Who Always Stays." *The New York Times*, December 31, 2006. www.nytimes.com/2006/12/31/magazine/31pole.t.html.

Fraser, C. Gerald. "Anaïs Nin, Author Whose Diaries Depicted Intellectual Life, Dead." *The New York Times*, January 16, 1977. www.nytimes.com/1977/01/16/archives/anais-nin-author-whose-diaries-depicted-intellectual-life-dead.html.

Johnson, Joyce. "BODY AND SOUL ANAIS NIN AND HENRY MILLER." *The Washington Post*, December 20, 1987. www.washingtonpost.com/archive/entertainment/books/1987/12/20/body-and-soul-anais-nin-and-henry-miller/0fcbb41b-11ee-4fb1-9803-56f83d34a9c4/.

Seymour, Miranda. "Truth Wasn't Sexy Enough." *The New York Times*, October 17, 1993. www.nytimes.com/1993/10/17/books/truth-wasn-t-sexy-enough.html.

Weil, Martin. "Anaïs Nin, Author, Diarist, Dies at 73." *The Washington Post*, January 16, 1977. www.washingtonpost.com/archive/local/1977/01/16/anais-nin-author-diarist-dies-at-73/9dc5d5d5-f3d7-41ad-9178-b59c855327e6/.

CHAPTER 9—LILLIAN HELLMAN

Churchwell, Sarah. "The Scandalous Lillian Hellman." *The Guardian*, January 22, 2011. www.theguardian.com/stage/2011/jan/22/lillian-hellman-childrens-hour-sarah-churchwell.

Emerson, Gloria. "Lillian Hellman: At 66, She's Still Restless." *The New York Times*, September 7, 1973. www.nytimes.com/1973/09/07/archives/lillian-hellman-at-66-shes-still-restless-the-right-place-an.html.

"LILLIAN HELLMAN, PLAYWRIGHT, AUTHOR AND REBEL, DIES AT 79." *The New York Times*, July 1, 1984. www.nytimes.com/1984/07/01/obituaries/lillian-hellman-playwright-author-and-rebel-dies-at-79.html.

Wright, William. "Why Lillian Hellman Remains Fascinating." *The New York Times*, November 3, 1996. www.nytimes.com/1996/11/03/theater/why-lillian-hellman-remains-fascinating.html.

CHAPTER 10—JOSEPHINE BAKER

Glover, Kaiama L. "Postmodern Homegirl." *The New York Times*, June 3, 2007. www.nytimes.com/2007/06/03/books/review/Glover-t.html.

Griffith, Joanne. "Josephine Baker: From Exotic Dancer to Activist." *BBC Culture*. BBC, December 30, 2014. www.bbc.com/culture/article/20141222-from-exotic-dancer-to-activist.

Haygood, Wil. "Her Life Was a Cabaret Josephine Baker Was Born into a Difficult, Racist Age. Through Song and Dance, She Sensuously Rose Above It." *The Washington Post*, December 24, 2006. www.washingtonpost.com/archive/lifestyle/style/2006/12/24/her-life-was-a-cabaret-span-classbankheadjosephine-baker-was-born-into-a-difficult-racist-age-through-song-and-dance-she-sensuously-rose-above-itspan/6b9b71e9-f4e9-4466-aeef-8a30f67cf184/.

"Josephine Baker Is Dead in Paris at 68." *The New York Times*, April 13, 1975. www.nytimes.com/1975/04/13/archives/josephine-baker-is-dead-in-paris-at-68.html.

Reed, Ishmael. "THE DIVINE JOSEPHINE." *The Washington Post*, October 15, 1989. www.washingtonpost.com/archive/entertainment/books/1989/10/15/the-divine-josephine/7770b5c8-f6ac-411b-8220-aec067c5cf3b/.

Venning, Annabel. "Rihanna Set to Play Josephine Baker in Biopic of Legendary Seductress." *Daily Mail Online*. Associated Newspapers, August 23, 2013. www.dailymail.co.uk/tvshowbiz/article-2400416/Rihanna-set-play-Josephine-Baker-biopic-legendary-seductress.html.

Waxman, Olivia B., and Liz Ronk. "Josephine Baker at 110: She Was More Than an Entertainer." *Time*, June 3, 2016. time.com/4342285/josephine-baker-birthday-anniversary-photos/.

CHAPTER 11—LEE MILLER

Conrad, Peter. "Observer Review: Lee Miller by Carolyn Burke." *The Guardian*, December 4, 2005. www.theguardian.com/books/2005/dec/04/biography.features.

di Giovanni, Janine. " 'What's a Girl to Do When a Battle Lands in Her Lap?' " *The New York Times*, October 21, 2007. www.nytimes.com/2007/10/21/style/tmagazine/21miller.html.

Hall, Chris. "Lee Miller, the Mother I Never Knew." *The Guardian*, March 19, 2016. www.theguardian.com/lifeandstyle/2016/mar/19/lee-miller-the-mother-i-never-knew.

Morrison, Blake. "Lee Miller: The Model, the Monster and the Mother." *The Guardian*, April 22, 2013. www.theguardian.com/artanddesign/2013/apr/22/lee-miller-war-peace-pythons.

Parker, Pat. "Lee Miller: The Woman in Hitler's Bathtub." *The Telegraph*, December 2, 2016. www.telegraph.co.uk/photography/what-to-see/lee-miller-woman-hitlers-bathtub/.

Paton, Elizabeth. "Lee Miller's Journey from Model to War Photographer." *The New York Times*, November 21, 2015. www.nytimes.com/2015/11/22/fashion/lee-miller-a-womans-war.html.

Rifkind, Donna. "Review | Lee Miller Was More than Man Ray's Muse." *The Washington Post*, February 7, 2019. www.washingtonpost.com/entertainment/books/lee-miller-was-more-than-man-rays-muse/2019/02/07/d53d441e-2598-11e9-ad53-824486280311_story.html.

Schappell, Elissa. "Look at Me." *The New York Times*, January 8, 2006. www.nytimes.com/2006/01/08/books/review/look-at-me.html.

Sheets, Hilarie M. " 'The Indestructible Lee Miller' Celebrates a Daring Surrealist and War Photographer." *The New York Times*, October 28, 2015. www.nytimes.com/2015/11/01/arts/design/the-indestructible-lee-miller-celebrates-a-daring-surrealist-and-war-photographer.html.

Sooke, Alistair. "As Rational as a Scattered Jigsaw." *The Telegraph*, November 28, 2005. www.telegraph.co.uk/culture/books/3648290/As-rational-as-a-scattered-jigsaw.html.

Thurman, Judith. "The Roving Eye." *The New Yorker*, January 14, 2008. www.newyorker.com/magazine/2008/01/21/the-roving-eye.

CHAPTER 12— ANTONINA ŻABIŃSKIS

Ackerman, Diane. *The Zookeeper's Wife: A War Story.* New York, NY: W.W. Norton, 2017.

Hoffman, Barbara. "How a Zookeeper's Hero Wife Saved Hundreds of Jews from the Nazis." *New York Post,* March 27, 2017. nypost. com/2017/03/25/how-a-zookeepers-hero-wife-saved-hundreds-of-jews-from-the-nazis/.

Max, D. T. "Antonina's List." *The New York Times,* September 9, 2007. www.nytimes. com/2007/09/09/books/review/Max-t.html.

Merry, Stephanie. " 'The Zookeeper's Wife': A True-Life Holocaust Tale Built around an Impossibly Perfect Heroine." *The Washington Post,* March 30, 2017. www.washingtonpost.com/goingoutguide/ movies/the-zookeepers-wife-a-true-life-holocaust-tale-built-around-an-impossibly-perfect-heroine/2017/03/30/56dbc988-1096-11e7-ab07-07d9f521f6b5_story.html.

CHAPTER 13—MARTHA GELLHORN

Anderson, Sarah. "Obituary: Martha Gellhorn." *The Independent,* October 22, 2011. www. independent.co.uk/news/obituaries/obituary-martha-gellhorn-1145325.html.

Lee, Hermione. "Review: Martha Gellhorn by Caroline Moorehead." *The Guardian,* November 1, 2003. www.theguardian.com/books/2003/nov/01/ featuresreviews.guardianreview8.

Lyman, Rick. "Martha Gellhorn, Daring Writer, Dies at 89." *The New York Times*, February 17, 1998. www.nytimes.com/1998/02/17/arts/martha-gellhorn-daring-writer-dies-at-89.html.

Thurman, Judith. "WAR REPORTER, EX-HEMINGWAY WIFE MARTHA GELLHORN DIES." *The Washington Post*, February 17, 1998. www.washingtonpost.com/archive/local/1998/02/17/war-reporter-ex-hemingway-wife-martha-gellhorn-dies/1afcdb68-286f-4c96-8dff-eeb8207b2865/.

Wagman-Geller, Marlene. *Once Again to Zelda: The Stories behind Literature's Most Intriguing Dedications.* New York, NY: Perigee Book, 2008.

Wheeler, Sara. "Angry, Every Minute." *The Telegraph*, October 12, 2003. www.telegraph.co.uk/culture/books/3604447/Angry-every-minute.html.

CHAPTER 14—LOUISE HAVOK

Abbott, Karen. *American Rose: A Nation Laid Bare: The Life and Times of Gypsy Rose Lee.* New York, NY: Random House Trade Paperbacks, 2012.

Ellis, Samantha. "Why Stripper Gypsy Rose Lee Owed It All to Mother." *The Guardian*, April 21, 2003. www.theguardian.com/stage/2003/apr/21/theatre.artsfeatures.

"Gypsy Rose Lee Memorial Service Tomorrow." *The New York Times*, April 28, 1970. www.nytimes. com/1970/04/28/archives/gypsy-rose-lee-memorial-service-tomorrow-burlesque-queen-was-noted.html.

Jacobs, Laura. "The Women Who Inspired Gypsy." *Vanity Fair*, March 3, 2003. www.vanityfair. com/hollywood/2003/03/inspiration-story-gypsy-musical.

McCabe, Vinton Rafe. "American Rose: A Nation Laid Bare: The Life and Times of Gypsy Rose Lee." *New York Journal of Books*, March 12, 2012. www.nyjournalofbooks.com/book-review/american-rose-nation-laid-bare-life-and-times-gypsy-rose-lee.

CHAPTER 15— CLARE HOLLINGWORTH

Addley, Esther. "Profile: Clare Hollingworth." *The Guardian*, January 17, 2004. www.theguardian. com/books/2004/jan/17/featuresreviews. guardianreview13.

Fisk, Robert. "Robert Fisk's Last Interview with Clare Hollingworth, Who Google Is Celebrating." *The Independent*, October 10, 2017. www. independent.co.uk/news/clare-hollingworth-birthday-google-doodle-robert-fisk-interview-hong-kong-life-career-ww2-a7992831.html.

Fox, Margalit. "Clare Hollingworth, Reporter Who Broke News of World War II, Dies at 105." *The New York Times*, January 10, 2017. www.nytimes.com/2017/01/10/business/media/clare-hollingworth-reporter-who-broke-news-of-world-war-ii-dies-at-105.html.

Garrett, Patrick. *Of Fortunes and War: Clare Hollingworth First of the Female War Correspondents*. London, UK: Thistle Publishing, 2016.

"Obituary: Clare Hollingworth Died on January 10th." *The Economist*, January 21, 2017. www.economist.com/obituary/2017/01/21/obituary-clare-hollingworth-died-on-january-10th.

Otis, John. "Clare Hollingworth, Reporter Who Broke News about Start of World War II, Dies at 105." *The Washington Post*, January 10, 2017. www.washingtonpost.com/world/clare-hollingworth-reporter-who-broke-news-about-start-of-world-war-ii-dies-at-105/2017/01/10/6aa9ca72-d73f-11e6-b8b2-cb5164beba6b_story.html.

Rowe, Dominique. "The Woman Who Scooped the World." *Time*, October 10, 2016. time.com/4520940/clare-hollingworth-war-correspondent-birthday-hong-kong/.

Simpson, John. "Clare Hollingworth." *The Telegraph*, January 10, 2017. www.telegraph.co.uk/clare-hollingworth/.

CHAPTER 16—NANCY WAKE

FitzSimons, Peter. "The White Mouse Who Roared." *The Sydney Morning Herald*, August 8, 2011. www.smh.com.au/world/the-white-mouse-who-roared-20110808-1ij2o.html.

Lichfield, John. " 'White Mouse,' the Feisty Heroine of the Resistance, Dies." *The Independent*, November 1, 2011. www.independent.co.uk/hei-fi/news/white-mouse-the-feisty-heroine-of-the-resistance-dies-2334293.html.

"Nancy Grace Augusta Wake." *Australian War Memorial*. Accessed September 6, 2020. www.awm.gov.au/collection/P332.

Stafford, David. "Nancy Wake Obituary." *The Guardian*, August 8, 2011. www.theguardian.com/world/2011/aug/08/nancy-wake-obituary.

Vitello, Paul. "Nancy Wake, Proud Spy and Nazi Foe, Dies at 98." *The New York Times*, August 13, 2011. www.nytimes.com/2011/08/14/world/europe/14wake.html.

Willsher, Kim. "Farewell to Nancy Wake, the Mouse Who Ran Rings around the Nazis." *The Guardian*, August 8, 2011. www.theguardian.com/world/2011/aug/08/nancy-wake-white-mouse-gestapo.

CHAPTER 17— FLORYNCE KENNEDY

Burstein, Patricia. "Lawyer Flo Kennedy Enjoys Her Reputation as Radicalism's Rudest Mouth." *People*, April 14, 1975. people.com/archive/lawyer-flo-kennedy-enjoys-her-reputation-as-radicalisms-rudest-mouth-vol-3-no-14/.

Busby, Margaret. "Obituary: Florynce Kennedy." *The Guardian*, January 10, 2001. www.theguardian.com/news/2001/jan/10/guardianobituaries1.

"Feminist Flo Kennedy, Civil Rights Lawyer, Dies." *The Washington Post*, December 24, 2000. www.washingtonpost.com/archive/local/2000/12/24/feminist-flo-kennedy-civil-rights-lawyer-dies/5688f66f-9dc9-41b8-abf7-fdfb918c0562/.

Grundhauser, Eric. "The Great Harvard Pee-In of 1973." *Atlas Obscura*, December 23, 2016. www.atlasobscura.com/articles/the-great-harvard-peein-of-1973.

Martin, Douglas. "Flo Kennedy, Feminist, Civil Rights Advocate and Flamboyant Gadfly, Is Dead at 84." *The New York Times*, December 23, 2000. www.nytimes.com/2000/12/23/us/flo-kennedy-feminist-civil-rights-advocate-and-flamboyant-gadfly-is-dead-at-84.html.

Randolph, Sherie M. *FLORYNCE FLO KENNEDY: The Life of a Black Feminist Radical*. Chapel Hill, NC: UNIV OF NORTH CAROLINA PR, 2018.

CHAPTER 18—BELLA ABZUG

Donoghue, Steve. "Bella Abzug: Liberal Trailblazer in a Broad-Brimmed Hat." *The Christian Science Monitor*, January 8, 2020. www.csmonitor.com/Books/Book-Reviews/2020/0108/Bella-Abzug-Liberal-trailblazer-in-a-broad-brimmed-hat.

Levy, Claudia. "FEMINIST, CONGRESSWOMAN BELLA ABZUG DIES AT 77." *The Washington Post*, April 1, 1998. www.washingtonpost.com/archive/local/1998/04/01/feminist-congresswoman-bella-abzug-dies-at-77/1502152a-e780-4768-bc01-47f2bcd7e316/.

MacPherson, Myra. "BELLA ABZUG, CHAMPION OF WOMEN." *The Washington Post*, April 2, 1998. www.washingtonpost.com/archive/lifestyle/1998/04/02/bella-abzug-champion-of-women/389bf3b8-20e5-44a1-86a5-d5e27eb2b991/.

Mansnerus, Laura. "Bella Abzug, 77, Congresswoman and a Founding Feminist, Is Dead." *The New York Times*, April 1, 1998. www.nytimes.com/1998/04/01/nyregion/bella-abzug-77-congresswoman-and-a-founding-feminist-is-dead.html.

CHAPTER 19—FRANÇOISE GILOT

Brockes, Emma. " 'It Was Not a Sentimental Love': Françoise Gilot on Her Years with Picasso." *The Guardian*, June 10, 2016. www.theguardian.com/artanddesign/2016/jun/10/francoise-gilot-artist-love-picasso.

Brown, Mick. "Picasso's Lover on Life with a Tempestuous Genius: 'It Was a Permanent Earthquake.'" *The Telegraph*, September 28, 2018. www.telegraph.co.uk/women/life/picassos-lover-life-tempestuous-genius-permanent-earthquake/.

Gilot, Françoise, and Carlton Lake. *Life with Picasso*. New York, Toronto, London: McGraw-Hill, 1964.

Kalter, Suzy. "At 57, Françoise Gilot Recalls Life with Picasso but Enjoys It with Scientist Jonas Salk." *People*, July 30, 1979. people.com/archive/at-57-francoise-gilot-recalls-life-with-picasso-but-enjoys-it-with-scientist-jonas-salk-vol-12-no-5/.

Kazanjian, Dodie. "Life After Picasso: Françoise Gilot." *Vogue*, April 27, 2012. www.vogue.com/article/life-after-picasso-franoise-gilot.

Wagman-Geller, Marlene. *Behind Every Great Man: The Forgotten Women behind the World's Famous and Infamous*. Naperville, IL: Sourcebooks, Inc., 2015.

CHAPTER 20—YAYOI KUSAMA

Adams, Tim. "Yayoi Kusama: The World's Favourite Artist?" *The Guardian*, September 23, 2018. www.theguardian.com/artanddesign/2018/sep/23/yayoi-kusama-infinity-film-victoria-miro-exhibition.

Fifield, Anna. "How Yayoi Kusama, the 'Infinity Mirrors' Visionary, Channels Mental Illness into Art." *The Washington Post*, February 15, 2017. www.washingtonpost.com/entertainment/museums/how-yayoi-kusama-the-infinity-mirrors-visionary-channels-mental-illness-into-art/2017/02/15/94b5b23e-ea24-11e6-b82f-687d6e6a3e7c_story.html.

Knight, Sophie. "Yayoi Kusama to Exhibit in London: at 85, 'the Ideas Just Keep Coming.' " *The Telegraph*, August 31, 2014. www.telegraph.co.uk/culture/art/art-features/11059373/Yayoi-Kusama-to-exhibit-in-London-at-85-the-ideas-just-keep-coming.html.

Loughrey, Clarisse. "Yayoi Kusama: How the Instagram Generation Fell in Love with the World's Top-Selling Living Female Artist." *The Independent*, October 6, 2018. www.independent.co.uk/arts-entertainment/art/features/yayoi-kusama-documentary-gallery-exhibition-victoria-miro-world-top-selling-living-female-artist-a8570121.html.

Swanson, Carl. "Yayoi Kusama's Return to the Art World—New York Magazine—Nymag." *New York Magazine*, July 6, 2012. nymag.com/arts/art/features/yayoi-kusama-2012-7/.

CHAPTER 21—BARBARA HILLARY

Katz, Brigit. "Barbara Hillary, a Pioneering African-American Adventurer, Dies at 88." *Smithsonian*, November 27, 2019. www.smithsonianmag.com/smart-news/barbara-hillary-pioneering-african-american-adventurer-has-died-180973663/.

Manby, Christine. "Remembering Barbara Hillary, the First Black Woman to Reach the North and South Poles." *The Independent*, December 18, 2019. www.independent.co.uk/news/obituaries/barbara-hillary-death-explorer-north-south-poles-african-american-a9230581.html.

McFadden, Robert D. "Edmund Hillary, First on Everest, Dies at 88." *The New York Times*, January 10, 2008. www.nytimes.com/2008/01/10/world/asia/11cnd-hillary.html.

Seelye, Katharine Q. "Barbara Hillary, 88, Trailblazer on Top (and Bottom) of the World, Dies." *The New York Times*, November 26, 2019. www.nytimes.com/2019/11/26/us/barbara-hillary-dead.html.

CHAPTER 22—MIRIAM MAKEBA

Aizlewood, John. "World Music Review: Miriam Makeba." *The Guardian*, September 19, 2001. www.theguardian.com/culture/2001/sep/20/artsfeatures3.

Cowell, Alan. "Miriam Makeba, 76, Singer and Activist, Dies." *The New York Times*, November 10, 2008. www.nytimes.com/2008/11/11/world/africa/11makeba.html.

Ewens, Graeme. "Obituary: Miriam Makeba." *The Guardian*, November 11, 2008. www.theguardian.com/music/2008/nov/11/miriam-makeba-obituary.

Gaylord, Chris. "Miriam Makeba: The Fame and Exile of 'Mama Africa.'" *The Christian Science Monitor*, March 4, 2013. www.csmonitor.com/Technology/Tech-Culture/2013/0304/Miriam-Makeba-The-fame-and-exile-of-Mama-Africa.

Haider, Arwa. "Pata Pata: The World's Most Defiantly Joyful Song?" *BBC Culture*. BBC, September 11, 2019. www.bbc.com/culture/article/20190911-pata-pata-the-worlds-most-defiantly-joyful-song.

Lusk, Jon. "Miriam Makeba: Singer Banned from Her Native South Africa for Fighting." *The Independent*, October 23, 2011. www.independent.co.uk/news/obituaries/miriam-makeba-singer-banned-from-her-native-south-africa-for-fighting-apartheid-1009604.html.

Nelson, Jill. "MAKEBA'S TORMENTED MELODY." *The Washington Post*, April 1, 1988. www.washingtonpost.com/archive/lifestyle/1988/04/01/makebas-tormented-melody/2eaa7dc3-7547-4d3f-88d8-67b7962d2c63/.

Pareles, Jon. "Books of The Times; South African Singer's Life: Trials and Triumphs." *The New York Times*, March 8, 1988. www.nytimes.com/1988/03/08/books/books-of-the-times-south-african-singer-s-life-trials-and-triumphs.html.

---. "Taking Africa With Her to the World." *The New York Times*, November 10, 2008. www.nytimes.com/2008/11/11/arts/music/11appr.html.

CHAPTER 23—DIANE DI PRIMA

"Diane di Prima, Poet of the Beat Era and Beyond, Dies at 86." *The New York Times*, October 28, 2020. www.nytimes.com/2020/10/28/books/diane-di-prima-dead.html.

Fitzpatrick, Anna. "What We Can Learn from Diane di Prima." *Harper's Bazaar*, October 29, 2020. www.harpersbazaar.com/culture/art-books-music/a34511902/diane-di-prima-obituary/.

Langer, Emily. "Diane di Prima, feminist poet of the Beat Generation, dies at 86." *The Washington Post*, October 26, 2020. www.washingtonpost.com/local/obituaries/diane-di-prima-feminist-poet-of-the-beat-generation-dies-at-86/2020/10/26/4a2be0fe-1797-11eb-befb-8864259bd2d8_story.html.

Lichtenstein, Grace. "Bohemian Rhapsody—Review of RECOLLECTIONS OF MY LIFE AS A WOMAN." *The Washington Post*, June 10, 2001. www.washingtonpost.com/archive/entertainment/books/2001/06/10/bohemian-rhapsody/a7940ed7-f61a-4a99-9e7f-08f7bd68948d/.

Seymour, Corey. "Why You Should Know About Diane di Prima, the Beat Poet Decades Ahead of Her Time." *Vogue*, October 27, 2020. www.vogue.com/article/diane-di-prima-obit.

Tamblyn, Amber. "The Undying Voice of Diane di Prima." *The New Yorker*, November 9, 2020. www.newyorker.com/culture/postscript/the-undying-voice-of-diane-di-prima.

Whiting, Sam. "Diane di Prima, prolific Beat poet, dead at 86." *San Francisco Chronicle*, October 26, 2020. datebook.sfchronicle.com/books/diane-di-prima-prolific-beat-poet-dead-at-86.

CHAPTER 24—JANE GOODALL

Abraham, Amelia. "Primatologist Jane Goodall: 'Tarzan Married the Wrong Jane.' " *The Guardian*, November 14, 2017. www.theguardian.com/lifeandstyle/2017/nov/14/primatologist-jane-goodall-tarzan-married-the-wrong-jane.

Baker, KC. "Dr. Jane Goodall Opens Up About Her 2 Marriages: 'How I Could Do It Twice? I Don't Know.' " *People*, July 24, 2020. people.com/human-interest/dr-jane-goodall-opens-up-about-2-marriages/.

Coronado, Kris. "Jane Goodall Became a Champion for Chimpanzees. It Started with a 10-Year-Old's Dream." *The Washington Post*, July 8, 2020. www.washingtonpost.com/lifestyle/kidspost/jane-goodall-became-a-champion-for-chimpanzees-it-started-with-a-10-year-olds-dream/2020/07/06/514c2dfe-a1e9-11ea-81bb-c2f70f01034b_story.html.

Lampert, Nicole. "The Ape Crusader: The Extraordinary Story of Jane Goodall." *Daily Mail Online*. Associated Newspapers, March 2, 2018. www.dailymail.co.uk/femail/article-5440531/The-ape-crusader-extraordinary-story-Jane-Goodall.html.

McKie, Robin. "Jane Goodall: 50 Years Working with Chimps | Discover Interview." *The Guardian*, June 26, 2010. www.theguardian.com/science/2010/jun/27/jane-goodall-chimps-africa-interview.

Tullis, Paul. "Jane Goodall Is Still Wild at Heart." *The New York Times*, March 13, 2015. www.nytimes.com/2015/03/15/magazine/jane-goodall-is-still-wild-at-heart.html.

CHAPTER 25—BRIDGET ROSE DUGDALE

Amore, Anthony M. *The Woman Who Stole Vermeer: The True Story of Rose Dugdale and the Russborough House Art Heist*. New York, NY: Pegasus Crime, 2020.

Bain, Mark. "British Heiress Was behind 1974 Unsolved Art Theft for IRA: Book." *Belfast Telegraph*, September 7, 2020. www.belfasttelegraph.co.uk/news/northern-ireland/british-heiress-was-behind-1974-unsolved-art-theft-for-ira-book-39507922.html.

"British Millionaire's Daughter Sentenced to 9 Years in Art Thefts for I.R.A." *The New York Times*, June 26, 1974. www.nytimes.com/1974/06/26/archives/british-millionaires-daughter-sentenced-to-9-years-in-art-thefts.html.

Shuster, Alvin. "Heiress in Art Theft a Social Rebel." *The New York Times*, May 7, 1974. www.nytimes.com/1974/05/07/archives/heiress-in-art-theft-a-social-rebel-the-heiress-in-art-theft-was-a.html.

Solly, Meilan. "The Heiress Who Stole a Vermeer, Witchcraft in Post-WWII Germany and Other New Books to Read." *Smithsonian*, November 5, 2020. www.smithsonianmag.com/history/heiress-who-stole-vermeer-witchcraft-post-wwii-germany-and-other-new-books-read-180976204/.

CHAPTER 26—SHERE HITE

Bindel, Julie. "Shere Hite Obituary." *The Guardian*, September 15, 2020. www.theguardian.com/society/2020/sep/15/shere-hite-obituary.

---. "Shere Hite: 'We Need to Make a Film about Me.'" *The Guardian*, May 13, 2011. www.theguardian.com/books/2011/may/13/shere-hite-film-feminist-sex.

Langer, Emily. "Shere Hite, Author of Taboo-Breaking 'Hite Reports' on Human Sexuality, Dies at 77." *The Washington Post*, September 12, 2020. www.washingtonpost.com/local/obituaries/shere-hite-author-of-taboo-busting-hite-reports-on-human-sexuality-dies-at-77/2020/09/11/0c60e96e-f397-11ea-b796-2dd09962649c_story.html.

Seelye, Katharine Q. "Shere Hite, Who Challenged Myths of Female Sexuality, Dies at 77." *The New York Times*, September 11, 2020. www.nytimes.com/2020/09/11/books/shere-hite-dead.html.

"Shere Hite, Author Whose Bestselling Hite Report Transformed the Way We Think about Sex—Obituary." *The Telegraph*, September 13, 2020. www.telegraph.co.uk/obituaries/2020/09/13/shere-hite-controversial-researcher-author-transformed-way-think/.

CHAPTER 27—ELAINE BROWN

Bray, Rosemary L. "A Black Panther's Long Journey." *The New York Times*, January 31, 1993. www.nytimes.com/1993/01/31/magazine/a-black-panthers-long-journey.html.

Brown, DeNeen L. " 'I Have All the Guns and Money': When a Woman Led the Black Panther Party." *The Washington Post*, June 12, 2020. www.washingtonpost.com/news/retropolis/wp/2018/01/09/i-have-all-the-guns-and-money-when-a-woman-led-the-black-panther-party/.

Brown, Elaine. *A Taste of Power: A Black Woman's Story.* New York, NY: Anchor Books, December 1, 1993.

Campbell, Duncan. "Brown Is the New Black." *The Guardian*, April 14, 2002. www.theguardian.com/books/2002/apr/14/society.politics.

Nelson, Jill. "The Outsider's Inside Story." *The Washington Post*, February 1, 1993. www.washingtonpost.com/archive/ lifestyle/1993/02/01/the-outsiders-inside-story/ dd236b7c-9dd2-452f-849a-226fc9c51933/.

Wallace, Michele. "Her Life at the Top." *The New York Times*, January 31, 1993. www.nytimes. com/1993/01/31/books/her-life-at-the-top.html.

CHAPTER 28—JANIS JOPLIN

Brown, Mick. "How Never-Seen-before Letters Reveal the Inner World of Janis Joplin." *The Telegraph*, January 28, 2016. www.telegraph.co.uk/music/ artists/how-never-seen-before-letters-reveal-the- inner-world-of-janis-jo/.

Garner, Dwight. "A New Biography of Janis Joplin Captures the Pain and Soul of an Adventurous Life." *The New York Times*, October 25, 2019. www. nytimes.com/2019/10/25/books/review-janis- joplin-biography-holly-george-warren.html.

"Goodbye, Janis Joplin." *Rolling Stone*, June 25, 2018. www.rollingstone.com/music/music-news/ goodbye-janis-joplin-68526/.

Helmore, Edward. "Janis Joplin's Creed Was 'Get Stoned, Stay Happy' but the Highs Had a Dark Side." *The Guardian*, November 22, 2015. www. theguardian.com/music/2015/nov/22/janis- joplin-teenage-traumas-little-girl-blue.

Holden, Stephen. "Review: In 'Janis: Little Girl Blue,' Exploring Joplin's Demons." *The New York Times*, November 26, 2015. www.nytimes.com/2015/11/27/movies/review-in-janis-little-girl-blue-exploring-joplins-demons.html.

"Janis Joplin Dies; Rock Star Was 27." *The New York Times*, October 5, 1970. www.nytimes.com/1970/10/05/archives/janis-joplin-dies-rock-star-was-27-janis-joplin-rock-singer-27.html.

CHAPTER 29—INGRID NEWKIRK

Cadwalladr, Carole. "Peta's Ingrid Newkirk: Making the Fury Fly." *The Guardian*, March 31, 2013. www.theguardian.com/world/2013/mar/31/peta-ingrid-newkirk-making-fur-fly.

Specter, Michael. "Michael Specter Meets Ingrid Newkirk, Founder of Peta." *The Guardian*, June 22, 2003. www.theguardian.com/lifeandstyle/2003/jun/22/fashion.beauty.

Wagman-Geller, Marlene. *Eureka!: The Surprising Stories behind the Ideas That Shaped the World.* New York, NY: Perigee, 2010.

CHAPTER 30—MALALAI JOYA

Boustany, Nora. "An Afghan Voice That Fear Won't Silence." *The Washington Post*, March 17, 2006. www.washingtonpost.com/archive/politics/2006/03/17/an-afghan-voice-that-fear-wont-silence/e2f6f0e2-84d5-4233-820a-fd8c72058047/.

Brothers, Caroline. "An Afghan Politician Pushes for a Comeback." *The New York Times*, March 15, 2010. www.nytimes.com/2010/03/15/world/asia/15joya.html.

"Female Afghan Politician Malalai Joya Speaks Out." *The Guardian*, December 31, 2008. www.theguardian.com/world/2008/dec/31/afghanistan-human-rights.

Joya, Malalai. *A Woman Among Warlords: The Extraordinary Story of an Afghan Who Dared to Raise Her Voice*. New York, NY: Scribner, October 1, 2009.

"Malalai Joya: The Woman Who Will Not Be Silenced." *The Independent*, October 23, 2011. www.independent.co.uk/news/world/malalai-joya-the-woman-who-will-not-be-silenced-1763127.html.

Waldman, Amy, and Carlotta Gall. "A Young Afghan Dares to Mention the Unmentionable." *The New York Times*, December 18, 2003. www.nytimes.com/2003/12/18/world/a-young-afghan-dares-to-mention-the-unmentionable.html.

CHAPTER 31—MEGAN RAPINOE

Allen, Scott. "Megan Rapinoe Delivers Yet Again for USWNT—This Time with Rousing Parade Speech." *The Washington Post*, July 10, 2019. www.washingtonpost.com/sports/2019/07/10/megan-rapinoe-speech/.

Bobb, Brooke. "Giant Sunglasses Are Becoming Badass Megan Rapinoe's Signature Accessory." *Vogue*, July 18, 2019. www.vogue.com/vogueworld/article/megan-rapinoe-world-cup-parade-sunglasses.

Boren, Cindy. "Megan Rapinoe Is Sports Illustrated's Sportsperson of the Year, Only the Fourth Woman Chosen Alone." *The Washington Post*, December 10, 2019. www.washingtonpost.com/sports/2019/12/09/megan-rapinoe-is-sports-illustrateds-sportsperson-year-only-fourth-woman-chosen-alone/.

Brockes, Emma. "Megan Rapinoe: 'We're Everything Trump Loves—except That We're Powerful Women.'" *The Guardian*, August 17, 2019. www.theguardian.com/football/2019/aug/17/megan-rapinoe-everything-trump-loves-except-we-are-powerful-women.

Graham, Bryan Armen. " 'They're Icons': US Women's Champion Team Take Victory Parade in New York." *The Guardian*, July 10, 2019. www.theguardian.com/football/2019/jul/10/us-womens-soccer-team-world-cup-champions-new-york-parade.

Helmore, Edward. "Why Megan Rapinoe Is America's Badass Sweetheart." *The Guardian*, July 13, 2019. www.theguardian.com/us-news/2019/jul/13/megan-rapinoe-us-womens-football-performer-entertain-trump-piers-morgan.

Longman, Jeré. "For Megan Rapinoe, Boldness in the Spotlight Is Nothing New." *The New York Times*, June 27, 2019. www.nytimes.com/2019/06/27/ sports/megan-rapinoe-trump-world-cup.html.

Vrentas, Jenny. "Megan Rapinoe: Sports Illustrated's 2019 Sportsperson of the Year." *Sports Illustrated*, December 9, 2019. www.si.com/ sportsperson/2019/12/09/megan-rapinoe-2019-sportsperson-of-the-year.

CHAPTER 32—BILLIE EILISH

Coscarelli, Joe. "Billie Eilish Is Not Your Typical 17-Year-Old Pop Star. Get Used to Her." *The New York Times*, March 28, 2019. www.nytimes. com/2019/03/28/arts/music/billie-eilish-debut-album.html.

Eells, Josh. "Billie Eilish and the Triumph of the Weird." *Rolling Stone*, October 10, 2019. www. rollingstone.com/music/music-features/billie-eilish-cover-story-triumph-weird-863603/.

Haskell, Rob. "How Billie Eilish Is Reinventing Pop Stardom." *Vogue*, February 3, 2020. www.vogue. com/article/billie-eilish-cover-march-2020.

Weiner, Jonah. "How Billie Eilish Rode Teenage Weirdness to Stardom." *The New York Times*, March 12, 2020. www.nytimes.com/ interactive/2020/03/11/magazine/billie-eilish-profile.html.

CHAPTER 33—GRETA THUNBERG

Alter, Charlotte, Suyin Haynes, and Justin Worland. "Greta Thunberg: TIME's Person of the Year 2019." *Time*. Accessed November 3, 2020. time.com/person-of-the-year-2019-greta-thunberg/.

Epstein, Kayla, and Juliet Eilperin. "Greta Thunberg Had One Question at the U.N. Climate Summit: 'How Dare You?.'" *The Washington Post*, September 23, 2019. www.washingtonpost.com/climate-environment/2019/09/23/greta-thunberg-vows-that-if-un-doesnt-tackle-climate-change-we-will-never-forgive-you/.

Hallett, Vicky. "Teen Activist Greta Thunberg Is Now a Fashion Icon, Whether She Likes It or Not." *The Washington Post*, April 14, 2020. www.washingtonpost.com/lifestyle/magazine/teen-activist-greta-thunberg-is-now-a-fashion-icon-whether-she-likes-it-or-not/2020/04/13/833ce1fe-6d33-11ea-aa80-c2470c6b2034_story.html.

Witt, Emily, and Carolyn Kormann. "How Greta Thunberg Transformed Existential Dread into a Movement." *The New Yorker*, April 6, 2020. www.newyorker.com/books/under-review/how-greta-thunberg-transformed-existential-dread-into-a-movement.

Zraick, Karen. "Greta Thunberg, After Pointed U.N. Speech, Faces Attacks from the Right." *The New York Times*, September 24, 2019. www.nytimes.com/2019/09/24/climate/greta-thunberg-un.html.

About the Author

Marlene Wagman-Geller received her BA from York University and her teaching credentials from the University of Toronto and San Diego State University. Currently, she teaches high school English in National City, California. Reviews from her first three books (Penguin/Perigree) have appeared in *The New York Times,* and the *Associated Press* article appeared in dozens of newspapers such as the *Chicago Tribune,* the *Huffington Post,* and *The Washington Post.* She also penned a review for a Penguin Publishers title.

Mango Publishing, established in 2014, publishes an eclectic list of books by diverse authors—both new and established voices—on topics ranging from business, personal growth, women's empowerment, LGBTQ studies, health, and spirituality to history, popular culture, time management, decluttering, lifestyle, mental wellness, aging, and sustainable living. We were recently named 2019 and 2020's #1 fastest growing independent publisher by Publishers Weekly. Our success is driven by our main goal, which is to publish high quality books that will entertain readers as well as make a positive difference in their lives.

Our readers are our most important resource; we value your input, suggestions, and ideas. We'd love to hear from you—after all, we are publishing books for you!

Please stay in touch with us and follow us at:

Facebook: Mango Publishing
Twitter: @MangoPublishing
Instagram: @MangoPublishing
LinkedIn: Mango Publishing
Pinterest: Mango Publishing
Newsletter: mangopublishinggroup.com/newsletter

Join us on Mango's journey to reinvent publishing, one book at a time.